The Living Tree

*The Changing Meaning
of Being Chinese Today*

Contributors

Myron L. Cohen

Mark Elvin

Ambrose Yeo-chi King

Leo Ou-fan Lee

Victor Hao Li

Vera Schwarcz

Tu Wei-ming

Wang Gungwu

L. Ling-chi Wang

David Yen-ho Wu

Zhu Hong

The Living Tree

The Changing Meaning of Being Chinese Today

Edited by Tu Wei-ming

Stanford University Press

Stanford, California 1994

© 1991, Preface and Chapters 8 and 10 © 1994,
by the American Academy of Arts and Sciences
Originally published in the Spring 1991 issue of
Daedalus, Volume 120, Number 2, of the
Proceedings of the American Academy
of Arts and Sciences

Reprinted, with a Preface and two new chapters,
in 1994 by Stanford University Press
Printed in the United States of America

CIP data appear at the end of the book

Stanford University Press publications
are distributed exclusively by
Stanford University Press within
the United States, Canada, and Mexico;
they are distributed exclusively by
Cambridge University Press
throughout the rest of the world

Preface to the Stanford Edition

Growing out of a special issue of *Daedalus* (Spring 1991), the *Proceedings of the American Academy of Arts and Sciences*, this book explores the changing meaning of being Chinese from significantly different but mutually illuminating perspectives. An underlying theme of our collaborative effort is the emergence of a cultural space (a symbolic universe) that both encompasses and transcends the ethnic, territorial, linguistic, and religious boundaries that normally define Chineseness.

Surely a salient feature of being Chinese is to belong to a biological line traceable, as the legend goes, to the Yellow Emperor. This ethnic identification, mythologized in the idea of the "dragon's seed," evokes strong sentiments of originating from the same progenitor. Since China proper, the Central Country (*Zhongguo*), is clearly identifiable on the map of the world, another salient feature of being Chinese is simply being born in the Divine Land (*shenzhou*), a poetic name for China. We may surmise that being Chinese also means the ability to speak the language (preferably Mandarin, but any of the scores of "dialects" will do) and hence participate in the Chinese linguistic world. Furthermore, for those who are politically sensitive, being Chinese implies the practice of a code of ethics (e. g., loyalty and filial piety) toward one's homeland, the "mother country" (*zuguo*). Indeed, from the interpretive stance of either an outside observer or an inside participant, Chineseness entails common ancestry, homeland, mother tongue, and basic value orientation. The essays in this book, however, raise fundamental questions about these conventional assumptions and offer radically different ways of addressing this subject.

While fully acknowledging that Chineseness is always intertwined with and often inseparable from race, land, language, and faith, we are critically aware of and deeply intrigued by its fluidity. We have chosen to come to terms with the elusive quality of our inquiry by allowing the tension generated by a wholesome conflict of interpretation to persist, rather than seeking a premature reconciliation. Our main task is to inspire a continuous conversation on the meaning of being Chinese by trying to explode stereotypes. We have not attempted to offer disinterested descriptions; we hope that the record of our wrestling together with this engrossing issue will serve as a point of departure, if not a source of inspiration, for our potential conversation partners.

Race may be a biological reality, but ethnicity, as experience and consciousness, is mediated by a complex of social and political factors and thus cannot be reduced to mere empirical facts. Similarly, territoriality in itself may be seen as a solid, objective reality; but, as it is experienced or imagined as a fatherland, it can engender great psychic energy. The potential for language, especially in its incarnation as the mother tongue, to evoke sympathetic responses or great indignation is even stronger. This matter is compounded by the fact that written Chinese (*hanzi, kanji* in Japanese), as a distinct cultural symbol significantly different from an alphabet, gives literate Chinese a strong sense of membership in a unique discourse community. These primordial ties—ethnic, territorial, linguistic—are so invested with personal feelings that they almost never present themselves simply as unambiguous conditions of human life. Considering the explosive power embedded in religion, not to mention a variety of fundamentalist movements throughout the world today, the capacity of our beliefs to prompt us to individual or collective action cannot be overestimated. The highly politicized code of ethics of either the Nationalist or the Communist variation can be quite demanding.

The idea of being Chinese is further complicated by China's turbulent modern history: from the imagined universally recognized cultural center (the "Central Country") to the humiliating status of backwardness in virtually all areas of human endeavor. Responding to unprecedented exogenous forces threatening to reduce China to a mere geographic expression, nationalism emerged as the strongest Chinese revolutionary ideology in the twentieth century. The burning desire to "save the nation" (*jiuguo*) spawned passionate patriotic sentiments among the military, the working class, the peasantry, and the merchants, as well as the intelligentsia. The violence embedded in this mercurial situation has affected all aspects of being Chinese. The combination of "heavenly disasters and human calamities," imposed from outside and manufactured from within, made China synonymous with an abyss of misery. The untold suffering of the Chinese people—caused by Western imperialism, the Taiping Rebellion, the collapse of the Manchu dynasty, the internecine struggle of the warlords, Japanese aggression, the conflict between the Nationalists and the Communists, and the misguided policies of the People's Republic of China—contextualized the meaning of Chineseness in a new symbolic structure. Marginality, rootlessness, amnesia, anger, frustration, alienation, and helplessness have gained much salience in characterizing the collective psyche of the modern Chinese. The China that evokes historical consciousness, cultural continuity, and social harmony, not to mention centeredness and rootedness, already seems a distant echo.

Accordingly, this book does not presume to define or describe what Chineseness, in a static sense, really means. Such a "nonproblematized" approach is neither engaging nor illuminating; moreover, some of us find this kind of presentation not only intellectually bland but ideologically repugnant. Defining a Chinese as belonging to the Han race, being born in China proper, speaking Mandarin, and observing the "patriotic" code of ethics may seem innocuous, but this oversimplified conception conceals as much as it reveals. Indeed, it can easily produce unintended and unfortunate consequences. A focus on the Han race would inadvertently marginalize over ninety million members of Chinese minorities; requiring birth in the Divine Land excludes most of the 36 million or so overseas Chinese; emphasizing proficiency in spoken Mandarin, which is unintelligible to millions of Han Chinese, may make speakers of Cantonese or Fujianese feel inadequate; and the parochialism of imposing a "patriotic" code of ethics, no matter how broadly defined, is too obvious to need elaboration. Yet hegemonic discourse, charged with an air of arrogance, discriminates not only by excluding but also by including. Often, it is in the act of inclusion that the art of symbolic control is more insidiously exercised. Indeed, learning to be truly Chinese may prove to be too heavy a psychological burden for minorities, foreign-born, non-Mandarin speakers, or nonconformists; for such people, remaining outside or on the periphery may seem preferable.

Our joint venture has been to explore the fluidity of Chineseness as a layered and contested discourse, to open new possibilities and avenues of inquiry, and to challenge the claims of political leadership (in Beijing, Taipei, Hong Kong, or Singapore) to be the ultimate authority in a matter as significant as Chineseness. The eleven essays that follow, offering a variety of approaches, make an effort to provide "insiders' perspectives" on the changing meaning of being Chinese. We believe that such an immensely complex subject requires the collaboration of concerned intellectuals worldwide, as well as reflective minds in peripheral Chinese communities throughout the globe. While we have tried to uncover the dimensions of this rich field, we are fascinated by its fruitful ambiguities and humbled by its profound implications. The traces of our endeavor, presented here in our own idiosyncratic sequence, are, therefore, an open invitation as well as an interim report.

This book begins with my essay on "cultural China," the interaction of three symbolic universes: (1) mainland China, Taiwan, Hong Kong, and Singapore, (2) overseas Chinese communities throughout the world, and (3) the international communities of scholars, students, officials, journalists, and traders who provide a global forum for China-related matters. Intended as an introduction and a conceptual framework for our project, the discussion focuses on the role of the intellectual and envisions the emergence of a communal critical self-consciousness among the reflective minds in all three symbolic universes in cultural China. It concludes with the suggestion that, in the process of accumulating symbolic capital and in the exercise of spiritual and moral influence, the geopolitical periphery may have already become a new cultural center. Being Chinese, as a result, is as much an attainment as a given.

The following essays originally in the *Daedalus* issue explore vitally important areas in all three symbolic universes, giving rich texture and vibrant character to cultural China as imagined community. While China's legacy may have been fundamentally transformed, its grammar of action, embedded in the Sinic mentality, often unacknowledged and even unconscious, continues to define and redefine Chineseness (Mark Elvin). Yet, ironically, the China that is thought to have been blessed with the longest continuous history in the world is suffering from a sort of collective amnesia, incapable of coming to terms with her cultural tradition in recent times. Is this loss of memory, "no solace from Lethe," confined to members of the intelligentsia, asks Vera Schwarcz. Might it not have been the case, suggests Myron Cohen, that the wellspring of cultural creativity of the Chinese farmer, despite repeated misappropriation by the ill-informed and wrong-headed Nationalist and Communist regimes, has never been depleted and is again pouring out fresh water with new dynamism in economy and polity?

Perhaps a deep structure underlies the psychocultural life of the Chinese, a structure that is so ingrained in the "habits of the heart" that, tumultuous modern transmutation notwithstanding, it has not lost its enduring strength. To be sure, social relations are present in all communities, but, as Ambrose King argues, the density, intricacy, and self-reflexivity in the *kuan-hsi* (*guanxi*, networking) mechanism give a special tonality to the Chinese polyphony of human interaction. The global networking of overseas Chinese in trade, investment, and finance, a phenomenon that has begun to attract attention from the international business and scholarly community, is an indication that the Chinese merchant culture, seasoned in *guanxi*, has not only survived the challenge of "radical otherness" in foreign countries but, as Wang Gungwu shows, flourished in alien and often hostile environments throughout the world.

Still, learning to be Chinese, especially for minorities and the foreign-born, is an attainment rather than a given. Since identity is culturally constructed and, not infrequently, imposed or encouraged by political considerations, the meaning of being Chinese, even in mainland China, is constantly changing. The situation in Southeast Asia or the Pacific Islands is of course much more fluid. As a result, according to David Wu, Chineseness can be a social stigma, a financial liability, or a political asset. The communal remembrances of things past for Chinese Americans help us to take stock of the experience and identity of overseas Chinese as a tiny minority in North America. The sojourner mentality, which defines our existence in terms of perpetual rootlessness, is undergoing a major transformation. Increasingly, overseas Chinese (*huaqiao*) have chosen to be Chinese (*huaren*) in their adopted countries. As emigrants, they have voluntarily severed their political ties with their mother country and, as immigrants, they have deliberately opted to settle down in the new land. They may work against overwhelming obstacles to obtain citizenship in the United States or Canada, but, in an unprecedented way, a large number of Chinese from the mainland, Hong Kong, Taiwan, and Southeast Asia have made the transition. Leaving home, even a home adopted for several generations, is a tormenting experience, but staying is insufferable. In either case, the psychological cost, says Ling-chi Wang, is high.

If it is not easy to be Chinese in modern times, learning to be a Chinese intellectual in the first symbolic universe must be more agonizing. The cultural tradition that impelled a Confucian literatus to assume the central role of defining the meaning of being Chinese and the contemporary radical politics that relegates the "knowledgeable elements" (*zhishi fenzi*) to the background with neither power nor influence make it painfully difficult for Chinese intellectuals to define themselves. The emergence of a new phenomenon whereby *"the center is nowhere and the periphery is everywhere"* may create a public sphere for Chinese intellectuals to reconstitute themselves as a cultural force, imagining the future by reanimating the past. In this regard, as Leo Lee points out, marginality may turn out to be liberating, if not salvific.

Two new essays have been added to the original *Daedalus* issue. Victor Li offers a personal reflection on the Chinese American "diaspora," underscoring the role of bridge that the overseas Chinese may perform in this dawning of the Asian-Pacific century. Zhu Hong helps us to hear a different voice, challenging the idea of cultural China as a "gendered" conceptualization. I am grateful to the two new authors for generously sharing their insights and to the original contributors, especially to those who on their own decided to revise their papers for the book. We are deeply indebted to Laurence and Mary Rockefeller for their generous grant in support of the Dialogue of Civilizations Project at the East-West Center in Honolulu and to David Xiaokang Chu of the Center, who helped organize and direct the conferences in support of the *Daedalus* issue. Stephen Graubard, editor of the American Academy of Arts and Sciences and of *Daedalus*, deserves special thanks from all of us in Chinese studies for his wise leadership and editorial guidance for making *The Changing Meaning of Being Chinese Today* of interest and concern to the intellectual community in North America.

T.W.M.

Contents

Contributors

Myron L. Cohen is Professor of Anthropology at Columbia University. He has carried out research in Taiwan, Hebei, Shanghai County, and Sichuan. His research interests are family and lineage organization, popular religion, economic culture, and the cultural problems of modern Chinese nationalism. Among publications resulting from his Taiwan research are *House United, House Divided: The Chinese Family in Taiwan* (1976) and "Shared Beliefs: Corporations, Community and Religion Among the South Taiwan Hakka During Ch'ing," *Late Imperial China* 14 (June 1993): 1–32. Publications based upon fieldwork on the mainland include "Lineage Organization in North China," *Journal of Asian Studies* 459 (August 1990): 509–34, and "Family Management and Family Division in Contemporary Rural China," *China Quarterly* 130 (June 1992): 357–78. He is also the editor of *Asia Case Studies in the Social Sciences: A Guide for Teaching.*

Mark Elvin is Professor of East Asian History in the Division of Pacific and Asian History in the Research School of Pacific and Asian Studies of the Australian National University, Canberra. Trained in history and Chinese at Cambridge University, he is best known for *The Pattern of the Chinese Past* (1973) and *A Cultural Atlas of China* (1983), co-authored with Caroline Blunden. His current interests include the history of the emotions in modern China, of which the piece in the present volume forms a part, and the history of the environment in China, on which he recently organized the first international conference in collaboration with Professor Liu Tsui-jung of the Academia Sinica, Taipei.

Ambrose Yeo-chi King is Pro-Vice-Chancellor and Chair Professor of Sociology at the Chinese University of Hong Kong. He received his B.A. from National Taiwan University, M.A. from National Cheng Chi University, and Ph.D. from the University of Pittsburgh. He has been Visiting Fellow at the Center of International Studies, Massachusetts Institute of Technology, and Visiting Professor at the University of Wisconsin and the University of Heidelberg. His publications include *From Tradition to Modernity: An Analysis of Chinese Society and Its Change*, *The Politics of Three Chinese Societies*, and *Salient Issues of Chinese Society & Culture*. He has been an editorial board member of *The Journal of Applied Behavioral Science* and *The China Quarterly*. He has held many advisory positions to the Hong Kong government, including Independent Commission Against Corruption and The Law Reform Commission.

Leo Ou-fan Lee is Professor of Chinese Literature at Harvard University. He received his Ph.D. in history and East Asian languages from Harvard University and has taught at the University of California at Los Angeles, the University of Chicago, Indiana University, Princeton University, and the Chinese University of Hong Kong. Among his many publications in both English and Chinese are *The Romantic Generation of Modern Chinese Writers*, *Voices from the Iron House: A Study of Lu Xun*, and *Zhongxi wenxue de huaixiang* (Rambling thoughts on Chinese and Western literatures). He is currently exploring culture and media in a Pan-Chinese context.

Victor Hao Li is Co-Chairman of the Asia Pacific Consulting Group in Honolulu. He was President of the East-West Center from 1981 to 1990. He taught at Columbia Law School and the University of Michigan Law School and was the Shelton Professor of International Legal Studies at Stanford Law School from 1972 to 1981. He is Acting Professor of Law at Stanford Law School and a member of the New York bar. His current interests are Pacific trade and investment, U.S. relations with the Asia-Pacific region, China's legal system, and the cultural dimension in economic and political development.

Vera Schwarcz is the Mansfield Freeman Chair Professor in East Asian Studies and Professor of History at Wesleyan University. She received her Ph.D. in history from Stanford University and was awarded research grants from the American Council for Learned Societies, the Committee for Scholarly Communication with the People's Republic of China, and the American Philosophical Society. Her long-term intellectual dialogues with major Chinese thinkers, notably Liang Shuming, Zhang Shenfu, and Li Zhehou, enables her to take an active part in shaping the discourse on "Cultural China." She is the author of *Long Road Home: A China Journal* (1984), *The Chinese Enlightenment* (1986), and *Time for Telling Truth Is Running Out* (1993). She just completed a study of the Chinese and Jewish commitment to historical memory and has begun research on art and suffering during the Cultural Revolution.

Tu Wei-ming was born in Kunming, China, and educated in Taiwan and North America. Before joining Harvard as Professor of Chinese History and Philosophy in 1981, he taught at Princeton University and the University of California at Berkeley. He has also lectured on Confucian thought at Peking University, Taiwan University, the Chinese University of Hong Kong, and the University of Paris. He is the president of *Contemporary*, an intellectual monthly published in Taipei, and a fellow of the American Academy of Arts and Sciences. He is the author of *Confucian Thought: Selfhood as Creative Transformation* (1985) and *Way, Learning and Politics: Essays on the Chinese Intellectual* (1989) and the editor of *China in Transformation* (1994) and *Confucian Traditions in East Asian Modernity* (forthcoming).

Wang Gungwu graduated from the University of Malaysia and obtained his Ph.D. from the University of London's School of Oriental and African Studies. He is Vice-Chancellor of the University of Hong Kong and was Professor of History at the University of Malaya and Professor of Far Eastern History and the Director of the Research School of Pacific Studies at the Australian National University in Canberra. He has published extensively in the field of Chinese and Southeast Asian history, and his most recent publications include *Lishi di gongneng* (The Function of History; 1990), *China and the Chinese Overseas* (1991), *The Chineseness of China* (1991), and *Community and Nation: China, Southeast Asia and Australia* (1992).

Ling-chi Wang is Associate Professor of both Ethnic Studies and Asian American Studies at the University of California at Berkeley. Born in Xiamen, China, he received his undergraduate degree in music and graduate training in comparative Semitic languages in the United

States. Since the late 1960's he has combined his research and teaching on Asian American history with civil rights activism in Asian American communities. He lectures and writes extensively on Asian American history, race relations in the United States, bilingual education, and the Chinese Diaspora.

David Yen-ho Wu is Chair of the Department of Anthropology at the Chinese University of Hong Kong and was a Senior Fellow with the East-West Center in Honolulu from 1974 to 1993. He grew up in Taiwan and received his Ph.D. in cultural anthropology from Australian National University. His research interests are childhood socialization, indigenous minorities, mental health, and ethnic and national identity. He has conducted field work in Taiwan, mainland China, Papua New Guinea, and the Chinese communities in Southeast Asia and Hawaii. His publications include *The Chinese in Papua New Guinea* (1982), *Ethnicity and International Interaction* (1982), *Chinese Culture and Mental Health* (1985), *Preschool on Three Cultures* (1989), and *The Paiwan People* (1993).

Zhu Hong is Research Professor at the Institute of Foreign Literature, Chinese Academy of Social Sciences in Beijing, and is currently Visiting Professor at Boston University where she teaches contemporary Chinese women's writing. She has collected and translated into English two volumes of contemporary Chinese short stories—*The Chinese Western* and *The Serenity of Whiteness*—and has edited *The Stubborn Porridge and Other Stories* by Wang Meng. A researcher in nineteenth-century English fiction by training, she has been the recipient of fellowships and awards from the Humanities Research Centre in Canberra, the British Academy in London, the Harvard-Yenching and the Bunting Institute at Harvard, and the National Humanities Center in North Carolina for her work in literary interpretation, and is the author of several books of critical writings published in China.

The Living Tree

*The Changing Meaning
of Being Chinese Today*

I

Cultural China:
The Periphery as the Center

Tu Wei-ming

> The inscription of the Tang's basin reads, "If one day you truly
> renew yourself, day after day you will renew yourself; indeed,
> renew yourself every day." In the "Announcement to the Prince
> of Kang" it is said, "You shall give rise to a renewed people." In
> the Book of Poetry it is said, "Though Zhou is an old state, the
> Mandate it holds is new." For this purpose, the profound person
> exerts himself to the utmost in everything.
>
> —The Great Learning[1]

China, one of the longest continuous civilizations in human history,
"may be visualized as a majestic flowing stream."[2] Chinese culture, the
generic term symbolizing the vicissitudes of the material and spiritual
accomplishments of the Chinese people, has undergone major interpretive phases in recent decades and is now entering a new era of critical
self-reflection. The meaning of being Chinese is intertwined with China
as a geopolitical concept and Chinese culture as a lived reality.

For China, Chinese people, and Chinese culture, the image of the
twentieth century as an atrocious collective experience of destructiveness and violence emerges with fulgent salience as we approach the
fin-de-siècle rumination. Stability has often meant a delicate balance
for a few years; even a decade of peaceful coexistence evokes memories of permanence. The fluctuating Chinese political landscape since
the mid-nineteenth century, precipitated by external events unprecedented in Chinese history, has become so restless in the last decades
that not only the players but the rules of the game have constantly
changed. For instance, in the eight decades since the end of the Qing
Dynasty in 1911, a succession of different versions of the state consti-
tution were drafted and promulgated in both the Republic of China

and the People's Republic of China. Not just revisions or amendments, each new version superseded the previous one.[3] Indeed, virtually no institution of significance (university, church, press, professional society, or civic organization) has lasted for more than a generation. The two major parties (the Nationalist and the Communist) seem to have endured in form, but they both have been so substantially and radically restructured that a sense of cynicism and uncertainty prevails among their members. The most devastating rupture, however, occurred within the intellectual community.

Although China has never been subjected to the kind of comprehensive colonial rule experienced by India, China's semicolonial status severely damaged her spiritual life and her ability to tap indigenous symbolic resources. Chinese intellectuals have been much more deprived than their Indian counterparts ever were. While Indian intellectuals have continued to draw from the wellsprings of their spiritual life despite two centuries of British colonialism, the Western impact fundamentally dislodged Chinese intellectuals from their Confucian haven. Having lost their moorings in a society that for most of two millennia had provided a secure and respected anchorage for their predecessors, they desperately tried to find a niche in a cruel new world defined in terms of power with or without wealth. Their sense of impotence, frustration, and humiliation, prompted by a curious mixture of political nationalism and cultural iconoclasm, framed the context for their quest for identity not only as Chinese but as thinking and reflective Chinese in an increasingly alienating and dehumanizing world.

QUESTION

The question of Chineseness, as it first emerged in the "axial age" half a millennium prior to the birth of Confucius in 551 B.C., entails both geopolitical and cultural dimensions. While the territory of China has substantially expanded over time, the idea of a cultural core area first located in the Wei River Valley, a tributary of the Yellow River, and later encompassing parts of the Yangtze River, has remained potent and continuous in the Chinese consciousness. Educated Chinese know reflexively what China proper refers to; they may not be clear about the periphery but they know for sure that the center of China, whether Xi'an or Beijing, is in the north near the Yellow River. The archaeological finds of recent decades have significantly challenged the thesis that China grew from the Wei River Valley like a light source radiating from the center. Even in neolithic periods, there were several centers spreading across present-day China. The Central Country came into being as a confederation of several equally developed cultural areas rather than growing out of an ever-expanding core.[4] Yet regardless of this persuasive scholarly explanation of the origins of Chinese civilization, the impression that geopolitical China evolved through a long process centering around a definable core remains deep-rooted.

If the presumed core area was instrumental in forming a distinctive Chinese identity, Chinese culture as symbol of a living historical presence made the sense of being Chinese even more pronounced; it signified a unique form of life profoundly different from other styles of living often condemned as barbarian. The expression *hua* or *huaxia*, meaning Chinese, connotes culture and civilization. Those who lived in China proper were, inter alia, cultured and civilized, clearly differentiable from those barbarians on the periphery who had yet to learn the proper ways of dressing, eating, dwelling, and traveling. On the surface, the classical distinction between Chinese and barbarians was predicated on the divergence of two drastically different modes of life: the agrarian community of the central plains and the nomadic tribes of the steppes.[5] But the rise of Chinese cultural consciousness was occasioned by primordial ties defined in ethnic, territorial, linguistic, and ethical-religious terms. Although it is often noted that culture, rather than ethnicity, features prominently in defining Chineseness, the cultured and civilized Chinese, as the myth goes, claim a common ancestry. Indeed, the symbol of the "children of the Yellow Emperor"[6] is constantly reenacted in Chinese literature and evokes feelings of ethnic pride.

This idea of being Chinese, geopolitically and culturally defined, is further reinforced by a powerful historical consciousness informed by one of the most voluminous veritable documentary records in human history. Indeed, the chronological annals have flowed almost uninterruptedly since 841 B.C.; based on archaeological evidence and bronze inscriptions, Sinologists have been able to specify an exact date for the Zhou conquest in the eleventh century B.C.;[7] and the current debate over Confucius's birthday has been confined to two days (September 26 or 28, 551 B.C.). The collective memory of the educated Chinese is such that when they talk about Tu Fu's (712–770) poetry, Sima Qian's (died

c. 85 B.C.) *Historical Records*, or Confucius's *Analects*, they refer to a cumulative tradition preserved in Chinese characters, a script separable from and thus unaffected by phonological transmutations. An encounter with Tu Fu, Sima Qian, or Confucius through ideographic symbols evokes a sensation of reality as if their presence was forever inscribed in the script. Whether or not it is simply a false sense of continuity, the Chinese refer to the Han (206 B.C.–A.D. 220) and Tang (618–907) dynasties as if their greatness still provides practicable standards for contemporary Chinese culture and politics.

The Middle Kingdom syndrome or Central Country complex[8] may have made it psychologically difficult for the Chinese leadership to abandon its sense of superiority as the center and join the family of nations as an equal partner; but we must also remember that China had never been thoroughly challenged by an alien equal—if not superior—civilization until the penetration of the West in the mid-nineteenth century. The "Buddhist conquest of China"[9] entailed the introduction, domestication, maturation, and development of Indian spirituality in China for more than six hundred years, culminating in the intense Sinification of Buddhist teachings in distinctively Chinese schools of Tiantai, Huayan, and Chan.[10] The military and political domination of the Central Country by the Jurchens, the Khitans, the Mongols, and the Manchus in the last millennium was compensated, in cultural terms, by the Sinicization of the Jin, Liao, Yuan, and Qing into legitimate Chinese dynasties. China survived these "conquests" as a geopolitical entity and Chinese culture flourished. Nevertheless, if we take seriously the image of "a majestic flowing stream," we must acknowledge that these great outside influences altered this stream at various points. "As the stream moves on, the new forces may move forward more or less intact, swerve off into small eddies and side pools, form new currents through interaction with older ones, or be overwhelmed by newer currents entering farther down the stream."[11] Thus China, or Chinese culture, has never been a static structure, but rather a dynamic, constantly changing landscape.

In the Chinese historical imagination, the coming of the West, however, could be seen as more "decentering"; it was as if the Buddhist conquest and the Mongol invasion had been combined and compressed into one generation. It is understandable, therefore, that it has thoroughly destroyed the "pattern of the Chinese past"[12] and fundamentally redefined the *Problematik* for the Chinese intellectual. The convulsive disturbances that geopolitical China has suffered since the Opium War (1839–1842) are well-documented,[13] but the effervescences in Chinese culture that eventually brought about the intriguing paradox of iconoclasm and nationalism of the May Fourth (1919) generation (as well as subsequent generations) are so elusive that scholars of modern thought are still groping for a proper explanatory model to probe them.[14]

A radical manifestation of this ambivalent May Fourth legacy is the recent advocacy of comprehensive modernization qua Westernization in the People's Republic of China after the official closure of the devastating Cultural Revolution decade (1966–1976). This new rhetoric is deceptively simple: since China's backwardness, fully acknowledged by the Chinese intelligentsia in response to the open-door policy of the new reform era, had deep roots in Chinese polity, society, and culture, a total transformation of Chineseness is a precondition for China's modernization. Strategically, the most painful yet effective method of achieving this total transformation is to invite the modern West with all of its fruitful ambiguities to "decenter" the Chinese mentality. This wishful thinking—liberation through a willing and willful confrontation with radical otherness—has become a powerful countercultural thrust against both ossified Marxism–Leninism and the still vibrant "habits of the heart"[15] molded by the Confucian tradition.

River Elegy, a controversial, interpretive, six-part television series on Chinese cultural roots and ethos, straightforwardly advocated the necessity of embracing the blue ocean as the only way to save the "Yellow Earth."[16] Shown twice in 1988, *River Elegy* provoked a heated nationwide debate on tradition, modernity, change, China, and the West.[17] From the top Party leaders and intellectuals to workers, soldiers, and farmers, from the metropolitan areas of Beijing, Shanghai, and Wuhan to the sparsely populated great Northwest, perhaps several hundred million citizens were affected by the central message: China, behind even west African countries in per capita income, would soon be disfranchised as a player in the international game.[18] The intellectuals were stunned by the poignance of the question it posed: "Whither China?" Overwhelmingly siding with the radical Westernizers, they have accepted that reform requires the courage to restructure China fundamentally by importing proven models of success. The sacred symbols of the ancestral land stand condemned. The dragon, the symbol of Chinese ancestry, is condemned as outmoded imperial authoritarianism;[19] the Great Wall, the symbol of historical continuity, is condemned as a manifestation of close-minded conservatism; and the Yellow River, long regarded as the cradle of Chinese civilization, is condemned as the symbol of unmitigated violence against innocent people. The unstated message, obvious to most, gives a warning, indeed an outright challenge, to the powerholders in the Party: speed up the reform or else! Chineseness, under scathing assault, is ironically made to stand for the modus operandi of an authoritarian, conservative, and brutal ruling minority.

The paradox embedded in the message of *River Elegy* evokes memories of the May Fourth intellectuals' dilemma: the intertwining of nationalism (patriotism) and iconoclasm (antitraditionalism).[20] This leads inevitably to a whole set of thought-provoking questions. If Chinese intellectuals in China proper are so thoroughly disgusted with Chinese culture, can they define their Chineseness as an exclusive commitment to wholesale Westernization? If their condemnation of things Chinese is total, does this mean that they have voluntarily forfeited their right to be included in a definition of Chineseness? For the Chinese intellectuals living in China proper, can the meaning of being Chinese be sought in the limbo between the past that they have either deliberately relegated to fading memory or have been coerced into rejecting or forgetting, a present that they have angrily denounced, and the uncertain future that must follow their commitment to an alien unknown? The way these issues are formulated may appear relevant only for a tiny minority—the articulate and self-reflective intelligentsia—but the emotional intensity provoked by the debate has affected the Chinese populace in general.

CHALLENGE

The rise of Japan and the so-called Four Mini-Dragons (South Korea, Taiwan, Hong Kong, and Singapore) as the most dynamic region of sustained economic development since the Second World War raises challenging questions about tradition in modernity, the modernizing process in its different cultural forms. Does it suggest the necessity, indeed the desirability, of a total iconoclastic attack on traditional Chinese culture and its attendant comprehensive Westernization as a precondition for China's modernization?[21] From the perspective of economic organization, does this new capitalism, labeled *guanxi* (net-work, connections) capitalism, contrasted with the classical capitalism of Western Europe, signal a new age—the age of the Pacific Rim? [22] Or is it a mere epiphenomenon that can be explained in terms of exist-ing European and American development models? Politically speaking, are we witnessing a process of democratization based more on consen-sus formation than on adversarial relationships, giving a new shade of meaning to the concept of participatory democracy? Or are we observ-ing the continuing presence of an authoritarian political elite operating under the guise of majority rule? [23] Socially, do family cohesiveness, low crime rates, respect for education, and a high percentage of savings, relative to other industrial societies, indicate an ethos different from individualistic "habits of the heart"? [24] Or do they simply reflect an earlier stage of modern transformation, one that will lead eventually to the anomie and alienation experienced in the West? Culturally, do these societies symbolize successful examples of advanced technology in combination with age-old ritual practices, or are they merely the passing phases of traditional societies? [25] In short, how does the rise of East Asia challenge our deep-rooted conceptions of economic growth, political development, social transformation, and cultural change?

These questions are significant for interpreting the meaning of being Chinese; they are potentially provocative to the overwhelming majority of the Chinese intellectuals in mainland China who believe that Chineseness is incongruous with the modernizing process, defined purely in terms of science and democracy. If, indeed, the "Sinic World" [26] or the "Post-Confucian" [27] region has succeeded in adopting a form of life definitely modern, distinctively East Asian—by implication Chi-nese as well—the sharp dichotomy between tradition and modernity must be rejected as untenable, as useless in analyzing developing coun-tries as in its application to more highly industrialized or postindustrial societies. Any attempt to measure modernization with a linear develop-mental scale is thus shown to be simpleminded. Although this point has been repeatedly argued by the culturally sophisticated modernization theorists since the early 1970s, [28] the existence of empirically verifiable counterexamples should settle the argument. [29]

Since traditional features of the human condition—ethnicity, mother tongue, ancestral home, gender, class, and religious faith—all seem to be relevant in understanding the lifeworlds of societies, both modern and developing, the search for roots, despite the pervasiveness of global consciousness, is a powerful impulse throughout the world today.[30] If there is an alternative path to capital formation, then democracy, technology, and even modernization may indeed assume different cultural forms. The most radical iconoclastic assertion espoused by some of the articulate May Fourth intellectuals—that Chinese culture, not just Confucianism, but the ideographic language itself, would have to be abolished as a precondition for China's modernization—is now regarded as completely outdated. Even the most ardent Westernizers in Beijing and Shanghai chose to see their ideas circulated in the Chinese journals printed in Chinese characters. To Chinese intellectuals in industrial East Asia, the awareness that active participation in the economic, political, social, and cultural life of a thoroughly modernized community does not necessarily conflict with being authentically Chinese implies the possibility that modernization may enhance rather than weaken Chineseness. Still, the meaning of being Chinese is itself undergoing a major transformation.

A recent economic phenomenon with far-reaching political and cultural implications is the great increase in intraregional trade in the Asian-Pacific region. The annual volume of $200 billion already exceeds trans-Pacific trade (which is now significantly larger than trans-Atlantic trade). Since the Four Dragons are providing 31 percent of all foreign investments in the countries of the Association of Southeast Asian Nations (ASEAN), notably Malaysia, Indonesia, the Philippines, and Thailand, the participation of "diaspora" Chinese is vitally important; they are responsible for the largest transfer of capital in this region, exceeding that of both Japan and the United States. A predictable result is the evolving image of the Chinese. Just as the popular image of a Chinese in the United States has changed from laundryman to engineer, the image of Chinese as economic animals is likely to be further magnified in Southeast Asia, changing perhaps from that of trader to that of financier. The Chinese merchant culture underlying Chinese behavior as trader, banker, and entrepreneur adds vibrant color to the impressive reality that the Chinese constitute not only the largest peasantry in the world, but also the most mobile merchant class.[31]

Despite all these remarkable economic accomplishments in Asia and the Pacific region, the future is filled with uncertainties. As the United States reduces its budget deficit, it may not be the same catalyst for growth as it was in the 1980s, when an American import spree fueled much of the economic expansion in the region. Also, with the hope of a unified European Community and the West's preoccupation with Eastern Europe, not to mention the deterioration of the former Soviet economy and the on-going Middle East crisis, the West may well turn its attention away from Asia and the Pacific. Although it is unlikely that a "fortress Europe" or a Western hemisphere economic zone will push the Asian-Pacific region to move toward a Japan-anchored trading bloc, the hazards of protectionism in North America are certainly real.

Still, if the projection of a Pacific century is at all credible, the roles of Taiwan, Hong Kong, Singapore, and the Chinese communities in Southeast Asia ought not to be underestimated. Taiwan, for example, has the distinction of holding the largest reserve of foreign currency in the world (over $70 billion in 1990), surpassing that of Japan, the United States, and Germany. While this fact alone may not be particularly significant, the combination of government leadership, entrepreneurial ingenuity, and a strong work ethic has made Taiwan, despite its political isolation, an assiduous investor and innovator in international trade. Taiwanese merchants (predominantly in small and medium-sized industries) are a noticeable presence worldwide. To be sure, the perceived Taiwanization of Silicon Valley and parts of Los Angeles county is an exaggeration (there is nothing comparable to the Koreatowns of southern California or the Korean groceries of New York), but the Nationalist government has made a highly coordinated and strategically sophisticated effort, with the full cooperation of the business community, to make Taiwan a valued partner in many joint ventures in a number of key places in North America.

If the Taiwan "economic miracle" has attracted the most attention from the American public, the most fascinating and enduring feature of the Taiwan experience has been its conscious effort to chart a radically different course of development, a deliberate challenge to the socialist experiment on the mainland. As a result, the perceptual gap between the two sides of the Taiwan Straits has remained exceedingly wide; despite the rhetoric of unification, the two "countries" have vastly different economic structures, political systems, social conditions, and cultural orientations. The Taiwan independence movement has created perhaps the most controversial and explosive political issue on the island, but the democratization process initiated by the top Nationalist leadership under pressure in 1987 has undoubtedly caught the spirit of the moment. If Taiwan (the Republic of China) becomes truly democratic, the question of Taiwan's Chineseness will inevitably become a matter of public debate. Much attention has already been focused on what may be called sedimentations of Taiwanese history. For the intelligentsia, especially those now under forty who were born and raised in Taiwan, the recognition that there have been distinctive Dutch, Japanese, and American strata superimposed upon the Chinese substrate since the eighteenth century—not to mention the upsurge of nativist sentiments among the aboriginal peoples—makes the claim of Taiwan's Chineseness problematic.

Still, the very fact that nowadays more than a million Taiwan residents travel each year to the mainland to sightsee, do business, carry on scholarly communication, and hold family reunions has created a sort of "mainland mania" in the island, compelling the Nationalist government to deal with the mainland question in ways scarcely imagined even a few years ago. In late December 1990, the President of the Republic of China announced that its state-of-war "emergency" vis-à-vis the mainland would be terminated by May 1991. This has led to other once unthinkable activities. Nowadays, "natural economic zones" are being formed on the two sides of the Taiwan Straits. This new economic reality will certainly have political and cultural ramifications. Taiwan's official ideological claim to be the true inheritor of Chinese culture has taken a quizzical turn. In response to the threat of the independence movement, the government deems it advantageous to underscore Taiwan's Chineseness, but the challenge from the mainland prompts it to acknowledge how far Taiwan has already departed from the Sinic world.

The tale of the two city-states, Hong Kong and Singapore, is equally fascinating. All indications suggest that the average per capita income in Hong Kong had by 1990 surpassed that of its colonial ruler, England. And England, rather than Hong Kong, seems to be the principal beneficiary of their two-way investment relationship. Hong Kong's free-market capitalism, ably guided by government-appointed local leaders, exemplifies the "loose-rein" political philosophy characteristic of traditional Chinese statecraft. Even though Hong Kong's ruling style is noninterference, its approach to economic affairs is a far cry from laissez-faire capitalism as it is putatively practiced. The role of Hong

Kong in international finance and in the development of manufacturing and light industry appropriate to her specific geopolitical and cultural conditions provides an inspiring example for many developing
and developed societies. Lurking behind the scenes, of course, is the
overwhelming presence of mainland refugees and their experience of
persecution, loss, escape, renewal, and uncertainty. An estimated 1.5
million of Hong Kong's 5.5 million residents demonstrated in support of
the democracy movement in Beijing in May 1989; virtually every family
was represented in these demonstrations. Hong Kong's concern for and
involvement in the affairs of the homeland cannot be overestimated.
While Hong Kong residents still have a strong aversion to their colonial
status, the outpouring of sentiment urging the British government to
assure them of legal protection from Beijing suggests the emergence of
a new ethos. Ironically, only a fraction of middle-class professionals are
eligible for British legal protection. The well-grounded fear experienced
by the overwhelming majority of Hong Kong residents of an imminent
Communist takeover in 1997 overshadows any national commitment
to redress the humiliation of the Opium War: maintaining the status
quo of British colonial rule is far preferable to returning to the mother
country. For the majority of Hong Kong residents, being Chinese as a
British subject is, in human terms, arguably superior to being Chinese
as a citizen of the People's Republic of China.

The story of Singapore—which in less than two decades emerged
from an endangered entrepôt to become a major center in the Asian-
Pacific region in trade, high technology, petroleum, tourism, medicine,
and finance—is no less dramatic. The linguistic situation alone offers
a clue to the complexity of the human condition. Among the 75 percent of the inhabitants who are Chinese (15 percent are Malay and
7 percent Indian), at least six major groups who find each other's dialects unintelligible can be identified: "In 1980, for example, there were
800,000 Fujianese (locally called Hokkien and in turn subdivided into
the Amoy and the Fuzhou); 400,000 Chaozhouese locally called Teo-
chew; 300,000 Cantonese; 140,000 Hakka; and 130,000 Hainanese.
The Chinese lingua franca became Mandarin, which is for Singapore-
ans a dialect learned in this generation and devoid of deep family-
rooted ethnic significance."[32] Yet, Singapore as an independent state
and a safe society with its own unique blend of cultural eclecticism
has endured. Whether or not Singapore is practicing "capitalism with

socialist characteristics," [33] her success in providing adequate housing, transportation, education, security, and welfare for her citizens clearly indicates that, at least in the economic sphere, her leadership, in both government and business, has charted a course of action congenial to Singapore's situation.

Because omnipresent government intervention has transformed Singapore into an administrative state, with tight control of the press, mass media, and public discourse, a stigma is attached to Singapore in prominent English-language newspapers such as the *Far Eastern Economic Review* and the *Asian Wall Street Journal*. The fact that "the leading business entrepreneurs in Singapore are government bureaucrats," [34] not to mention the overwhelming power of the one-party political system, raises serious doubts about the state's commitment to democracy. Still, one has the impression that Singapore's government is efficient and uncorrupt; that the environment is fresh and clean; and that the people are healthy and hardworking. Singapore's Chineseness, in contrast to Hong Kong's, is not particularly pronounced; indeed, in a certain sense, it is artificially constructed. Despite the obvious fear that any emphasis on Chinese cultural identity will lead to racial disharmony, [35] Singapore is unmistakably a sanitized version of Chinese society. As Ezra Vogel notes, "If Hong Kong entrepreneurs thought of Singapore as a bit dull, rigid, and too tightly controlled, Singapore's leaders thought of Hong Kong as too speculative, decadent, and undisciplined." [36] In any case, both Hong Kong and Singapore have been instrumental in helping to define the character of a Pacific century. The Chinese communities in Malaysia, Thailand, Indonesia, and the Philippines are similarly participating in transforming these societies into newly industrial countries.

One striking aspect of all these scenarios is an absence—that of mainland China. For thirty years (1949–1979), hostile external conditions and self-imposed isolation made the People's Republic of China largely irrelevant to the rise of industrial East Asia. In the last decade, as the resumption of tourism, trade, and scholarly exchanges thrust new responsibilities upon the Beijing regime, the Chinese intellectual community as well as the official establishment was appalled to discover that while the periphery of the Sinic world was proudly marching toward an Asian-Pacific century, the homeland seemed mired in perpetual underdevelopment. Despite the insistence of the Beijing government on defining China's coming-of-age narrowly in terms of the "Four

Modernizations"—agriculture, industry, science and technology, and national defense—issues of political and social restructuring have been raised not only by dissidents, but also by intellectuals in state organizations, research institutions, and universities. The "barracks mentality" is no longer tenable.

This context is vitally important for understanding the question of Chineseness from the perspective of cultural China. Although the phenomenon of Chinese culture disintegrating at the center and later being revived from the periphery is a recurring theme in Chinese history, it is unprecedented for the geopolitical center to remain entrenched while the periphery presents such powerful and persistent economic and cultural challenges. Either the center will bifurcate or, as is more likely, the periphery will come to set the economic and cultural agenda for the center, thereby undermining its political effectiveness.

DISCOURSE

Cultural China can be examined in terms of a continuous interaction of three symbolic universes.[37] The first consists of mainland China, Taiwan, Hong Kong, and Singapore—that is, the societies populated predominantly by cultural and ethnic Chinese. The second consists of Chinese communities throughout the world, including a politically significant minority in Malaysia (35 percent) and a numerically negligible minority in the United States. These Chinese, estimated to number 36 million, are often referred to by the political authorities in Beijing and Taipei as *huaqiao* (overseas Chinese).[38] More recently, however, they have tended to define themselves as members of the Chinese "diaspora," meaning those who have settled in scattered communities of Chinese far from their ancestral homeland. While Han Chinese constitute an overwhelming majority in each of the four areas in the first symbolic universe, communities of the Chinese diaspora—with the exception of Malaysia already mentioned—rarely exceed three percent of their country's population. (An interesting evolving exception is Fiji, where the Chinese population is rapidly increasing owing to recent changes in government policy.)[39]

The third symbolic universe consists of individual men and women, such as scholars, teachers, journalists, industrialists, traders, entrepreneurs, and writers, who try to understand China intellectually and bring their conceptions of China to their own linguistic communities. For the last four decades the international discourse on cultural China has unquestionably been shaped more by the third symbolic universe than by the first two combined. Specifically, writings in English and Japanese have had greater impact on the intellectual discourse on cultural China than in Chinese. For example, Chinese newspapers abroad often quote the *New York Times* and Japan's *Asahi Shimbun* to enhance their credibility. The highly politicized Chinese media on both sides of the Taiwan Straits have yet to earn a reputation as reliable reporters and authoritative interpreters of events unfolding in their own domain. To be sure, it is worth noting that Mao's utopian socialism was a source of inspiration for student demonstrators in Berkeley and Paris in the late 1960s; and, for a while, even Lin Biao's strategy of using the countryside of the Third World to encircle industrialized Western Europe and North America was accepted as "theory" in revolutionary rhetoric. But while we must not overlook the power and influence of the third symbolic universe in shaping the international discourse on cultural China, the situation is rapidly changing. In cultural matters, the *New York Times* may be months out of date; *River Elegy*, not to mention the so-called cultural fever it inspired,[40] did not catch the attention of Western journalists for months after it had engulfed the Chinese-speaking world. Japanese reporting also suffers from a lack of systematic analysis of the cultural landscape. Still, foreign journalists continue to exert a strong influence on the discourse on cultural China. Sinologists in North America, Japan, Europe, and increasingly Australia have similarly exercised a great deal of power in determining the scholarly agenda for cultural China as a whole.

There is undoubtedly a whiff of Orientalism, à la Edward Said,[41] in the third symbolic universe, but it is simplistic to underscore foreign representations as if the cultural China constructed by non-Chinese Sinologists has become a dominant discourse obliterating indigenous visions. The picture is much more complicated, even if we focus our attention exclusively on the power play between foreign and native representations. The views of John King Fairbank, for instance, long prevailed in discussions of trade and diplomacy on the China coast.[42] Indebted to his Harvard mentor E. B. Morse, Fairbank's interpretive stance on the origins of the Opium War can mistakenly be viewed as primarily Europe-centered with little reference to the "local knowledge" of the Chinese. Unexpectedly, however, Jiang Tingfu, an eminent Chinese scholar-diplomat, also subscribed to this supposedly foreign representation. We may surmise that Jiang was Westernized in his outlook. Yet that view is confounded by the challenge to Fairbank's thesis by his student Paul Cohen, who vigorously argues for a China-centered perspective.[43] He is apparently Sinified! Furthermore, under Fairbank's supervision, Chang Hsin-pao published a monograph offering a self-consciously nativist understanding of the Opium War.[44] The confluence of several seemingly conflicting and even contradictory explanatory models makes the third symbolic universe rich and varied.

My tripartite division of cultural China is admittedly problematic. Hong Kong, Taiwan, and Singapore have much more in common with the Chinese diaspora than they do with mainland China. Despite Hong Kong's impending return to the homeland in 1997, an overwhelming majority of the working class as well as the business people and intellectuals, if offered a choice, would not elect to identify themselves as citizens of the People's Republic of China. Hong Kong is, at least in spirit, part of the Chinese diaspora. Although the Republic of Singapore established full diplomatic ties with the People's Republic of China in 1990, its leadership has had closer contact with the Nationalist government in Taipei than with the Communists in Beijing. After all, Singapore, as a full-fledged nation-state, is English-speaking and a loyal member of ASEAN; the overall linguistic proficiency of Singaporean Chinese seems not as high as that of the Chinese in Malaysia. Singapore is basically apprehensive about its Chineseness, for fear that its perceived ethnic and cultural chauvinism might alienate its own minorities and strain relations with its neighboring states. Nevertheless, Taiwan, Hong Kong, and Singapore are grouped together with mainland China as the first symbolic universe because the life orientation in these societies is based on Chinese culture. If we define being Chinese in terms of full participation in the economic, political, and social life of a Chinese community or civilization, the first symbolic universe offers both the necessary and the sufficient condition.

Divergences in economic development, political system, and social organization notwithstanding, the four members of the first symbolic universe share a common ethnicity, language, history, and worldview. To be sure, ethnic awareness has been diluted by the admixture of a variety of races in the generic Han people; linguistic cohesiveness is threatened by the presence of numerous mutually incomprehensible spoken "dialects" (in the case of Singapore, the situation is further complicated by multilingualism); historical consciousness has been undermined by varying interpretations of "Confucian China and its modern fate."[45] (In the case of Singapore again, one can surely claim that her history began in 1819, when Stamford Raffles landed on the island, for there were only about 120 Malay and thirty Chinese inhabitants then.)[46] And, with increasing rapidity, worldviews have been affected by the importation of radically different belief systems. Still, if we view cultural China as being a psychological as well as an economic and a political nexus, then the dynamics of the interaction between mainland China, especially the coastal areas of Guangdong, Fujian, Jiangsu, Zhejiang, and Shanghai on the one hand, and Hong Kong, Taiwan, and Singapore on the other, offer grounds for grouping them together as constituent parts of the first symbolic universe. For the last ten years, the cultural impact that Hong Kong has had on mainland China as a whole—and metropolitan Guangzhou (Canton) and the Shenzhen Special Economic Zone in particular—has been profound; Hong Kong's transformation of mainland China is likely to become even more pronounced in the decade ahead. The effects on the modernization of China traceable to recent visitors from Taiwan and Singapore—scholars, teachers, advisors, traders, journalists, and tourists—indicate clearly the potential for Taiwanization or Singaporization of selected geographic regions and social strata of the mainland in the coming decades.

This does not necessarily mean that perceived convergence will eventually lead to a reintegrated China as a civilization-state. It is more likely that, as the peripheral regions of mainland China become "contaminated" by Hong Kong, Taiwan, and Singapore, relative economic prosperity and cultural richness will bring about a measure of political independence. The Pudong project, the planned development of a Special Economic Zone comparable in size to Singapore in metropolitan Shanghai, is a case in point. As similar projects develop along the coast northward to the Shandong peninsula and Manchuria, the economic and cultural influence of South Korea and Japan will become more pronounced. Without accepting the post-Tiananmen speculation about military warlordism, we can expect a rise in economic and cultural regionalism. Whether by choice or by default, a significantly weakened center may turn out to be a blessing in disguise for the emergence of a truly functioning Chinese civilization-state. Of course, the destructive power of the center is such that the transformative potential of the periphery can easily be stifled. The unpredictability of the Beijing leadership and the vulnerability of the status quo in Hong Kong, Taiwan, and Singapore make the first symbolic universe fluid and a fruitful interaction among its members difficult. Despite the so-called Central Country syndrome, a Chinese civilization-state with a variety of autonomous regions (including Tibetan, Mongolian, Zhuang, and other minority areas) or even a loosely structured Chinese federation of different political entities, remains a distinct possibility.[47]

Nevertheless, we are well-advised to heed the observation of Lucian Pye, who maintains that "China is not just another nation-state in the family of nations," but rather "a civilization pretending to be a state."[48] Actually, Pye writes, "the miracle of China has been its astonishing unity." In trying to find an analogy in Western terms, Pye says of China today, it is "as if the Europe of the Roman Empire and of Charlemagne had lasted until this day and were now trying to function as a single nation-state."[49] We may not accept Pye's assertion that "the overpowering obligation felt by Chinese rulers to preserve the unity of their civilization has meant that there could be no compromise in Chinese cultural attitudes about power and authority"; but his general point is well taken: "The fact that the Chinese state was founded on one of the world's great civilizations has given inordinate strength and durability to its political culture."[50] The beguiling phenomenon of China as a civilization-state requires further elucidation.

The idea of the modern state involving power relationships based on competing economic and social interests is anathema to the Chinese cultural elite as well as to the Chinese ruling minority. To them, the state—intent on realizing its historical mission to liberate China from threats of imperialist encroachment and the lethargy and stagnation of the feudal past—symbolizes the guardian of a moral order rather than the outcome of a political process. The state's legitimacy is derived from a holistic orthodoxy informed by Sinified Marxism-Leninism, rather than from operating principles refined by political praxis and codified in a legal system. The state's claims on its people are comprehensive and the people's dependence on the state is total; the state exemplifies the civilizational norms for the general public and the leadership assumes ideological and moral authority. The civilization-state exercises both political power and moral influence.

It should be acknowledged, however, that for all her power and influence, China as a civilization-state often plays a negligible part in the international discourse on global human concerns. The marginalization of the Central Country is so accepted a fact in the contemporary world that it is virtually taken for granted, even by those of us committed to Chinese studies in the West. It may be an overstatement to say that China has been irrelevant in many of the geopolitical discussions at the annual Economic Summit, but it is undeniable that for decades intellectuals in North America and Western Europe have been involved in supposedly global and ecumenical discussions of psychology, politics, society, religion, and philosophy without any apparent need to take China into serious consideration. Despite the persuasiveness of the third symbolic universe in determining the agenda for international discourse on cultural China, even the most prominent Sinologists lament the relegation of their intellectual pursuits to the backwaters of the modern academy. Generations of college students from leading Western universities have graduated without any exposure to East Asia, not to mention China. Some of the most impressive grand theories about the human condition make no reference to China, past or present. The asymmetry between its centrifugal pull in cultural China and its marginal role in the "global village" as a whole makes the first symbolic universe a challenging issue for analysis and contemplation.[51]

DIASPORA

The second symbolic universe, the Chinese diaspora, presents equally intriguing conceptual difficulties. Diaspora, which literally means the scattering of seeds, has most often been used to refer to Jews outside Palestine after the Babylonian exile or to Jews living in a Gentile world. Until the establishment of the modern nation-state of Israel, the salience of faith in Jehovah and the attendant observance of law and ritual, rather than membership in a political entity, characterized the distinctive features of the Jewish religious community.[52] By contrast, the state, or more precisely China as a civilization-state, features prominently in the Chinese diaspora. Because the Chinese diaspora has never lost its homeland, there is no functional equivalent of the cathartic yearning for Jerusalem. Actually the ubiquitous presence of the Chinese state—its awe-inspiring physical size, its long history, and the numerical weight of its population—continues to loom large in the psychocultural constructs of diaspora Chinese. For many, the state, either Nationalist or Communist, controls the symbolic resources necessary for their cultural identity. Although dual citizenship is no longer possible, both Beijing and Taipei routinely expect the loyal support of their *huaqiao* (overseas Chinese). Few diaspora Chinese ever speculate about the possibility of China's disintegrating as a unified civilization-state. The advantage of being liberated from obsessive concern for China's well-being at the expense of their own livelihood is rarely entertained. The diaspora Chinese cherish the hope of returning to and being recognized by the homeland. While the original meaning of scattering seeds suggests taking root and producing offspring elsewhere, many diaspora Chinese possess a sojourner mentality and lack a sense of permanence in their adopted country. Some return "home" to get married or send their children back for a Chinese education; they remain in touch with relatives and friends who keep them informed of the economic and political climate at home.[53]

The Chinese settlers who are scattered around the world come, historically, from a few well-defined areas along the southeast coast of mainland China—notably Guangdong and Fujian. For specific groups of settlers, the province was too extensive and diffuse an entity to provide a point of emotional identification with their homeland. Until the recent waves of immigration to North America, which began after 1949, the overwhelming majority of Chinese Americans identified themselves not as Cantonese—too cosmopolitan a term to evoke any real sense of roots—but as natives of subprovincial districts such as Taishan, Zhongshan, or Panyu. Similar phenomena occurred in Europe and Southeast Asia. As a rule, mutual aid associations in Malaysia, Thailand, and Indonesia were organized according to county or village, rather than provincial, affiliations.[54] Secret societies that crossed local boundaries were either politically oriented or economically motivated. It is understandable, then, that the Chinese diaspora was for decades so fragmented that there was little communication between groups within a host nation, let alone any transnational cooperation.

Nevertheless, despite apparent parochialism, the overseas Chinese have managed to adapt themselves to virtually all types of communities throughout the world. The impression that the overall cultural orientation of Chinese settlers has been shaped predominantly by the magnetic power of the homeland is simplistic. The reasons why overseas Chinese rarely consider themselves thoroughly assimilated in their adopted countries are complex. In the United States, racial discrimination against the Chinese was, until recently, blatant; and the Chinatown mentality, as a response to the hostile environment, may be seen as a psychosocial defense and adaptation. The post–1949 immigrants from Taiwan and Hong Kong have developed entirely different patterns of assimilation. The arrival of "boat people" and refugees from the mainland has initiated yet another process whereby new-style Chinatowns have emerged in such unlikely places as the deep South and the Midwest in the United States.

The situation in Southeast Asia is radically different. The case of the Philippine Chinese, perhaps the smallest Chinese population of any major Southeast Asian country, merits special attention:

The history of the Chinese in the Philippine population is one of regular intermarriage with ethnic Filipinos and the generation, thereby, of an historically important body of Chinese mestizos. When waves of Chinese immigration have receded and the Chinese community was not replenished for a time, these mestizos have flourished in business pursuits. And, as in Thailand, Chinese-Filipino intermarriage has produced, over long periods of time, much of the political, social and cultural leadership of the country.[55]

"In common with most of the rest of Southeast Asia," Edgar Wickberg writes, "the Philippines has had little replenishment of its Chinese population since 1949." He further notes: "Other things being equal, then, we would expect such a population to be increasingly oriented towards the Philippines and Philippine culture and decreasingly interested in things Chinese."[56] This seems to be incongruent with the perceived phenomenon that the Chinese in the Philippines, unlike those in Thailand, have not yet been fully assimilated into the mainstream of Filipino society. In fact, their distinct Chineseness makes them vulnerable to nativist assaults. Wickberg explains that, prior to 1975, "the Philippine policy of restricting certain occupations to citizens but making it difficult for Chinese to become citizens put the Chinese in an almost impossible situation."[57] It appears, then, that the push of local conditions as well as the pull of the homeland impels the Chinese to become inassimilable.

However, the story is complicated by the fact that relations between China and the Philippines figure prominently in determining the fate of the Chinese settlers. For example, in the 1950s and 1960s, when the

Nationalist government in Taiwan exerted profound influence in the Philippines, "the Philippine government, on the whole, gave over to Taiwan the responsibility for defining the nature of the Chinese culture to be taught in the Philippine Chinese schools."[58] As part of the united, anti-Communist front between the Nationalist government and the Marcos regime, Chinese schools were allowed to fly the Republic of China flag, to display pictures of Sun Yat-sen and Chiang Kai-shek, and to use textbooks from Taiwan. The recognition of Beijing in 1975 facilitated the Filipinization of the Chinese schools and prompted the Marcos government to grant full citizenship to more than 100,000 Chinese Filipinos, about one-sixth of the entire Chinese population in the Philippines. More recently, President Corazon Aquino's unusual symbolic gesture in making a pilgrimage to the village of her paternal ancestors in Fujian, joined by Cardinal Jaime Sin's public acknowledgment of his Chinese ancestry, helped popularize "a favorable image of things Chinese and people of Chinese background."[59] Their effort to underscore the heuristic value of the life of the Philippines' first saint— Lorenzo Ruizo—who was of Chinese extraction, offered a new perspective on Chineseness in the public sphere.

Perhaps the most encouraging sign was the approach of the newly established intellectual organization Kaisa Para Sa Kaunlaran, which advocated "the understanding and retention of one's Chinese culture while fully identifying oneself with the Philippines and with Filipinos of non-Chinese backgrounds."[60] Conceived in the 1970s by young university graduates of Chinese ancestry, the Kaisa vision intends to create a narrow bridge between cultural chauvinism and total assimilation. One of the most threatening issues confronting the Chinese Filipino community is its public perception; although the Chinese are beneficiaries of the political and economic system, their contribution to social welfare is limited and their participation in the cultural life of the land is minimal. The resentment of the local population against the conspicuous consumption of some rich Chinese (for example, elaborate tombs in the style of miniature world-class hotels), which in the past often led to anti-Chinese riots against the peddlers and retailers in Chinatowns, remains a haunting memory.

The precariousness of being Chinese in Southeast Asia is amply demonstrated by the institutionalized mechanisms of de-Sinicization in Malaysia and Indonesia. For political reasons, the Malaysian and Indonesian governments consider Chineseness a potential threat to national security, not to mention national integration. Among the most tragic events in the second half of the twentieth century were the atrocities committed against the native population in Indonesia in 1965, which were brought on by the perceived threat of a Communist takeover supported by China. An estimated 250,000 to 750,000 people (including thousands of Chinese) died in a matter of months, partly as the result of a coup d'état engineered by President Suharto. The holocaust inflicted upon both Indonesians and the Chinese minority received little attention in the first symbolic universe of cultural China. The mainland was embroiled in its own holocaust, the Cultural Revolution; Taiwan condoned the heavy-handed attack on Communism; Hong Kong was too remote to be affected; and Singapore's proximity to Indonesia—both geographically and politically—made it too vulnerable to offer a protest. It was actually in the same period that growing anti-Chinese sentiment in Malaysia pushed Singapore to become an independent state. Intent on demonstrating its good faith as a member of ASEAN, Singapore declared that it would establish a full diplomatic relationship with the People's Republic of China only if Indonesia chose to do so as well.[61]

The second symbolic universe, the Chinese diaspora, was too fragmented and isolated even to take notice of the tragedy. Malaysian Chinese, Thai Chinese, Philippine Chinese, and American Chinese were aware of what happened, but there was neither the infrastructure nor the resources to mount a transnational demonstration. The word *Chinese* qualified by Malaysian, Thai, Philippine, or American did not signify any underlying consciousness of ethnic or cultural identity; these terms were used generically to designate communities that were culturally and racially similar but were otherwise unrelated. It is ironic that it was the third symbolic universe—consisting primarily of non-Chinese students, scholars, and journalists who were committed, informed, and often sympathetic observers of things Chinese—that reacted most strongly to the holocaust and exposed it to the world at large.

Recent events have greatly improved the atmosphere for the Chinese in Southeast Asia, although the "Chinese question" continues to be a sensitive subject. In Malaysia and Indonesia, being Chinese remains a stigma; things Chinese, especially symbols of Chinese high culture such as the written script, are viewed with suspicion. The economic success of the Chinese makes them hungry for cultural expression, and the host countries, while tolerating their prosperity, are adamant about imposing cultural prohibitions. Signs of a Kaisalike solution to the conflict between political loyalty and cultural identity of Chinese in Malaysia and Indonesia are yet to be found.

After having been ostracized from the diplomatic community of ASEAN for more than a decade, Taiwan is now returning as an investment giant. Records show that Taiwanese investments in the Philippines, Malaysia, Thailand, and more recently Vietnam have increased dramatically and, in some cases, have surpassed Japanese investments by a respectable margin. Taiwan's presence in Indonesia is significant enough to have persuaded the Suharto government to relax its prohibition against Chinese schools, Chinese video cassettes, and publications in Chinese, which has inspired a new vitality in Indonesian Chinese communities. Furthermore, with the full collaboration of merchants of Chinese origin in Bangkok, Taiwanese capital has also contributed to the economic dynamism of Thailand. An obvious consequence for the second symbolic universe is the latent tension and visible conflict between Taiwan's economic strength and the mainland's political clout. The drama of competition between the mainland and Taiwan is not confined to ASEAN countries; the conflict is felt by Chinese communities in Tokyo, Paris, New York, San Francisco, Toronto, and Sydney. Although it is too early to tell whether a depoliticized cultural agenda will emerge as a result of this confrontation, it seems that Singapore may play a vital role in addressing economic and cultural issues and transcending the political animosity emanating from both sides of the Taiwan Straits. For example, by hosting the first international convention of Chinese entrepreneurs in 1991, the Chinese Chamber of Commerce of Singapore hoped to foster an institutional structure within which discourse on cultural China could proceed despite political differences.

Another example of the impact of the first symbolic universe on the second is the emigration of professionals from Hong Kong to North America and Australia. As 1997 draws near, Hong Kong emigrants with substantial capital and professional expertise are making their presence felt in Chinese communities in Toronto, Vancouver, Los Angeles, San Francisco, New York, and Sydney. This seems to be part of a broader pattern: Chinese immigrants in these cities are also coming from mainland China, Taiwan, Singapore, Malaysia, Indonesia, the Philippines, and Vietnam. What we are witnessing, then, is a new era in the Chinese diaspora.

This phenomenon, which historian Wang Gungwu, vice-chancellor of Hong Kong University, aptly describes as the remigration of Chinese to North America, Europe, and Australia, is unprecedented and requires closer examination.[62] These financially secure Malaysian, Indonesian, Filipino, and Vietnamese Chinese have ostensibly emigrated from their adopted homelands of several generations to escape from anti-Chinese discrimination. In other words, to escape the pressure to assimilate imposed by the new nation-states of Southeast Asia and to preserve a measure of Chineseness for their descendants, they have opted to emigrate to modern Western-style nations with strong democratic traditions of human rights, freedom of speech, thought, religion, and assembly, and due process of law. By disappearing into a big country, the reasoning goes, they can avoid becoming targets of discrimination, and they and their children will have a better chance of making a decent living and of keeping their Chineseness. The irony of their not returning to their ancestral homeland but moving farther away from China with the explicit intention of preserving their cultural identity seems perplexing, but as Wang Gungwu perceptively remarks, the transformation from a sojourner mentality to deliberate emigration is a new phenomenon.[63]

As recently as the 1960s, the decision to renounce Chinese nationality (whether Nationalist or Communist) and to take up local citizenship was, for many Chinese in the diaspora, an agonizing matter.[64] The massive exodus of many of the most brilliant Chinese intellectuals from the mainland during the last decade clearly shows that the civilization-state has lost much of its grip on the Chinese intelligentsia, and the Tiananmen tragedy may have irreversibly severed the emotional attachment of the diaspora Chinese to the homeland. The meaning of being Chinese, an issue that has haunted Chinese intellectuals for at least three generations, has taken on entirely new dimensions. The conscious and, for some, impulsive choice to realize one's Chineseness by moving far from one's homeland is one of them. Yet the sojourner mentality lingers on. *Shijie ribao* (World Journal), arguably the most widely circulated Chinese-language newspaper in the Chinese diaspora, in its obituary of Qian Gechuan, professor emeritus of English literature at National Taiwan University, states forthrightly that he was a genuine Chinese because for eighteen years as a New York resident he dutifully kept on renewing his Republic of China passport; this was regarded as a clear manifestation of his faith in and commitment to the legitimacy of the Nationalist government in Taiwan.[65]

PARADOX

In 1988, plans for the publication of a monthly magazine bearing the name *Wenhua Zhongguo* (Cultural China) were made by a group of Hong Kong–based Chinese intellectuals who had extensive professional connections in Beijing. The idea of simultaneous publication in Hong Kong, Beijing, and Taipei was explored and concrete steps taken for implementation. An international advisory board involving scholars primarily of Chinese origin from the mainland, Hong Kong, Taiwan, Singapore, and North America was also organized. Even though the Tiananmen tragedy of June 1989 derailed the plan, at least temporarily, the very undertaking signals the emergence of a transnational Chinese intellectual community.[66]

The term "cultural China," coined in the last decade or so and often seen in intellectual journals outside mainland China, is itself an indication of the emergence of a "common awareness" (*gongshi*) among Chinese intellectuals throughout the world. The presence of such an awareness prior to the opening up of mainland China in the late 1970s is made clear in the deliberate use of *huaren* (people of Chinese origin) rather than *Zhongguoren* (citizens of the Chinese state) to designate people of a variety of nationalities who are ethnically and culturally Chinese.[67] *Huaren* is not geopolitically centered, for it indicates a common ancestry and a shared cultural background, whereas *Zhongguoren* necessarily evokes obligations and loyalties of political affiliation and the myth of the Central Country. By emphasizing cultural roots, Chinese intellectuals in Taiwan, Hong Kong, and North America hoped to build a transnational network to explore the meaning of being Chinese in a global context. For these intellectuals, the relevant political center that influenced their lives was the Nationalist government in Taiwan. Their efforts to depoliticize the cultural movement were an attempt to maintain a critical distance from the official anti-Communist line of the Guomindang (the Nationalist Party).

The "patriotic" events that unfolded first in North America and then in Hong Kong and Taiwan, commonly known as the Diaoyu-tai Movement, in the early 1970s, was as much an anti-Guomindang as an anti-Japanese protest. The coalition forged by Chinese of different political persuasions, linguistic groups, and social backgrounds in the United States to show moral indignation toward the perceived Japanese encroachment upon a small island chain between Japan and Taiwan, regarded as legitimate Chinese territory, strongly suggests that the symbols of *huaren* were powerful enough to form a unity in diversity without appealing to an existing geopolitical center. The inability of the Nationalist government in Taiwan, fearful of straining relationships with Japan, to steer the Diaoyutai Movement away from anti-Guomindang activities may give the impression that leftists sympathetic to Beijing were behind the movement; but the ability of the student organizers to enlist the support of virtually all Chinese communities in North America and the lack of any evidence that Beijing even knew about the nature of the movement suggest otherwise. Beijing may have been the beneficiary, for the movement did mobilize human and material resources that were helpful for its international policy, yet the underlying cooperative spirit of the Diaoyutai Movement was grounded in culture and ethnicity in a way that was not easily manipulated by any political interest group.

In the 1980s, with the advent of mainland China as an active participant in the discourse on cultural China, the symbol of *huaren* assumed a new significance: how could overseas Chinese help the homeland to modernize? On the intellectual side, an unintended consequence of Deng Xiaoping's economic reforms was "cultural fever," brought on by the revival of communication in the social sciences and humanities between scholars in mainland China on the one hand, and Hong Kong, Taiwan, Singapore (the first symbolic universe), the Chinese diaspora (the second symbolic universe), and North America, Japan, and Europe (the third symbolic universe), on the other. The Diaoyutai mentality, a commitment to the dignity of China as a civilization and a critique of political regimes that privatized the public sphere for their own interests, reemerged as a defining characteristic of the "common awareness" of Chinese intellectuals. The Tiananmen tragedy of June 4, 1989, symbolizes the near-total alienation of the Chinese intelligentsia from the ruling minority on the mainland. It is highly unlikely that the political regime that brutally massacred peaceful demonstrators and bystanders will ever win back the hearts and minds of the intellectuals and those citizens who are committed to the dignity of China as a civilization.

The potential for mainland intellectuals to perceive their mission as cultural transmitters rather than political propagandists, as guardians of the well-being of the people rather than party functionaries, and as articulators of universal human values rather than servants of the state, a potential that has been brilliantly realized time and again by heroic individuals since the April Fifth Movement of 1976,[68] was, nevertheless, for most of a generation, not even an imagined possibility. The fate of the Chinese intelligentsia in the People's Republic of China unavoidably elicits the horrifying question, how could the scholar, honored as a paradigm of the personality ideal in Chinese culture, have stooped so low for so long?

The answer, in part, lies in the coexistence of political nationalism and cultural iconoclasm among the most articulate intellectual elite. The decline of China, for centuries the Central Country, to being the "Sick Man of East Asia" in just two generations (from the Opium War of 1839 to the collapse of the Hundred Days' Reform in 1898), in conjunction with the disintegration of the Chinese political order, created such spiritual turmoil among the Chinese intelligentsia that the reconstruction of a political center became an overriding concern. Intent on creating the optimal conditions for China to recapture its position of wealth and power, Westernized intellectuals launched a frontal attack on the Confucian tradition: Confucianism was perceived to have nurtured a "national character" (*guominxing*) detrimental to China's modernization. The desire to increase China's chance of survival was therefore linked to an all-out attack on the tradition that had shaped Chineseness throughout history.

Their assertion—that we must totally reject that which has made us who we are—enabled the most forward-looking Chinese intellectuals to be receptive to foreign ideologies while still maintaining their nationalist objectives. The May Fourth patriots experienced a keen sense of liberation when they confronted the national crisis by embracing virtually all major Western philosophical currents of thought, including Dewey's pragmatism, Bergson's vitalism, Bakunin's anarchism, and Russell's empiricism and logicism. What was conspicuously absent was any persuasive form of fundamentalism or nativism that glorified Chinese culture for its own sake. However, underlying this intellectual

commitment to alien Western values was a powerful surge of fundamentalist and nativist sentiments, which throughout the country was
dangerously volatile among the Chinese populace.

An unintended and unfortunate consequence of this period of
wholesale Westernization and anti-Confucianism was the marginalization of the intelligentsia from the center of the political arena. The
thrust of their intellectual quest was the establishment of a political center; yet such a focus relegated them to the background. Furthermore,
their demand for action was so overwhelming that the seeds of their
own decline were embedded in the logic of the intellectual discourse.
Hu Shi (1891–1962), the American-educated liberal thinker, may have
discovered the pernicious implications of the rhetoric on ideology for
the liberal exchange of ideas, but his advocacy of a problem-solving
attitude was easily drowned out by impassioned pleas for this or that
"ism" to save the nation. It is not surprising that Marxism-Leninism
triumphed in the marketplace of ideologies; it met the requirements of
both cultural iconoclasts and political nationalists: it was Western to
the core as the cultural iconoclasts had strongly recommended, and its
anti-imperialist stance was precisely what the political nationalists had
demanded.

What the Chinese intelligentsia did not expect—and is still struggling to understand—is that inherent in the Marxist-Leninist-Maoist
praxis is the assertion that the Party is not only the embodiment of
socialist truth but also the bearer of the correct method for its eventual
realization. The birth of the Chinese Communist Party, mainly in response to the intellectuals' aspiration, seemed to offer the perfect match
of cultural iconoclasm and political nationalism. The actual struggle
undertaken by the masses (the peasants, the workers, and the soldiers)
was too rooted in Chinese soil to benefit from a sophisticated intellectual consciousness framed in Western liberal democratic terms. The rise
of Mao Zedong to the trinity of political leader, ideological teacher,
and moral exemplar, though unprecedented in Chinese history, can be
explained in terms of a fundamentalist-nativist challenge to the Westernization process as envisioned by the May Fourth intellectuals. In
examining Mao Zedong's ideology we find, among other things, a combination of iconoclasm and nationalism; however, the iconoclasm is
layered with numerous sediments of nativist pathos, and the nationalism is imbued with fundamentalist claims to China's uniqueness. Since

his death, Chinese intellectuals may have radically changed their minds about Mao as the savior of the Chinese people, but for decades they were awed by his sagacity and, on occasion, charmed by his earthiness. The demonic power of destruction, which Mao unleashed repeatedly, stunned the intellectuals to such a degree that they lost their ability even to describe it. Indeed, they have yet to develop adequate conceptual frameworks to analyze that phenomenon, including their own roles as participants (willing or otherwise) and as victims.

Collective amnesia is so pervasive in China that the national memory has difficulty extending back even to the decade of the Cultural Revolution (1966–1976), let alone to the disaster of the Great Leap Forward (1958–1960) or the brutality of the Anti-Rightist Campaign (1957–1958). Virtually all intellectuals of note were purged during the Anti-Rightist campaign that followed the short-lived domestic liberalization in the wake of Khrushchev's de-Stalinization in the Soviet Union. The Great Leap Forward—an ill-conceived utopian experiment intended to enable China to surpass the West in industrial productivity within fifteen years—in combination with natural disasters led to mass starvation, killing an estimated 30 million people.[69] Subsequently, neither the Party, nor the leadership, nor Mao was held accountable. Indeed, Mao, disgusted with the inertia of the leadership and the bureaucratism of the Party, managed to rouse the Chinese youth to a crescendo of iconoclasm and nationalism by launching the Cultural Revolution in 1966. The dramaturgy of the Red Guards, composed of the zealous, the repressed, and the naive, shamelessly displayed all the nativist sediments and fundamentalist claims of the Chinese psyche. To paraphrase a depiction of Lu Xun's consciousness, the gate of darkness was opened and hell broke loose. Iconoclasm was decoded to mean "rebellion is justified," and nationalism degenerated into cannibalistic tribalism against fellow Chinese. Yet, as some of the most perceptive minds in China have confessed, their faith in the truth of Marxism-Leninism, in the credibility of the Chinese Communist leadership, and in the legitimacy of the Party was not shaken until the mid-1980s.[70]

Traditionally, in the Confucian symbolic universe, the cultural elite never fully identified itself with the ruling minority. No matter how powerful the emperor, he always relied upon his chief ministers to administer the central bureaucracy, the gentry to exercise local control, and the comprehensive ritual system involving the participation of Heaven, gods, and ancestors to rule the land. It was taken for granted that political power and cultural influence were separable. The respected teachers in the realm, though marginal to the center of power, were often more influential than the ministers. Moreover, through control of classical learning, scholars monopolized the most important channels of upward social mobility. In addition, even illiterate parents performed vital functions in society as oral transmitters of education.

The intellectuals, either as scholar-officials or as members of the local gentry, tapped a rich wellspring of symbolic resources to define their worth. They acted as cultural transmitters because they were the guardians of the cumulative tradition that set standards of inspiration for the civilized world; they represented the well-being of the people because while they were trained to become the most articulate members of society, they were meant to be neither philosophers nor prophets but the conscience of the multitude; and they styled themselves as emissaries of the Mandate of Heaven, which always "sees as the people see and hears as the people hear."[71] This highly idealized and seemingly romanticized view of the traditional Confucian intellectual serves to make a critical point: only recently could the *zhishi fenzi* (intellectuals, a modern term, literally meaning "knowledgeable elements") in mainland China even begin to imagine what was taken as the birthright of the *ru* (scholar or minister of the moral order).[72] Understandably, what would have been considered highly routinized Confucian expressions of political protest in imperial China are often viewed with awe as a courageous act of defiance against the all-powerful state in the People's Republic of China. The total politicization of culture and the totalization of the political process, as manifested in the notorious *danwei* (work unit) system, destroyed any healthy space between culture and politics. As a result, the intellectual lost his or her bearings as cultural transmitter, conscience of the people, and emissary of Heaven.

It is therefore instructive to note that the simplistic dichotomies culture/politics, public/private, intelligentsia/ruling minority, and good/evil became lived realities in the spring of 1989. For the first time, Chinese intellectuals worldwide developed a truly new, communal, critical self-consciousness, in which the agenda of iconoclasm and nationalism is reversed; a search for cultural roots and a commitment to a form of depoliticized humanism became a strong voice in the discourse on cultural China.

PROSPECTS

China has witnessed much destructiveness and violence in her modern transformation. The agonizing question for us all in the three symbolic universes is raised with great pungency by Stevan Harrell: "Why does a culture that condemns violence, that plays down the glory of military exploits, awards its highest prestige to literary, rather than martial, figures, and seeks harmony over all other values, in fact display such frequency and variety of violent behavior, that is of the use of physical force against persons?"[73] Echoing Harrell's puzzlement and frustration, Andrew Nathan, in a thought-provoking review essay, cites the condemnation of the authors of the aforementioned *River Elegy*: "What Confucian culture has given us over the past several thousand years is not a national spirit of enterprise, a system of laws, or a mechanism of cultural renewal, but a fearsome self-killing machine that, as it degenerated, constantly devoured its best and its brightest, its own vital elements."[74] This is reminiscent of Lu Xun's bitter satire against the Confucian legacy, which he mordantly denounced as cannibalistic ritualism.[75]

Lu Xun's distress over the human condition in China was truly exercised when he learned about the massacre of 47 demonstrating young patriots in Peking (Beiping) on March 18, 1926: "I am always ready to think the worst of my fellow countrymen, but I could neither conceive nor believe that we could stoop to such despicable barbarism."[76] As an afterthought or, perhaps, a desperate attempt to make some sense of a senseless situation, Lu Xun philosophized: "As for any deeper significance, I think there is very little; for this was only an unarmed demonstration. The history of mankind's battle forward through bloodshed is like the formation of coal, where a great deal of wood is needed to produce a small amount of coal."[77] This caustic remark, tinged with a strong elitist hue, prompted Andrew Nathan to conclude his insightful article with a rhetorical question: "Much human wood lies under the ground of Chinese history, but how much coal?"[78] In the aftermath of the Tiananmen tragedy, Nathan was truthfully reporting "the consensus of Chinese outside officialdom": the answer to the loaded question, What has been acquired in exchange for all this misery, is plainly "nothing."[79]

In retrospect, what the Chinese intelligentsia has collectively experi-

enced in the twentieth century is what Mark Elvin pointedly characterizes as the "double disavowal" of both Confucianism and Marxism.[80]
The same indignation that Lu Xun's generation felt about Confucian
authoritarianism is now being expressed against Marxist totalitarianism. Many intellectuals strongly believe that the collusion of the feudal
past and the socialist present makes China a victim of a double betrayal. This conviction explains the vehemence with which the authors
of *River Elegy* attacked the Confucian legacy and their enthusiastic embrace of the modern West. The matter, however, is complicated: the
real challenge to mainland Chinese intellectuals is not the modern West
per se, but the modern West mediated through industrial East Asia.
Surely the Yellow River must flow into the blue sea, but as it enters the
ocean, it first encounters the Pacific.

While Lu Xun's generation, despite Spengler's warning, never entertained the possibility of a path to modernity other than Westernization, the authors and producers of *River Elegy* could not but explore
courses of action more congenial to the Chinese situation. If Japan,
South Korea, Taiwan, Hong Kong, Singapore, and Chinese communities throughout the world have shown not only the relevance of Confucian ethics to their modus operandi but also the dynamics of the
Confucian tradition in shaping their forms of life, then the existential
predicament of the mainland intellectual caught between a contempt-
ible past and a brutal present is not indissoluble. Notwithstanding that
"the inner strength of the Chinese intelligentsia has been sapped by the
collusion of feudal Chinese traditionalism (the remnants of a politicized Confucian moralism) and the modern Western collectivism (the
outmoded practice of Leninist dictatorship),"[81] the fruitful interaction
between Confucian humanism and democratic liberalism in cultural
China has already occurred. The authors and producers of *River Elegy*,
some now as scholars in exile, have also begun to explore traditional
symbolic resources (including those in Confucian humanism) in order
to reformulate their strategy for China's cultural reconstruction.[82]

The so-called "Third Epoch of Confucian Humanism"[83] may have
been the wishful thinking of a small coterie of academics, but the emergence of a new, inclusive humanism with profound ethical-religious
implications for the spiritual self-definition of humanity, the sanctity
of the earth, and a form of religiousness based on immanent transcendence has already been placed on the agenda in cultural China. The

real challenge to this new humanism is the Enlightenment mentality of the modern West narrowly conceived—an aggressive anthropocentrism, informed by instrumental rationality and fueled by a Faustian drive to conquer and destroy. Although the modern West has created virtually all major spheres of value for the twentieth century (a partial list includes science, technology, the free market, democratic institutions, metropolises, and mass communication), the painful realization that it has also pushed humanity to the brink of self-destruction engenders much food for thought. The question of whether humankind is, in fact, a viable species is being asked with an increasing sense of urgency.

It is ironic that, for the first half of the twentieth century, a major concern of Chinese political leaders—notably Sun Yat-sen, Chiang Kai-shek, and Mao Zedong—was the very survival of the children of the Yellow Emperor. The fear, far from that of a population explosion, was actually the depletion of the Chinese race in the Social Darwinian sense. With a view toward the future, notwithstanding the danger of evoking fears of the "Yellow Peril," we need to ask, what form of life should the Chinese pursue that is not only commensurate with human flourishing but also sustainable in ecological and environmental terms? Of course, in helping the Chinese to articulate this critical concern, we need also heed the prophetic warning of Edwin Reischauer: "Americans, Europeans, and Japanese on a per capita basis are polluting the world and using up its resources at a rate anywhere from 10 to 15 times higher than the citizens of the less developed nations."[84] That observation was made in 1973; we may now want to add in the negative contribution to the environment and the ecosystem that the Four Mini-Dragons, with their economic miracles, have made in the last two decades.

What mainland China eventually will become remains an overriding concern for all intellectuals in cultural China. She may try to become a mercantilist state with a vengeance; she may continue to be mired in inertia and inefficiency for years to come; or she may modernize according to a new holistic humanist vision. Saddled with a population burden approaching 1.2 billion, can this state succeed at any of these ambitions without finding a workable means to liberate the energies of the people? Although realistically those who are on the periphery (the second and third symbolic universes plus Taiwan, Hong Kong, and Singapore) are seemingly helpless to affect any fundamental transformation of China proper, the center no longer has the ability, insight, or legitimate authority to dictate the agenda for cultural China. On the contrary, the transformative potential of the periphery is so great that it seems inevitable that it will significantly shape the intellectual discourse on cultural China for years to come. It is perhaps premature to announce that "the center is nowhere, the periphery is everywhere,"[85] but undeniably, the fruitful interaction of a variety of economic, political, social, and cultural forces at work along the periphery will continue to shape the dynamics of cultural China.

The exodus of many of the most brilliant minds from the mainland, the emigration of Chinese professionals from Hong Kong, and the remigration of middle-class Chinese from Southeast Asia to North America and Australia suggest that it is neither shameful nor regrettable to alienate oneself voluntarily from a political regime that has become culturally insensitive, publicly unaccountable, and oppressive to basic human rights. The meaning of being Chinese is basically not a political question; it is a human concern pregnant with ethical-religious implications.

Is it possible to live a meaningful life as a Chinese individual if the dignity of one's humanity is lost? Does citizenship in a Chinese polity guarantee one's Chineseness? As a precondition for maintaining one's Chineseness, is it necessary to become a fully participating citizen of one's adopted country? While the overseas Chinese (the second symbolic universe) may seem forever peripheral to the meaning of being Chinese, can they assume an effective role in creatively constructing a new vision of Chineseness that is more in tune with Chinese history and in sympathetic resonance with Chinese culture? Is it possible or even desirable for someone in the third symbolic universe who is not proficient in the Chinese language and who has no Chinese family ties of birth or marriage to acquire an understanding of Chinese culture such that he or she can greatly shape the intellectual discourse on cultural China and significantly contribute to the definition of being Chinese? An obvious No to the first two and a resounding Yes to each of the remaining questions, and an understanding of the implications of these answers, will give rich texture to the provocative inquiry into the meaning of being Chinese.

2

The Inner World of 1830

Mark Elvin

If we are to understand what it means to be "Chinese" today, we need some conception of what it meant to be Chinese around 1830, before the Western invasion of Chinese culture. This essay, therefore, sketches an impression of the inner world of thought and feeling that has been— variously—transformed, distorted, and destroyed in the modern age. It focuses on a few crucial domains of perception and emotion, and on their internal complexities and seeming contradictions, since it is rare that any simple formula can do justice to the subtleties of the Chinese experience.

The categories examined are: the concepts of causation, both material and moral, to the limited extent that these two aspects can be disentangled; the central cultural dream or inspirational "story" that gave meaning to the Confucian life, both public and private—again to the extent that these two domains can be separated; the two basic concepts of the "self"—Confucian and Daohist-Buddhist; the interplay of what was seen as conventional and what as fundamental in Chinese and any society; the conceptions of political action and of social discipline (sometimes mistakenly labelled "law"); the governing ideas of the nature of technology and economics, and of scholarship. The sketch ends with a consideration of intellectual recreations, seen as an indication of the kind of mental activity that was appreciated and understood.

Conveying the feeling, and the believability, of another "inner world" is difficult within a limited compass. The methods of the novel-

ist, rather than those of the conventional historian, are often best suited
to this task. The compromise adopted here is to treat one topic, namely
the relatively unfamiliar one of the perception of causation, more ex-
pansively than the others in the hope that it may, to some extent, serve
as an illustration of what would be possible given more time (on the
part of the reader) and more space (on the part of the publisher).

The approach used here is also unconventional. Quite simply, the
thought world of a single remarkable novel, Lii Rurzhen's* *Destinies
of the Flowers in the Mirror,*[1] is summoned back into a fleeting re-
existence. There are three reasons for going about the matter in this
way. The book is a microcosm of the educated Chinese mind around
the year 1830, when it was published. It is also self-aware, to the extent that it could be described as imaginative armchair anthropology;
the Chinese were already conscious, by this time, of being "Chinese."
Last, it constrains interpretative fancy by compelling a systematic look
at everything that is in it, and inhibiting that scholarship *en brochette*
that takes a morsel from here and a morsel from there simply as it feels
inclined.

The *Flowers* is a mixture of fantasy and realism, of iconoclasm and
conventionality. Swiftian irony tears at such conventionally accepted
horrors as the binding of women's feet at the same time as a most un-
ironic enthusiasm exalts accepted virtues like filial piety and loyalty to a
superior. It extols Confucianism and the drama of the world history of
humanity unfolding uniquely in China since the time of the sages. It de-
values it by subordinating it to the vision of a reincarnational Daohism
that sees our earthly lives as mere repetitive forays into the arena of
illusion. Its purported setting is the reign of the usurper Empress Wuu
in the seventh century; but the society it shows is that of the late eighteenth and early nineteenth centuries. The viewpoints supported by its
characters frequently differ from one another, clearly as a result of the
author's intent, not inadvertence, and define the polarities of problems,
not fixed positions.

The book's structure is a single cycle of life, symbolizing one turn
of the wheel of reincarnation. The human world is shown as embedded

---

*Tonalized *pinyin* is used here for transcription. The rising and falling tones are
marked by the postvocalic insertion of a silent *r* and silent *h* respectively. The low dip-
ping tone is marked by doubling the main vowel, as in the convention already used for
Shaanxi province. Standard forms may be recovered simply by omitting these additions.

within a supernatural world that is all around it, yet at the same time almost wholly hidden. The celestial story opens in Heaven. As a punishment for a misdemeanor, the Spirits of the Flowers, and the Immortal of the Hundred Flowers, who rules them, are scattered to live as mortal girls in the world below. The first half of the earthly story is set in the strange "Lands Beyond the Seas," sociological foils to China, where Tarng the Roamer, a disillusioned official now searching for immortality, gains merits by gathering together the separated flower spirits. The second half takes place in China, the "Land Within the Seas." The reunited sisterhood of the young ladies triumphs in the first imperial examinations for women (a historical fiction, of course), and thereafter celebrates at a prolonged party at the Capital, which becomes for a moment an Earthly Paradise. Their leader is Tarng's daughter, originally Little Hill, now renamed Servant of Tarng, the incarnation of the once and future Immortal of the Hundred Flowers. The book closes with the war of the loyalists of the Tarng dynasty against the Empress, and the break of the sisterhood even as victory is being won. A few depart to illustrious careers. Many more commit virtuous suicide to follow their slain warrior-husbands. Two pass back directly to immortality. For all, their time in the human world is done.

To take such a mixture of fantasy and polemic as a guide to psychological reality clearly has its hazards. It is to be hoped that it proves its worth in practice.

CAUSALITY

There was a lack of rigor in the Chinese universe. Rules could be broken precisely because they were not laws of nature. A drama of rewards and punishments based on karma ran through all sentient action, human and nonhuman alike, but—in contrast to the Buddhism from which it was borrowed—it was more bureaucratic than inexorable.

The Immortal of the Hundred Flowers is asked, at the birthday party of the Queen Mother of the West, to make all species of flower bloom at the same time. She refuses this as improper:

"God on High gives strict orders for flowers, and He checks up in the most minute detail. An illustrated register has to be submitted a month in advance, showing all the flowers supposed to open a month later. All such matters as an increase, or reduction, in the stamens or petals, or a change of colors, have to wait for His decision. God tells the Jade Maiden Cloaked in Fragrance to make an attentive decision. . . .

"If a flower has been without error, this is noted in the Cloud Tallies and the Golden Memoranda. The year following, it is moved, perhaps inside some carven balustrade, or to the front of some decorated doorway, so that it may be fed on pure soil, be watered from a clear spring, attract the admiration of poets, and give pleasure to distinguished guests. . . .

"If there are some who transgress, the Magical Inquisitor asks in a memorial that separate decrees be issued for the punishment of each. In the most serious cases, a flower . . . will have to bear with people pulling it up, or snapping it off. . . .

"Since there are all these sorts of inspection, I can only pay heed, humble Immortal that I am, to the orders that I receive. I dare not act irregularly." (1:5)

Some of the other Immortals disagree, by no means believing that it is impossible to act contrary to Heaven.

With a twist characteristic of court politics, the Immortal of the Hundred Flowers is then spitefully predestined to be guilty of being responsible for a breach of the very principles she holds dear. In due course her flowers obey the order of the earthly Empress to bloom all at once in winter, and for this the Immortal, since she bears the responsibility though she herself gave no such command, is punished. The point is that preserving the celestial hierarchy preempts the preservation of the natural order.

This view of a universe operating through a bureaucratic and hence somewhat capricious causation conflicted with another conception, namely that causes worked automatically, even calculably. These two views appear side by side in a discussion about thunder held during the party:

"Mathematicians often boast without justification," said Jade Brooch, "and make everything into the opposite of what it is."

"That's not true," retorted Orchid Fragrance. "I can even calculate from how many miles away this thunder is coming."

[She] . . . pointed to a chiming clock on the table and said: "Simply look at the second hand. Then it can be calculated."

An instant later there was a flash. A short while afterward came the rumble of thunder.

"The thunder arrived here 15 seconds after the flash," observed Jade Iris. "Work it out, elder sister."

Orchid Fragrance did some figuring. Then she said:

"It's a fixed rule that in one second the sound of thunder travels 1285 feet and seven inches [Chinese measure]. If we reckon on this basis, the thunder was ten miles and 1280 feet distant [1285.5]."....

Some time later the sky became very calm. The husband of Precious Cloud's old wet nurse had just brought two jars of Cloud-Mist tea ... so she asked him how things were at home....

"If you do wicked things," the man replied, "you may fool people, but don't forget the Thunder God can pay you back if you do wrong. There was a storm just now at Ten Mile Hamlet. A clap of thunder ... struck a man dead.... He was a bad man, who did every sort of wickedness."

"How far away is Ten Mile Hamlet?" asked White Cloud.

"Only ten miles from here," answered the wet nurse's husband. "He was struck down a little more than half a mile outside it." (79:589–90)

The scientific method is, in a rough sense, latent in Fragrant Orchid's point of view, and this mixture of "modern" with "premodern" elements is characteristic of many aspects of late imperial China.

The characters in the book are also persistently concerned with how far future events are predetermined. They often make remarks such as, "Since the ethers and numbers [i.e., fate] were as they were, there was nothing to be done about it." Omens are an obsession, being seen as transtemporal links between the future and the present. Much of the drama in the second half of the novel comes from the working out of the cryptic prophecies that Little Hill has found on a stele in Little Pernglair, a lesser Land of the Immortals. Late in the party, a mysterious Daohist nun appears and tells the girls: "Today's gathering is in no way accidental. The karmic forces at work in it cannot be told in a short space of time." Then she recites to them a long, riddling poem partly about the past and partly about the future. She tells them that "the slightest trifles are predetermined from the beginning," and concludes with two somewhat scientific metaphors: "In all these cases the roots determine the blossoms, just as the magnet is drawn toward the iron." (90:687–88)

Many Chinese believed that the otherwise fated course of events *could* be altered. One technique was that of sepulchral geomancy, that is to say, the art of improving one's own fortune by burying the remains of one's parents or grandparents in a site suitably selected to tap the forces running in the veins of the earth. Many years often passed with the bones unburied while a descendant looked for the perfect location. Lii Rurzhen has one of his characters from the Land of Gentlemen attack this practice with a typically Confucian blend of skeptical rationality, familistic ethics, concern for the prudential management of life, an appeal to the Confucian scriptures as reliable authorities for facts on which arguments could be grounded, and belief in the magical power of moral behavior:

"Don't men who are skilled in geomancy have parents? If they find a good location, why don't they keep it for their own use? If it is the case that, having found such a place, they can advance in the world, then consider—how many skilled in geomancy have in fact done well for themselves? . . .

"None of these people understand that 'if a man has been great, the ground he lies in will be magically efficacious.' . . . The grave mounds of the sage-king Furxi, of King Wern, and of Confucius all grow milfoil that has a high degree of magical efficacy for oracular prediction [by casting its stalks]. The quality of the milfoil found elsewhere is less good, and the omen taking not so effective. . . .

"These days people choose a shady spot [that is, one dominated by the Dark or Female Principle] because they want their sons and grandsons to prosper. . . . If we consider flourishing and decay, then in the case of the lineage of Duke Lih of Chern . . . there was the oracle of 'male and female phoenix in flight, singing like tinkling bells.' . . . Was this caused by fate, or by ground dominated by the Female Principle? Since the oracle spoke of events that were to come, it is evident that the excellence, or otherwise, of ground dominated by the Female Principle had no effect. In general, in the affairs of this world, only great goodness can convert a [predestined] disaster into good fortune." (12:72)

An example of this last point is provided during a later discussion of astrology by "the response of Heaven-Nature to a moral influence," with the result that the visible brightness of the constellations changes, and the otherwise correctly predicted demise of the Empress Wuu is postponed for a few years. (57:426–27) Even a generation or so after the *Flowers* was written the real Chinese Emperor was still issuing decrees in the tradition of what may be called "meteorological religion," apologetically linking bad weather to his own lack of virtuous conduct.

The belief in the magical powers of morality to affect the fate of the individual was also deeply rooted. When the merchant Seafarer Lirn and the helmsman-scholar Duo the Ninth discuss this, Lirn says that if a tiger eats a man this is always because "his previous lives determined that he should suffer in the tiger's jaws." Duo disagrees, arguing that tigers only eat men if their own immoral behavior, in this life, has made them the equivalent of beasts. If the virtuous appear to suffer, this can only be because their outer goodness is a sham that conceals a secret wrongdoing. (10:61)

Later, though, Job's problem is confronted in a different way. The following conversation takes place between the Daohist nun and Little Spring:

Little Spring: If all of us sisters are going to die so many sorts of ill-omened death, can it really be that every one of us has done some sin in her lifetime great enough to meet with such retribution?

Nun: If it is tragic to be disembowelled, would you argue that in ancient times Lord Gan of Bii [put to death by the evil last emperor of the Shang on account of his honest criticisms] also committed some sin? To those in this universe who are endowed with feelings of loyalty and purity, the question of whether they live or die is irrelevant.

Little Spring: There are always many good people in this world who, even so, do not come to a good end, and some bad people enjoy excellent fortunes. What does this mean?

Nun: It is said in *The Analects* that "the superior person's anxiety is that he may die without leaving a good name behind him." . . . If one merely schemes to save one's own neck, one leaves behind a foul repute for many years afterward. . . . Isn't it better to meet death with a smile, and leave behind a good name in perpetuity? (90:687–88)

Others of the girls then join the debate, but the issue is not resolved.

Virtue had its own powers. Thus, Helmsman Duo recounts how his intensely filial great-grandfather cured his great-great-grandmother's dysentery by the traditional means of making her a soup from a piece cut out of his own thigh, and later obtained the prescription for a cure for a relapse from an immortal on a nearby mountain as a result of his filial self-torture. (27:195) The hagiographical chapters of the local histories of the Mirng and Qing dynasties are full of similar tales of such devotion. These *miracula* had the social status of facts, and were ethically "rational."

The nature of the interaction between the physical world and human actions, moral or immoral, was nonetheless controversial. During the Hahn dynasty, a Judas tree belonging to the Tiarn family was said to have withered when they were at the point of committing an offense against the ideals of kinship—dividing up the family property and separating—but to have recovered when they changed their minds and stayed together. Orchid Talk comments on this:

"You can hardly argue that the tree had a certain knowledge of human affairs, and died merely because they were about to split up the family property. It happened simply as the result of a blast of perversely violent matter-energy-vitality that emanated from the Tiarn family on this occasion." (71:522)

Purple Mushroom counters with the more conventional view that "the Judas tree . . . itself desired to die, so as to warn them." Orchid Talk reasserts her materialism based on the idea of matter-energy-vitality:

"From ancient times down to the present day, a great deal of family property has been divided up. Why have we never heard of other families having a tree warn them not to do it? . . . Even if trees and grasses have the power of consciousness, they are definitely not going to put an end to their own lives to 'rescue others by falling into the well themselves.'"

Purple Mushroom then asks why violent matter-energy-vitality has not been emitted when other families have divided up their property. Orchid Talk replies that these things are unknowable as "violent matter-energy-vitality is something without form," but the fact that the tree later came back to life shows that "harmonious matter-energy-vitality causes good fortune." (71:522)

The weakness in the analysis made by the young ladies is not a lack of rationality, but an inadequate repertoire of facts and an inadequate notion of what a fact might be. They work as best they can with historical and scriptural data they cannot validate, and with their own experiences. A "fact" is a complex cultural creation that only fully emerged in the West during the seventeenth century, and its absence in China may have been linked with the different conceptions of trial and evidence in the two cultures.

Ethical rationality was, however, incomplete. Magical powers could emanate from evil sources as well as from good ones, and good and bad could be mixed up in ways that a Westerner can find confusing. An example is the episode in which Little Hill (the reincarnated Immortal of the Hundred Flowers) and her companions are captured by four demons who have the intention of fermenting them into "naked-body wine." They are rescued by a nun who is the Immortal of the Hundred

Fruits, a close friend from a previous life, in disguise. She reveals that the demons are the emanations of four fruit pips that once lodged in the mouths, respectively, of an ancient femme fatale, a catamite minister, a virtuous and many-talented statesman, and a disciple of Confucius. The influences of two depraved and of two highly moral historical figures have alike nourished evil. The only difference is that the first two demons can assume the actual faces of these personages who "used their physical beauty to seduce their lords into delusion," whereas the others have to be content with faces that resemble an orange and a date. (46:336–37)

Particular evils were not seen as the manifestations of a central source of evil. They were widespread and harmful, like diseases or dangerous animals. There was no Master Adversary behind them. Yarnluor, ruler of the Chinese hells, was not a tempter but a judge, and part of a single celestial-infernal supernatural bureaucracy.

If the source of moral destruction lay anywhere it was, in the late traditional Chinese view, deep in the self of the individual as a sort of "original weakness." This can be seen at the end of the novel, when the loyalist warriors who have married the reincarnated flower spirits attempt to overthrow the Empress Wuu. To reach the Capital they have to pass through four "enchantments of self-destruction" conjured up against them by the Empress's brothers. These four are wine, anger, women, and money. Most of the warriors cannot resist the allurements of these four temptations and bring their own deaths upon themselves. When Hero Lirn loses his temper with an insolent waiter in a restaurant, "in an instant the nameless fires inside him drew forth the evil in the enchantment. . . . He tripped, toppled over, and lost consciousness." (98:751–52) In the fourth enchantment, beneath a huge golden coin suspended in space there is a multitude of people of every class engaged in every sort of evil for the sake of gain, and the corpses of the destroyed lie about in heaps. In some respects it resembles Bunyan's *Vanity Fair*, but what is different is that it is an illusion, a conjurer's spell, and power to resist the seduction can come only from a lonely personal moral fortitude, or the piercing vision of enlightened understanding. (99:757) Delusion is the principal proximate cause of evil. The Daohist Nun tells the girls at the party:

"The life of a person in this world is a thousand schemes, a thousand anxieties. He gambles for victory and struggles to be the strongest. Illusion follows illusion as he dies and is born again. It is no more than a game of chess. Because he cannot see through this soul-befuddling spell, he is deluded by it." (90:689)

And this, she adds of the novel itself, is the "main theme of this dream."

The last problem is that of free will. One immortal tells the Immortal of the Hundred Flowers that she was punished because she neither controlled herself nor fulfilled her duties (6:33), and this implies that she had the freedom to do so. Nonetheless, individuals come into the world with different "predestined affinities" bequeathed to them from their previous existences. The concept of the predestined affinity is many-sided. Someone seeking immortality needs a predestined affinity with the magical foods that confer longevity or eating them will only make him sick. The banishment of the flower spirits is their "predestined affinity with the dust." (88:666) Little Hill escapes from the fruit demons because of her predestined affinity with the Immortal of the Hundred Fruits. Likewise, she can read an inscription that tells of the future when her friend Flowerlike, with no appropriate predestined affinity, sees only an incomprehensible archaic script. Flowerlike, however, says that it is better to have the "freedom" that comes from being without the burden of predestination.(49:361) In short, the Chinese believed that underlying the complexities of life, and its seemingly capricious twists and turns, lay a vast skein of these predestined affinities linking lives once lived and lives yet to come, transtemporal bonds between past, present, and future.

THE CONFUCIAN INSPIRATION

The central cultural dream of traditional Chinese society was that China was the center of world civilization, the only place where life was lived properly, in its full humanity, and that the influence of her values and learning radiated out to all other nations, transforming them for the better. In the Land of the Black Teeth, Tarng the Roamer and Helmsman Duo observe that the modest and proper demeanor of its inhabitants is due to the influence of the neighboring Land of Gentlemen, which in its turn owes its high moral quality to China, and Duo declares that "the fact of the matter is that our China must be regarded as the root of all other countries." (16:109) The modern West was, simply by making China conscious of its existence, to destroy this self-ennobling vision, and so to devalue a history. The comparatively rational and "this-worldly" justification of Confucian culture (since Heaven, when It responded, responded only here below) made it doubly vulnerable to apparent empirical failure.

Educated Chinese in late imperial times thus saw themselves as participants in the latest chapter of a story that was essentially the story of civilization. This civilization depended on a pattern of human relations, interconnecting humanity with itself internally and with the pattern of normative natural forces externally, that was fragile, precious, and in need of fine tuning every few hundred years as times altered. (52:383) Confucianism was the body of doctrines and the complex of activities responsible for the maintenance and renewal of this pattern.

The characters of the *Flowers* devote many pages to enthusiastic discussion of ritually correct behavior, and it is close to impossible for a reader who has not spent years of self-induction into premodern Chinese ways of thought to share their concern for the almost countless specific details. What he (or she) can perhaps imagine is the Chinese sense of how easily superficially small deviations by the ruler or other leaders could lead to the undermining of the psychological orientations on which vital parts of the system depended. Thus, Servant of Tarng declares, "In the case of Duke Wern of Luu [in the second quarter of the first millennium B.C.E.], who sacrificed improperly in his ancestral temple by placing his father's soul tablet above that of his father's predecessor [since his father, though the *elder* brother, had only been the son of a *concubine*, and had first served as the *minister* of his *younger brother,* the previous ruler who was the son of the *principal wife*] . . . the rituals of mourning were done away with." (52:385) The preservation of the proper hierarchy required an almost scientific precision, like the movements of the constellations or the seasonal flowering of plants.

Two Confucian virtues were preeminent, namely filial devotion and loyalty to the lord whom one served (rather than to an ideal or to a collectivity). A third virtue, the fidelity of a widow to her deceased husband, grew in importance during the last few centuries of the empire. Lii Rurzhen celebrates the first two, and takes the third for granted. An unusual twist, and one that has made Lii's book famous, is given to the theme of filiality by showing daughters performing heroic feats that would normally have been thought of as more appropriate for sons. (Thus, one girl kills tigers to avenge her mother's death in the jaws of one of these beasts.) The late traditional reader could relish conventional morality in a somewhat unconventional setting.

Little Hill makes two dangerous voyages inspired by the filial emotion driving her to find her father, now an immortal in Little Pernglair. The author's intention seems to be, so far as we can tell, to convey admiration for her worthy determination while at the same time covertly indicating that it is but a creation of her own thoughts—"There is nothing," says Duo of her attitude, "that is not made what it is by the heart-mind" (43:320–21)—and that it is an irrelevance in the world of the immortals.

The nobility of the burden of loyalty also receives sympathetic treatment at Lii's hands. Here is the aged loyalist Governor Wern Yiin speaking to his nephew:

"I am old, myself, sick and debilitated. I seem no more than a candle that gutters in the wind. . . . If you want to know why I prolong my last few breaths in office, to no good use . . . it is, first of all, because His Majesty has not yet been restored to his throne, and, second, because internal disorder has not yet been suppressed. If I were to retire, I would not share my sovereign's sorrow during my years of life, and so fail in the pure fidelity required of ministers. Even after my death, how could I face the rulers of the past in the world below? . . . Every time my thoughts turn to His Majesty, before I know it, my internal organs seem to be on fire! Since not long is now left to me in the world of men, . . . I can only urge my descendants to take up my purpose as their inheritance." (57:425)

All three virtues in their premodern forms were to vanish in the modern era. The belief of the educated in the fidelity of widows went the soonest, as it had come the latest, and disappeared the most completely, in broad terms, by the second quarter of this century. The ideal of personal loyalty was on the whole transformed into faith in a country or a cause, even if it popularly often took the form of loyalty to those who seemed to embody them. Devotion to filial piety, once backed by the state with a determination that enabled it with a good conscience to have, for example, a military graduate who had repeatedly slapped his mother, skinned alive in public, or exile a son for a lifetime at the mere request of his father, softened into a mixture of social support for filial respect and various forms of obligation. What little is now left is of slight intensity compared with what once was.

THE INDIVIDUAL

The Chinese "self" had two aspects. In the Confucian domain one was one's parents' child. One came into the world with obligations defined by what was, ideally at least, a unique place in a network of kinship. As life progressed, one acquired further obligations toward teachers, friends, and relatives by marriage. A person in this Confucian sense was largely defined by his or her relationships, which created a field of obligations and feelings in which the self found its meaning and its orientation.

On the other hand, one was also a reincarnated soul. As such, one's links with one's earthly kin were contingent, though conditioned by the karma of past lives. Destiny was individual, pursued through rebirth after rebirth, with "immortalhood" as the ultimate goal.

Sometimes the two aspects clashed. When Tarng the Roamer has eaten a magical herb that seems not to be agreeing with him, Seafarer Lirn says wryly:

"You'll be an immortal before long, brother-in-law. Why have you suddenly begun to frown and look unhappy? Surely you don't mean to say that you can't give up family and homeplace, and are scared to play the part of a deathless spirit?" (9:54)

Not infrequently Lii Rurzhen makes it clear how the quest of one person for immortality wounds the hearts of those who are left behind at home. This is particularly true of Tarng's wife, who loses both her husband and her daughter in this way. Lii's personal view, though, is probably close to that expressed by Purple Twig:

"From the point of view of human affections . . . when husband and wife are united together, and so are father and son . . . then the chief matters of human life have been fulfilled. But to my way of thinking—what happens after . . . people have taken delight in being together? After a few tens of years they all go to their extinction. As the moment approaches, who can escape the grave mound?" (94:724)

She says she wishes to "escape from the bitter sea," indirectly indicating a search for immortality or enlightenment.

Lirn, the merchant, represents the average Chinese, except perhaps in his level of self-awareness. "I know well enough," he says, "that

man's life in this world is like a dream. . . . At ordinary times, when I
hear people talking about this, I too can feel a cold indifference. But,
when some critical occasion appears for grabbing a little prestige or a
little profit, my heart-mind cannot help being led astray by it. I rush
forward with my mind bent on nothing else, as if I were going to live
for an eternity." (16:107) His realistic comments often serve as a foil to
the idealism of his traveling companions. When they admire a mountain pheasant that dashes its brains out on a rock after being defeated
by a peacock in a display of dancing, Lirn demurs. "If all human beings
had the same heroic spirit," he says, "think how many would die! As
I see it, the best thing to do is to be hard-boiled about matters of face.
Then one can muddle through." (20:143)

The grander Confucian aspirations for life are summed up by Tirngtirng, the girl-scholar of genius, as her companions weep at the ending
of the party:

"If I and my three sisters were to stay in China or to go back to our own
countries, that would be unbearably commonplace—lives passed in emptiness.
Today we have received the Empress's decree to accompany Flowerlike back to
[the Land of Women]. This sort of opportunity occurs but rarely in a thousand
years. . . . We shall assist her to be a worthy sovereign, and leave behind for
ourselves a fine name as famous lady ministers. . . . Even if we stayed together
for another few decades, it would not be better than it is now. . . . There are no
feasts in the world that do not break up some time." (68:504–5)

The well-managed "Confucian" private existence required a subtle
combination of regard for principle, delicacy, and ingenuity. This is
shown in an intricate conversation between Tarng the Roamer and his
former tutor Yiin Yuarn, in which they each agree to arrange the marriages of each other's children. (15:101–2) It is too long to quote here
but it shows how an individual Chinese organized his actions in society.
Each move was based on an awareness of the relative statuses of the participants, and this was continually expressed in the language, notably
by terms of address and self-description. Each status carried its particular rights and obligations. In this conversation, Tarng and Yiin assume
quite comfortably that elders have the right and duty to arrange the lives
of their juniors, Tarng suavely switching around his son's prospective
wife for another when it seems strategically preferable to do so, with
no concern for the boy's possible feelings. He does pay close attention
to the proprieties though, raising the question of the possible conflict in

status terms of his former teacher's (and hence senior's) daughter and son becoming "junior relatives" of his through marriage, a problem that the other swiftly dismisses. It is also a concern of Tarng's that his own future daughter-in-law be filial.

Both of them act by mobilizing their connections into a pattern of social choreography. Tasks are "entrusted" to those with whom they have the appropriate links, and who owe some obligation. It is understood that a return request may in due course be made. All these arrangements are made with a surface diplomatic *politesse*, but each proposal is supported by a socially underwritten sense of what is proper and a concern to maintain a warm field of mutual rapport, and thus carries more force than is apparent at first sight.

By early modern European standards, the late imperial Chinese world was free of any ingrained sense of guilt or self-disgust. The person was worth cherishing and preserving. This was evident in the Confucian goal of refining one's character throughout one's lifetime, and the more Daohist concern to cultivate one's health—even to a point that can seem to us hypochondriacal—and to achieve longevity.

Chinese believed that qualities of character had physical correlates that were hard to counterfeit. When Seafarer Lirn has been obliged by circumstances to "make a pretense of Confucian elegance" in the land of the cultivated Black Teeth, he observes as he recovers, "Who would have thought that merely trying to put on airs would have given me backache, blurred vision, a sore neck, a dizzy head, a parched tongue, and a dried-out mouth?" (19:131) Conversely, defects of personality are liable to lead to bodily deformity. Those who are lazy and greedy develop lumps in their breasts; gluttonous fisherfolk grow preternaturally long arms; and the heads of the winged people swell "from their love of compliments and flattery." (27:191) Ideally, at least, moral worth is physically visible, as is illustrated by the Country of the Great, where people ride on clouds whose color corresponds to their inner nature. Shame is a great pressure for self-reform as a result, since "a black cloud is shameful." (14:91)

The author of the *Flowers*—and so, presumably, many of his readers—was obsessed with diet, medicines, and health. Tea is attacked as a slow-acting poison. Herbal remedies are listed with all their ingredients and their proper proportions. The value of physical exercise is extolled, so long as it is done in the proper way. The wrong style and use of the inner energy and a faulty posture can, on the other hand, be debilitating. (79:586) The effects of "burn-out," possibly a real danger in a society that was probably already overly competitive, are warned against by Duo in a passage on the Land of the Intelligent:

"They are addicted to astrology, divination, trigonometrical calculations, . . . and every kind of mechanical art. They compete against each other, and take risks to come off best. They use all their mental powers in their determination to surpass others, with anxious thoughts and ill-intentioned cogitations. . . . From the beginning of the day to its end they are only concerned with scheming until, eventually, the forces of their minds are worn out. . . . For this reason none of them reaches a great age." (32:229)

An even more cautionary tale is that of the Land of the Worried, who fear falling asleep will prove fatal, and go to the greatest and most painful lengths to stay awake, eventually perishing "like lamps that have used up their oil." Tarng the Roamer resolves, after hearing this, that he will "banish all care from this time on, and, with the relaxed attitude that comes from content, live for many more years." (27:193–94) The Chinese were unashamedly concerned with looking after themselves both physically and mentally.

SOCIETY

The Chinese of late imperial times were also able to look at themselves with an anthropological self-awareness. Lii Rurzhen caricatured the society of his day. Sometimes he does this directly in the form of his fictitious societies "beyond the seas." At others he has the members of these societies, using Chinese theoretical standards, make critical comments on actual Chinese practice. Though the tragic vision is never quite as deep as in the last part of *Gulliver's Travels,* or the ideological subversion as radical as in *Lettres Persanes,* there is more than a little of the nature of both these works in his pages.

His perception of cultural relativity is apparent in the visit that Tarng, Lirn, and Duo make to the Land of Women, where physical differences between the sexes are the same as elsewhere, but everything else is reversed: dress, social and economic roles, and political power. When Tarng comments that women in men's clothes seems to him a "perversion," Duo retorts, "I only fear that when they look at us they'll say, for their part, that we don't make very good women and are per-

verted in playing the roles of men." (32:231) Almost immediately afterward, they are warned by a male "woman" that their impropriety risks
having them flogged half to death. Lii's point is that while conventions
may be culturally arbitrary in many respects, they can be dangerous if
not respected.

Lii's disgust at the way women were turned into merely pretty objects, without being permitted a full personality or control over what
happened to their bodies, is displayed in his account of what happens to Lirn when he is captured for the female "king's" harem. His
feet are bound, his ears pierced, his most intimate bodily functions
monitored by palace "maids" with moustaches, and he is tortured—
including being hung upside down—until his spirit is broken and he
submits to the degrading process of being beautified for the royal bed.
(33–34:237–41) In the Country of Gentlemen, one Confucian worthy
comments on footbinding: "I thought these girls had in all likelihood
committed some improper action, and that their mothers, unable to
bear putting them to death, had therefore used this method to punish
them. Who would have thought that it was done to make them *beautiful*
to look at?!" (12:78)

Other social vices—as Lii sees them—are attacked in the *Flowers,*
some predictable, others less so. Thus, in the eyes of the Confucians
of the Country of Gentlemen, the stepmother, and the widower who
self-indulgently marries her, are figures of evil:

"She falsely accuses the [deceased former wife's] daughter of not listening to
her instructions. Or she falsely accuses the [previous wife's] son of disobeying
her. . . . She lays every sort of trap. . . . How can one count the numbers who
have died from such ordeals . . . or perished from a broken heart?" (12:77)

Likewise, the Chinese habit of dedicating children to be celibate monks
and nuns undermines the perpetuation of the family (one of the worst
Confucian sins), runs contrary to the proper pattern for the mating of
the sexes, and leads to adulterous liaisons by the majority who have
no religious vocation. Lii is also haunted by the fear that uncontrolled
sexuality will dissolve the bonds of society, and denounces the female
confidence tricksters, saleswomen, midwives, and others who arrange
covert sexual affairs—since in China, even an affair seems to have
needed a go-between. (12:76)

Other targets for his satire are snobbery, hypocrisy, and the quest
for social prestige. The dishonesty behind the external *politesse,* the

manners linked with the show of morality of which traditional China made so much, is symbolized by the Country of the Two-Faced. The visible countenance of these people is charming, at least toward those who are elegantly dressed, but they have a second set of features, at the back, hidden under a scarf, with ratlike eyes, a hawklike nose, a frown of disgust for anyone not judged important, and a mouth spewing foul vapor. (25:178–79) Likewise, the waste of money on banquets in the interests of socially conspicuous ostentation rather than delectable cuisine or the pleasure of the guests offends Lii and he has one of his Confucians conclude that "in the end it will become impossible to afford even a single banquet. One will be obliged to roast pearls, boil jades, simmer gold, or stew silver for the *pièce de résistance*." (12:76) Lying disgusts him, and he has Duo the Helmsman observe that liars have become so numerous since the passing of the Chinese golden age that the regular hell cannot hold them all, and that they have since been reincarnated—only the worst cases excepted—in a new location called Pigsnout Land, where they have the snouts of pigs and live on slop. (27:192) It is worth noting that many of these criticisms coincide with those made by the sharpest of the missionary observers, Arthur Smith, in his *Chinese Characteristics*.[2]

Lii was moved by what might be called the "romance of kinship," a feeling so little known in the West that there is no word for it. It is a delight among the Chinese to extend the network of one's relations, through marriage, adoption, the rediscovery of long-lost kin, or sworn brotherhood or sisterhood. The ever-expanding sorority of the flower spirits take particular pleasure in *always* sitting at banquets in the proper order of seniority, and hence always next to the same partners, except on the rare and precious occasions when a new member has been added. (53:397; 62:458) The abuse that corresponds to this delight is the forging of spurious kinship bonds. Lii denounces the prevalent vice of neglecting one's poorer relatives and creating fictitious relationships with the powerful and well-to-do as a form of social climbing, which is now, says one of his characters, "a common practice." (39:275)

Finally, Lii was convinced that animals, no less than people, were moral beings. His travelers on one occasion save some mermaids and are later rescued from a fire attack on their ship either by these or by similar beings repaying a debt of gratitude. He therefore deplores the butchering of beasts for food, especially the plow oxen to whom farmers owe so much, and describes it as an act that lays up a heavy burden of bad karma for its perpetrators. (12:74–75; 26:185–86)

POLITICS

The ideal Chinese state was one in which social status and moral worth were publicly labeled, and the ruler was the supreme labeling authority. This is both portrayed and gently satirized in the Land of Pure Scholars. Here all respectable citizens have passed at least one public examination and wear the dress of men of letters, subdivided by colors according to grade. Most of the houses are adorned with placards, bestowed by the king, on which golden letters proclaim such legends as "Understanding the Scriptures, Filial and Frugal." A few bear black characters and announce such themes as "Reforming Our Faults and Renewing Ourselves." These, the travelers learn from an old man, can only be removed if "the neighbors in the district where they live submit a petition on their behalf, or if the officials determine the facts of their case by a public inquiry." (24:170) Here is that enthusiasm for morality that gripped the Chinese mind in its Confucian mode, the importance of group approval in giving it effect, and the assumption that it was the state's obligation to define and to induce in its subjects a sort of externally supported conscience.

The public service examinations became an obsession with the educated classes, a romance and an agony that combined the individual quest for glory, the state's praiseworthy search for talented and moral officials, and the excitement of a sporting occasion. When the girl-scholar Hornghorng tells Servant of Tarng that in the Land of the Black Teeth success in the examinations depends on social position and intrigue, the latter is shocked and assures her friend that this never happens in China. "If anyone were to obtain a place by means of intrigue," she avers, "that would inevitably entail doing wrong to someone of real talent. If this were to happen, how would posterity be able to flourish?" (51:378) Lii Rurzhen then devotes the next thirty pages or so to describing an examination fraud in China, in which the brilliant but elderly Mrs. Black flouts the age restrictions for the women's examinations and comes in at the top of the prefectural level but has to feign sickness in order to avoid being detected. What is typical of his treatment of these events is the way in which indirect cynical comment about the true state of affairs and a hint as to why China may be in a decayed position is interwoven with an implied defense of these examinations as, above all, a way of determining the *moral character* of the candidates, not, in the first instance, their knowledge. The two examiners are shown as skilled readers of the heart and sensitive to Mrs. Black's "concentrated truthfulness and expression of experience" that "did not seem to come from the hand of a young person." (56:417) As so often, Lii's criticisms are at the service of an idealistic conservatism.

The actual process of politics was thought of in terms of the inter-action of a leader and the masses. There was no ideologically acceptable form of opposition. At most, subordinates could make loyal protests on grounds of principle. Examples of both good and bad leadership and of hostile and positive popular response can be found in the episode where Tarng tries to get Lirn released from the harem of the "king" of the Country of Women.

He begins by stirring up a crowd with promises of what he can do for their flood-stricken country as a water-control expert. "If you want the waterways to be controlled," he declares to them, "you must all go to the Court and appeal with your tears. If he is set free, I shall start the work at once." The mob gives a great shout and moves off to the palace. (35:247) Lust for Lirn the Seafarer has, however, diminished the king's sense of responsibility for her subjects' welfare. She orders the "Royal Uncle" to lie to the masses. "He" tells them it is too late. The marriage has been consummated. They are not convinced and begin to enter the palace. The king then turns on them:

Stirred by an impulse of hatred . . . she ordered the commandant on duty with-out further ado to exterminate the mob as rebels. . . . No sound was heard but the thundering of muskets and cannon . . . [but] the throng of commoners was in no mood to back off. . . .

The Royal Uncle saw that the situation created by the people might be-come . . . a rebellion. So she told the troops . . . not to hurt anyone. Then she repeatedly urged the commoners with these words:

"You must disperse. I shall of course present your case to His Majesty on your behalf and make sure that the person who took down the proclamation [offering a reward for solving the flood problem] will be detained here to repair the waterways. . . ."

When the crowd heard this, they slowly scattered. (35:248)

The public-spirited leadership given by Tarng evokes, in contrast, an enthusiastic mass response:

Since they had been afflicted by flooding for year after year, the inhabitants of the entire country came to contribute their efforts when the work was started. . . . Tarng gave the directions and supervised the operations. When the common people saw that he rose early in the morning and returned late, making painful efforts day and night, they were moved to admiration. Before long a few old "men" subscribed money to have an image made of Tarng. A "shrine to a living person" was set up for him, on which they erected an inscription in large golden letters that read "To whom the marshlands pay tribute and the rivers acknowledge mastery." (36:256)

Here, long before Chinese communism, is the paradigm of the ideal of Chinese communist leadership, both in its justification as being "for the service of the people" and its cult of personality. On the darker side, this episode also contains several choice bland-faced examples of Chinese administrative lying. Thus the Royal Uncle tells Tarng that "Your relative [Lirn] suddenly caught a severe illness while selling her goods in the palace. . . . The talk about her having been made a Royal Consort is a lie spread about by the lower orders of society." (35:251) It is not surprising, then, that the people are shown as disinclined to believe what their rulers say to them.

THE DISCIPLINE SYSTEM

Traditional China, seen from a Western perspective, lacked a social and an intellectual dimension—that of law, justice, and jurisprudence. Courts had little conception of the weighing and testing of evidence. Conviction required confession, and—unless protected by privileged status—accused and witnesses were tortured. There was no legal profession in the sense of qualified advocates who were heard by courts on behalf of litigants. Those who offered advice outside the courtrooms were regarded as social nuisances. In practice, the actual contents of a great part of the "law" and of "legal" precedents were inaccessible to those who were not officials. Subjects of the emperor were not equal before the law, such as it was, and this was most notable between seniors and juniors in a kinship structure. The objective of the system was not "justice"—a term for which there is no satisfactory traditional Chinese translation—but rather social discipline and the maintenance of the social structure, as with the rules governing a Western army, school, or church. Those who came nearest to pursuing justice in China were the so-called knights errant, moved by a "public-spirited righteousness" and "a heart-mind set on the Way of the General Good." (60:444) They were, almost by definition, impulsive and heroic beings outside the established system of social discipline.

There is only one trial in the *Flowers,* that held by two immortals of Sinful Dragon for abducting Tarng's daughter Little Hill and of Great Oyster for inciting him to do so. The case is too intricate for summary here, and perhaps is, in any event, too much of a fantasy for definite conclusions to be drawn from it. All the same it is interesting in that it shows common ground between the West and China in the concept of the offenses involved, namely abduction, incitement to abduct, and corruption of the mind of another, and at the same time applying different standards for the different creatures over whom Heaven rules. The Oyster was motivated by a desire to be revenged for his son, who had previously been murdered and his pearl stolen by "the filial daughter of the Liarn family" as a gift to Tarng after he had saved her life. It is only at the trial that the Oyster learns, belatedly, that Heaven had been using the girl as its means of executing his son, who was so gluttonous that he had become "the bane of sea creatures." (45:330–31) Both the girl (who was unaware of her role in Heaven's designs) and Oyster, by Western standards, had culpable intent and Oyster, arguably at least, better considerations for mitigation, but they are treated differently. Heaven, like the Emperor, was more concerned with discipline than fairness.

TECHNOLOGY AND ECONOMICS

Throughout the *Flowers* there is a delight in technology. Duo steers across the ocean with a magnetic compass. Several warriors carry the so-called linked-pearls musket, a kind of primitive machine gun. (95:731) The king of the Country of Women consults a striking clock to see if it is time for her nuptial banquet with Seafarer Lirn. Seagoing ships, chronometers, and firearms were European specialties in early modern times. They were not European monopolies.

The Chinese were proud of what they took to be their technological superiority to other nations, and the notion of Chinese technical assistance to less advanced peoples was one that took Lii Rurzhen's fancy, and—one may imagine—that of his readers. In the Country of Women, Tarng the Roamer teaches the female inhabitants how to make cast-iron tools and delivers a lecture on hydraulics. He explains that "when one wishes to use the flow of the water to scour away the silt deposited in a waterway, its course must be as straight as an arrow. Only then can the silt be carried downstream with the current. . . . Where you want it to be scoured away, the watercourse must also become narrower, . . . and have a downward gradient." He explains that it is a common error to think that "the wider it is, the more freely it will flow," since "when the water flows from narrow places to broad ones, it spreads itself and loses its power." (36:255) There follows a detailed account of the method of dredging using temporary cross-dikes and baskets on pulleys for hauling up the mud removed.

Ingenious machinery had a romantic appeal. When Flowerlike has to return in a hurry to the Country of Women to become its new monarch, she and three companions travel in "flying carriages":

[The pilots] raised the keys and set the mechanism in motion. All that could be seen were copper wheels, some upright, some horizontal, turning furiously. Some were the size of millstones, others of pulley wheels. [The carriages] seemed like pinwheels,[3] and each one rose up spinning. In an instant they were a few feet off the ground. Then they rose straight up to a height of more than a hundred feet and headed due West. (94:722)

The romance is checked by an awareness that changes in the technology could have disruptive economic effects. Pleasant muses: "If I could get hold of a flying carriage, then—if I wanted to go somewhere—I wouldn't have to stop for a meal or stay overnight in hostels." Little Spring then observes that "if this were so, the assistants in the hostels would have nothing to live on." (66:486–87)

For Lii, economics was a zero-sum game. One person's gain was another's loss. He does not conceive of the possibility of a general progress, sustaining itself with internal positive feedback. In Shaman Land, for example, we learn that people originally dressed in cotton, but then two girls arrived bringing with them silkworm eggs and the techniques of silk manufacture. Since the land has plenty of mulberry trees, silk production expands, and families who have lived by making cotton face bankruptcy. The travelers have to save the life of one of the girls who has introduced sericulture from the attack of a man who has been ruined by these "poisonous worms" and the spread of "these evil arts," and who tells them that "half the households that used to grow [cotton] have lost the livelihood they possessed for generations past." (28:198)

This passage, with its humor based on inversion, whereby silk becomes a social scourge, also expresses the view that circumstances determine value. Seafarer Lirn expounds the merchant's philosophy that
wherever one is, "one has to look and see what they're short of, and
make those items expensive." For Lirn, as for most Chinese businessmen, the essence of trade is arbitrage, not a regular relationship, and the
highest skill the opportunism that lets one "get an advantage without
making an effort to do so." (32:230–31; 20:139)

SCHOLARSHIP

In some respects late traditional Chinese scholarship was like a certain
type of television quiz. It required memorizing vast amounts of information, and to a great degree the answers were thought of as being
either right or wrong. Exchanges between scholars, though conducted
with surface politeness, were covertly aimed at establishing an academic pecking order, and could be enjoyed by the onlookers as a form
of intellectual fencing match.

The *Flowers* is obsessed with scholarship, and the reader is entertained with competitions like that between Helmsman Duo and Tirngtirng over the pronunciations of a certain Chinese character. (16:111–
12) But behind the rival displays of erudition, Lii has a serious purpose.
He is telling his reader to value the argument, and not the social standing of the person who puts it forth, and also to approach the Scriptures
with an open mind, using reason rather than authority to unravel their
meaning. He drives this point home by repeatedly using Tirngtirng, a
young, foreign female with a black face, to discomfit Duo, an elderly
Chinese male who holds an academic degree. When Duo cannot dis-
prove her contention that characters were pronounced differently in
ancient times, the best riposte he can make only causes him to appear
ludicrous:

"You would have to find some men from ancient times so that I could talk
with them, and hear what sort of a pronunciation they really had. . . . If not,
your lofty theory will have to wait till that time in the future when you have
discovered some people from the past and spoken with them." (17:115)

Even more important is Lii's rational approach to the Confucian
Scriptures as historical documents. His attitude, typical of much of

eighteenth-century scholarship, was the first stage of an unintended process of desacralization that began long before modern Western ideas began to undermine the thought structures of the Chinese. Thus, Duo and Tirngtirng dispute over how to gloss a sentence in *The Analects*, namely, "Yarn Luh asked Confucius for his carriage, so that he could make it into a *guoo* [the term at issue]."

Duo (smiling): All the commentators, ancient and modern, say that when Yarn Yuan [Confucius's favorite pupil] died, his father Yarn Luh was too poor to buy an *outer coffin*. He asked Confucius to *sell* his carriage so he could buy one. They all say this. On what do you need instruction?

Tirngtirng: Although Confucian scholars from former times explain it like this, do you have an alternative view, eminent worthy?

Duo: In my opinion, that is all there is to it. How should I presume to make a reckless show of cleverness, or give voice to disorderly disputation on this point? . . .

Tirngtirng: . . . . There would seem to be a different sense. If one explains it as Yarn Luh being too poor to buy an *outer coffin*, he ought to have asked the Master for financial help. Why should he specifically indicate that he wanted him to *sell* his *carriage*? Is it plausible to suppose he thought there was nothing in Confucius's home, apart from this carriage, that could be sold?

It's the same today. When people ask for financial help, they ask for assistance. How could it be proper for them to point specifically at the object they want someone to sell in order to furnish them with help? Even a commonplace idiot wouldn't make such a remark. How much less a worthy man who was the disciple of a sage!

When Confucius replied to this request he said that when previously his own son, Lii, had passed away, he had only had an inner coffin and no *guoo*. "I am not willing to go on foot," he declared, "to provide him with one." If we interpret this according to the commentaries you've quoted, it must in the same way have referred to *selling* a *carriage* in order to buy an *outer coffin*. How could it have been that when Yarn Yuan died his father boldly asked for the selfsame carriage that Confucius had earlier considered selling on behalf of his own son [but had decided not to]?

An outer coffin is not all that valuable or rare. Even an expensive one does not cost more than twice the price of an inner one. . . . What is more, in the later chapters the lavish burials of disciples are described. Why were the funds for these not used to buy an outer coffin? Why was it necessary to oblige Confucius to sell his carriage? . . . On the contrary, it would seem that what was meant was using the *timbers* of the carriage to construct an *outer surround* for the coffin [as a sort of memorial]. (17:116–17)

Faced with this logical onslaught, Duo can only say, fatuously, that if the meaning was not that Confucius had been asked to sell his carriage, "what need would there have been for the men of earlier times to write explanatory notes to that effect?"

Lii's criticism is thus the discontent of the enthusiast who still believes in the intrinsic importance of the Scriptures, and who wishes to use the powers of scholarly reason to understand them better. The potential for dissolving faith that was latent in the quest for the historical Confucius was as hidden from him as it is visible to us.

INTELLECTUAL RECREATIONS

A final insight into the mind of the educated Chinese of late traditional times is provided by intellectual amusements. Above all, it relished complexity, such as the mixture of literary, literal, and analogical thinking required to do crosswords in the West and, in China, the so-called lantern riddles. (32:229)

The supreme example of this type of thought was the two-dimensional poetic palindrome. The basically monosyllabic nature of the language and lack of inflections make it possible to construct matrices of characters that can be read as rhyming poems from right to left and left to right, downward and upward, along diagonals and around circumferences, and even alternately backward and forward. Lii devotes almost thirty pages to his reading of the most celebrated of all these palindromes, the 29-by-29 word square, with the graph for "heart" in its center, composed in the fourth century by Lady Su Huih in the attempt to win back her husband's affections from a concubine. Here, as an illustration, are two of the shortest poems, taken from a six-by-six submatrix and, in Chinese, consisting of exactly the same characters read in opposite directions:

> Alas! I sigh for my cherished one
> And the norms he has forsaken!
> Distant the road, and empty.
> Wounded my inmost feelings!
> Our family—without its lord,
> Chaste the room within the curtains.
>
> In painted splendor shining back
> My face within the looking glass.

Fallen pell-mell my sparkling jewels,
And luster gleaming from my pearls.
But, with thoughts of *him* before me,
What worth their glory?

Reversed, this becomes:

What, then is glory?
With thoughts of *him* so many. . . .
The loveliness of my lucent pearls?
The sparkle of my scattered jewels?
The shining mirror that shows back
My face embellished and bedecked?

Loveless within—the curtained room!
And my lord without his kin.
Inside my feelings, deep the wound.
Empty the road that winds away.
Through places where *he* was I pass,
And in my heart-mind sigh "Alas!" (41:293)

The effect is like that of shaking a kaleidoscope; the above are but two of over a thousand discoverable coherent poems.

But the Chinese could also think analytically. Lii himself was a keen phonetician, and his characters in the *Flowers* are made to wrestle, and his readers likewise, with the deciphering of a system of phonetic "spelling" used by the Double Tongues. The method, when its details are finally divulged, turns out to be a grid along whose vertical and horizontal axes are characters containing all the possible initial and final sounds for the syllables of the Chinese language. The idea is not original in its essentials, going back to the Tarng dynasty and having parallels in certain Morse Code–like drum signals used in Lii's own day. (28–31: 200–225 *passim*) What it shows is that the method of accounting for a wide range of phenomena by means of a limited set of elements plus a set of derivational rules was well established in the Chinese intellectual domain before the introduction of modern science.

CONCLUSIONS

What has changed in recent times in the meaning of being Chinese? To begin with, Scriptural Confucianism is defunct, even though certain deep-seated ways of perceiving and experiencing the world inherited from it are still powerful. Belief in reincarnation is almost dead, except perhaps in Tairwan, though the question needs research. The old "popular religion" is also nearly defunct, though it flickers fitfully into life again from time to time. The unique significance attributed to Chinese history has vanished. Though still impressive, it is neither the oldest nor the most important for humanity by most present estimations. On the other hand, the patterns of social action, of politics, and of social discipline sketched from Lii Rurzhen's pages are still vigorous, even if more complicated now than they were in the past.

And beyond that? Well, perhaps *The Destinies of the Flowers in the Mirror* provides evidence of a considerable capacity for self-awareness, self-criticism, and even self-mockery that the Chinese in late imperial times are not always credited with having possessed. It belies the notion that China on the eve of the Western cultural invasion was completely caught in a sealed psychological world of unalterable stereotypes.

In modern China, the cultural apparatus, so to speak, allowing one to identify with the Chinese nation, no longer exists. How does an average Chinese identify with the People's Republic of China? What is the cultural medium? What symbols and rituals are accepted that allow you to identify with the PRC? None. When I think about nationalism—a culturally elaborated nationalism—it provides the individual with an ability to identify with one's nation. What I am saying is that the traditional beliefs of China, labelled feudal superstition, provided a premodern form of identification with a clearly conceived Chinese nation. The Chinese had a traditional system which identified the Chinese nation, gave it dimensions, gave it a place in the world. . . . It was a total configuration that linked the people to the nation. It linked the people to the elite. This was destroyed by the same individuals who created modern Chinese nationalism, which has had the ironic effect of not providing a replacement.

Myron L. Cohen
From the Conference on the
Meaning of Being Chinese
Honolulu, October 1990

3

No Solace from Lethe: History, Memory, and Cultural Identity in Twentieth-Century China

Vera Schwarcz

And whether I go East or West,
Back against or gaze upon, It is always the River of Forgetting,
Always China on the other side of barbed wire—
A legend, a time-worn rumor
On some page, what page of my childhood?

— Yu Guangzhong, "River of Forgetting" [1]

One year after the shootings in Tiananmen Square, a Chinese dancer battles a rope on the stage of La MaMa theater in New York. The rough cord appears to have a life of its own as the young man pulls it, hangs from it, tries to but cannot undo its hold around his waist. The experimental piece is titled "Threshold: A Dance Theater of Remembering and Forgetting." [2] Produced collaboratively by eight Chinese artists from Hong Kong, the People's Republic, Taiwan, Singapore, and New York, this work is a meditation on the Beijing tragedy of 1989 and the more encompassing burden of Chinese historical consciousness.

From the balcony of the darkened room, the husky voice of a Chinese woman reads in halting English: "We are born in history. This is an attempt to escape it. . . . What I forget comes back to me in dreams. Cuts me open like a knife. . . . Mother? Motherland? Comrade." While the staccato voice draws near and flees from the memory of the Chinese mainland, the young man wars with his crimson rope on center stage. He's trying to make his way to a distant door, to cross its freedom-promising threshold. He tries to cut memory's umbilical cord, to be born anew. But he collapses on the way to the emancipation that lies beyond all mother tongues. The young man is left embracing the unbreakable tie—the history that cannot be forgotten, the dreams that cut like knives.

Away from China, away from the pain-ridden center where "comrades" just last year murdered students trying to show love for the "motherland," Chinese artists probe the meanings of their cultural identity. Exiled from the home country, they partake of the bittersweet feast of migrants throughout history: They pass beyond the fixed borders of inherited knowledge in search of new—even if dangerous—insights about the maternal world left behind. From the periphery of the Chinese world, these young artists expose and explore what psychoanalysts Leon and Rebecca Grinberg termed "the migratory impulse." According to the Grinbergs, who have studied exiles from Latin America and Eastern Europe, mankind as a whole is marked by a movement out of a native place toward another often alien world. This movement is part of a universal desire to "reach heaven," to reach forbidden zones of foreign knowledge. But as the Grinbergs point out, the myth of the Tower of Babel shows how frequently this desire is punished by "the confusion of tongues" and "the loss of the ability to communicate. Confusion may be experienced as punishment for the migratory impulse, for the desire to know a new world, a different world."[3] At home, historical memory is an all-pervading authority. It is synonymous with the native cultural tradition. Abroad, memory becomes an opportunity—however danger ridden—for a new kind of self-becoming that benefits from forcible distance from the mother tongue.

In New York, a year after the Tiananmen events, young Chinese artists seek to pass beyond the confusion of exile to a new understanding of their oldest dilemma: remembering and forgetting the Chinese cultural inheritance. They are beneficiaries of what the Grinbergs describe as "transitional space"[4]—a unique inner and outer marginality, a protected time away from native authorities that is not available to compatriots in the repression-burdened motherland. In this transitional space, Chinese abroad seek to create some continuity between past and present, between old selves imprinted by the mother tongue and new ones invented with painful freedom.

In Beijing, in Chinese, the events of 1989 are being drowned by the official lie that the student movement was nothing but "counterrevolutionary turmoil." In New York, in English, it is possible to recall, to mourn the students' patriotism as well as the dilemmas of memory and

forgetting. It is possible to express a wish to be rid of the endless con-
volutions of "Chineseness"—a code word that politicians on the mainland, in Taiwan, and in Singapore use whenever patriarchal authority
grows impatient with critical youth. In New York, it is also possible
to acknowledge that there will never be freedom from the Chineseness
inscribed in the heart.

"On some page, what page of my childhood?" asks the poet Yu
Guangzhong, who is the distant source of inspiration for the young artists in New York.[5] Born on the Chinese mainland in 1928, educated in
Taiwan, and writing some of his best poems from abroad, Yu Guangzhong provides younger intellectuals with a model of self-exploration
on the periphery of Chinese culture. Yu Guangzhong's marginality, like
that of the Chinese artists at La MaMa, is politically induced and culturally sustained. He was cut off, forcibly, from the mainland by the
events of 1949. The younger generation is now severed from China (or
more precisely, political authorities at home) by the Tiananmen massacre of 1989. And yet, Yu Guangzhong, like his latter-day admirers,
never reconciled himself to the reality of his—and his nation's—fragmented soul. On Memorial Day in 1966, for example, while riding in
his car on American highways, he brooded:

China, O China,
When shall we stop our quarrels?
China, O China you're big in my throat so hard to swallow!
The Yellow River flows torrential in my veins.
China is me. I am China.
Her every disgrace leaves a box print on my face. I am defaced.
China, O China you're a shameful disease that plagues me thirty-eight years.
Are you my shame or my pride, I cannot tell.[6]

Being in America, writing in Chinese but with the wild cadences of
spoken English in mind, did not soothe Yu Guangzhong's grief in the
1960s. For the Tiananmen generation, Yu is a pioneer in grieving, in
mourning, in remembering China from abroad. Though exiled from the
mainland since 1949, Yu Guangzhong continues to be riveted by it, to
gaze at it from beyond the border-barricading Shenzhen River (which
divides Hong Kong from the rest of South China). This river becomes
an internalized boundary for the exile. On one side lie the material remains of Chinese culture, on the other the unquenchable longing to
reclaim them with freedom.

The Shenzhen River acquires mythic proportions in Yu Guang-zhong's 1969 poem "The River of Forgetting." Overflowing its geographical boundary it now blends with the ancient Lethe,[7] the Greeks' border marker that divides the living from the shadowy Hades. Written at the height of the Cultural Revolution, "The River of Forgetting" is—like "Threshold" twenty years later—a dirge that circles around the wish and the impossibility of forgetting China.

The Greeks who drank from the Lethe were supposed to forget their life on earth. Why can't the Chinese poet partake of a similarly soothing amnesia? If not from the thirst-quenching Lethe, why not a sip from the Naihe, a river of forgetting in China's own folklore? On the Naihe bridge passersby are supposed to encounter Old Lady Meng who ladles out a soup of forgetting to prepare the soul for its new incarnation.[8] But no such relief, no such soup, no such nepenthe is available to Yu Guangzhong, the self-condemned rememberer:

> And whether I go East or West
> A great veil accosts me twenty years later
> What face of mercy hides behind barbed wire?
> What grief is the grief that cannot be rent? . . .
> And whether I go North or South
> Fringed lace decorates my terror
> A stranger abroad
> A prisoner at home
> It's all the same, inside and out of the net
> A fish destined for pain.[9]

Twenty years after the "loss of China" (not in the polemical sense used by supporters of Senator McCarthy in the 1950s, but in the emotionally charged sense of exile from the locus of Chinese historical origination), Yu Guangzhong cannot erase the memory of his homeland. It is there on the other side of barbed wire, a reminder that it is impossible to be Chinese except in some tension-filled relationship to the land of China and to Chinese time.

Like the young man with his rope on the stage of La MaMa, Yu Guangzhong wars with and ends up embracing the China he cannot forget. Like other Chinese intellectuals of the twentieth century, Yu Guangzhong seeks to redefine the meaning of Chineseness in a way that will sanction his quarrelsome love of tradition.

Critical-minded lovers of China have a common heritage in the twentieth century: the May Fourth Movement of 1919. This is the shared temporal anchor of those who would explore the meanings of Chinese identity from a critical perspective. It is the source of an ongoing effort to revitalize Chinese culture by a thorough immersion in the rapids of science, democracy, individual autonomy, and historical relativism.

The initial May Fourth Movement was an effort to brave these rapids by a conscious, systematic self-distancing from inherited Chinese values. In the same way as young Chinese artists in New York struggle with the burden of historical memory and Yu Guangzhong looks to the motherland as both a stranger and a lover sequestered behind barbed wire, May Fourth intellectuals sought a critical perspective on native traditions by turning to comparative perspectives offered by the modern West.

Their cultural movement was the first stage of an internal diaspora—a going into exile from traditional values long held to be true and "natural." By turning away, going "abroad"—first in their minds, then through actual study and work opportunities in Japan, France, and the United States—May Fourth intellectuals began the long, difficult process of denaturalizing, or rather reculturalizing, Chinese tradition.

The original event that sparked the May Fourth Movement of 1919 was a patriotic student movement. This movement was the first to articulate, combine, and propagate the twin goals of "science" and "democracy." Not content to defend Chinese national interest in political terms alone (at a moment when the Paris Peace conference of 1919 threatened to barter away Chinese sovereignty in the province of Shandong), students went on to become champions of a broader enlightenment movement. They sought to cure China's political and spiritual ills with a strong dose of doubt, reason, individualism, and a new vernacular language.[10]

The legacy of the May Fourth Movement of 1919 has inspired subsequent generations of Chinese intellectuals from the 1930s onward to the Beijing spring of 1989. "Science and Democracy" remains a powerful rallying call not only on the Chinese mainland but also in Taiwan, Hong Kong, and other places where Chinese intellectuals gather to ponder the fate of their troubled homeland. Commemorations of the event of 1919 provide a shared ground on which to stand whether the soil of China is near or far.

To commemorate the past is an act of repossession. It bestows on-going value, it claims unending relevance for the event that is being called to mind. In recalling May Fourth, Chinese intellectuals are re-consecrating themselves as critics and guardians of Chinese culture. The initial Chinese enlightenment came perilously close to uprooting tradi-tional values in its haste to wash away the encrustations of autocracy, prejudice, and unreason. It never had time to answer the question of what to keep and what to discard from the legacy of the past. Political revolution engulfed, emptied the space once occupied by enlightenment thought. And yet, the struggle goes on, the rope of history must be wrestled with, the waters of Lethe offer no solace to those who grew up on the time-weathered banks of the Yellow River.

To be Chinese, not unlike being Jewish, means to be inscribed in and by historical time. Though not immune to the wish to forget the past, Chinese culture demands the transmission of memory no less forcefully than the Jewish commandment *zachor*—"you shall remember." [11] From Confucius onward, the moral imperative of seeking the past (*qiugu*) has been the heart of China's spiritual continuity over time. Far from assuming that the past is fixed and readily knowable, both Chinese and Jewish traditions demand that it be sought after, reinterpreted, passed on, and thus preserved. [12]

In both traditions, attachment to ancestral language serves to tex-tualize the commitment to remembrance. In both traditions, core texts (the Bible, the Talmud, the *Analects*, the "Spring and Autumn Annals") enveloped by pages and pages of commentary fostered reverence as well as exegetical freedom. Even in the aftermath of the May Fourth lan-guage revolution (from classical to vernacular), even in the aftermath of the history-devouring Cultural Revolution, Chinese identity remains inseparable from the Chinese language, much as the future is insepa-rable from the past. The contemporary poet Bei Dao, a critical-minded patriot in the style of May Fourth intellectuals, has expressed the dual attachment to language and doubt, to the past and to the future, as follows:

> Let me tell you, world
> I—don't—believe!
> Even if a thousand challengers are at your feet,
> Count me as the thousand-and-first . . .
> New turns and sparkling stars

Stud the clear skies
The symbolic words of five thousand years.
The gazing eyes of generations to come.[13]

ON LETHE'S BANKS—ALMOST UNCHINESE

In the pivotal year of 1919, when a small group of Chinese intellectuals took the quarrel with inherited values from the pages of magazines onto the streets of Beijing, they appeared rather monstrous. In fact, radical thinkers were likened by conservatives to devils, hungry ghosts, evil spirits—all sorts of creatures from the repository of classical imagination—simply because they refused to suckle the teat of old-fashioned Confucianism as if it were China's only natural "mother."

This band of intellectuals saw itself, and was seen by others, as a force of destruction. Those who congregated around and wrote for *New Youth* and *New Tide* magazines described their mission as *ouxiang po-huai*—literally, idol smashing, or "iconoclasm."[14] According to these advocates of new thought, China was being strangled by old ideals "outworn, false notions" such as emperor worship, filial piety, the inferiority of women, and the sacredness of Confucian hierarchies. These ideas were deemed "idols" who had become so entrenched in the commoners' minds that truth could hardly find an entrance. Science was the only instrument that might ply open this closed, stuffy space—even though it carried the risk of spiritual havoc.

While science-minded iconoclasts prepared to manage the havoc caused by the dismantling of Confucian dogma, its defenders rallied with passion around the cause of the sage. Some of the cultural conservatives of the May Fourth era defended Confucianism on moral grounds—finding in it a last bastion of universal, humanistic ethics—others embraced the old ways of venerating the five "cardinal relationships" (between father and son, young brother and older brother, and so on) out of family loyalty. Some rallied around Confucianism simply because it was China's distinctive heritage in a world drenched by imperialist-sponsored cosmopolitanism.

One of the most articulate, most idiosyncratic defenders of Confucianism during the May Fourth period was the Penang-born, Edinburgh-educated Gu Hongming.[15] A latecomer to Chinese philosophy, Gu used his own circuitous path through Southeast Asia, Scotland,

and translations of Goethe to write—in eloquent English—a scathing indictment of the advocates of new culture. According to Gu's irony-tinged voice, May Fourth radicals were responsible for the moral failing of the nation as a whole. Armed with foreign degrees himself, Gu Hongming attacked others seeking this opportunity as spoilers of the "virtues" of the ordinary "Chinaman":

> I consider it a misfortune to his country that when a Chinese student . . . gets a degree from a foreign university for knowing vulgar [!] English, he immediately *denationalizes* himself . . . he cannot even understand the *nobility* of his own language—in fact, he does not know the value, the greatness of the moral and spiritual inheritance called the Chinese Civilization. . . . Just at this moment when civilization is threatened with bankruptcy, the real, the most valuable asset of civilization in the world is the *unspoiled, the real Chinaman*; and the real, unspoiled Chinaman is an asset to civilization because he is a person who costs the world little or nothing to keep him in order.[16]

Gu Hongming's charge—that to know English, to be interested in foreign ideas, to stir up the conscience of the Chinese people with new notions like "science" and "democracy" is tantamount to cultural betrayal—has been reiterated over and over again since 1919. The "unspoiled, the real Chinaman" has been the ideal with which nationalist leaders, whether of the Communist or Guomindang (KMT) persuasion, tried to whip cosmopolitan intellectuals into line. The whipping continues, more or less violently, in our own time, especially after the Beijing spring of 1989, which had been so strongly, so overtly identified with the spirit of May Fourth.[17]

And yet, despite Gu Hongming's unsparing attack on those who forgot "Chinese Civilization"—or maybe, because of it—the grain of truth in his accusation echoes through the decades after 1919: intellectuals of the May Fourth era had indeed tried to "denationalize" themselves. Giving full reign to the "migratory impulse" they had sought to denaturalize the moral supremacy of their culture's values upon their own lives. When they broke away from arranged marriages, when they advocated parliamentary democracy, when they propagated scientific rationality, they were indeed taking issue with China's traditional "moral nationality." They were trying to invent a new one.

Hu Shi, the American-educated liberal who was the main object of Gu Hongming's attacks, was intensely mindful of the spiritual and cultural dilemmas involved in creating a new Chinese morality, a new sense of Chinese nationality. Even as Hu Shi studied John Dewey, even as he translated Ibsen and wrote pamphlets on the importance of a new vernacular language, he knew himself to be engaged in a pressing yet dangerous task: the Nietzschean project of "transvaluation of values." Hu Shi used Nietzsche's term, mindful of the risks and not only of the glamour it entailed. To console himself during this undertaking, to give himself courage, Hu Shi sought moral companionship not only among fellow-minded Chinese intellectuals such as Li Dazhao and Chen Duxiu (who went on to found the Chinese Communist party in 1921 and left Hu Shi alone on the liberal platform) but also among contentious Westerners of the Renaissance.

Hu Shi was the epitome of the Chinese intellectual in diaspora: not only had he studied abroad (B.A. from Cornell, Ph.D. from Columbia, under John Dewey) but even after his return to China, Hu Shi continued to commune with ideas and minds alien to the Chinese soil. He loved and defended traditional Chinese culture—but always from the perspective of critical rationality. He was always aware that such "love" could be misread, dismissed in light of his other, Western-oriented affections. Therefore, Hu Shi took pains to explain the Chinese roots of the May Fourth Movement, which he liked to call the "Chinese Renaissance":

What pessimistic observers have lamented as the collapse of Chinese civilization, is exactly the necessary undermining without which there could not have been the rejuvenation of an old civilization. So, slowly, quietly, but unmistakably, the Chinese renaissance is becoming a reality. The product of this rebirth looks suspiciously occidental. But, scratch its surface and you will find the stuff of which it is made is essentially Chinese.[18]

Like Gu Hongming, Hu Shi expressed this passionate conviction, in English, to a foreign audience (in this case the Haskell Lectures delivered at the University of Chicago). And yet, beneath their shared appreciation of English for Chinese self-expression, Gu and Hu were divided in their view of the regenerative potential of iconoclasm. Hu Shi believed the rebirth of Chinese culture would follow after the ground-clearing task of iconoclasm. Gu Hongming embraced tradition as it was, as if it were an unquestionable inheritance—although he came to embrace Chinese tradition only after a thoroughly foreign upbringing and education in Southeast Asia and Scotland. Furthermore, the two men were separated by their belief in the utility of looking beyond China's borders for sources of Chinese renewal. Gu Hongming was, to use a psychoanalytical turn of phrase, "ocnophilic"—from the Greek root meaning "to grab hold of," to hold on to what is certain and stable. Hu Shi, on the other hand, might be described as "philobatic"—from the Greek root meaning "to walk on one's hands like an acrobat," as one who seeks the thrill of new experiences, situations and places.[19]

The gulf between "philobatic," outward-looking reformers and "ocnophilic," inward-gazing defenders of culture endures in China today. Authoritarian proponents of Chinese-style socialism are spiritual heirs of Gu Hongming, who promised foreigners a cheap way of keeping the "unspoiled Chinaman" subdued. Reformers in the tradition of Hu Shi, on the other hand, are critical-minded intellectuals who still try to pick and choose what to keep and what to discard from the Chinese cultural inheritance. In order to choose, however, they need to look abroad, to read Western books, to obtain Western degrees, to prepare themselves for the task of discriminating assimilation of both Chinese and Western traditions. Their training abroad is meant to provide them, and China, with what the Grinbergs described as the necessary transitional space for individual and cultural transformation.

Transitional spaces, however, were difficult to uncover and to maintain. By the late 1910s Hu Shi knew that the challenge of adapting traditional Chinese culture to the modern world would be an immensely difficult one. He was also intensely sensitive to the fact that this effort might seem to negate Chinese tradition, might make reformers appear as mindless rebels who have forsaken native culture, who have drunk too heartily from the waters of Lethe while abroad. As early as 1917 Hu Shi noted: "the real problem, therefore, may be restated thus: How can we best assimilate modern civilization in such a manner as to make it congenial and congruous and continuous with the civilization of our own making? . . . The solution to this great problem will depend solely on the foresights and the sense of historical continuity of the intellectual leaders of the New China."[20]

The leaders of new China, especially Mao Zedong and Chiang Kai-shek, answered Hu Shi's question in their own ruthless fashion. They appropriated the legacy of the May Fourth student movement, while showing repeated contempt for the proponents and the goals of the original enlightenment movement. Patriotism and nationalism were all fine and good, but the kind of critical, discriminating rationality that Hu Shi had hoped for in the 1910s was increasingly less tenable in the revolution and war-torn decades that followed the student movement of 1919.

The "sense of historical continuity" with which Hu Shi hoped to guide the process of cultural adaptation was in short supply as China rushed from one violent event to the next. Whether one looks at the breakdown of the first United Front between the Communist party and the Guomindang in 1927, or at the outbreak of war with Japan in 1937 or of civil war in 1947, the specter of terror is amply apparent on the Chinese intellectual scene. Time—quiet time for cultural reflectiveness, cultural selectivity, such as Europe had been blessed with in the centuries of Renaissance and Enlightenment before the French revolution—was unavailable in twentieth-century China. As a result, the Chinese enlightenment movement became an abrogated, unfinished project. It was and remains the stillborn offspring of an era of violent condensations: modernization, revolution, even reform were collapsed into one another and suffered the truncated fate of the May Fourth enlightenment.

Adherents of the original May Fourth ideology continued to work for enlightenment on the fringes of the Chinese revolution. Zhang Shenfu, for example, a contributor to *New Tide* magazine in 1919 and a founder of the Chinese Communist party in 1921, continued a passionate interest in mathematical logic and analytical philosophy through the 1920s and 1930s. In 1927, on the eve of the outbreak of the White Terror, he published the first Chinese translation of Wittgenstein's *Tractatus*.[21] In 1936, on the eve of the Sino-Japanese war, the bookstalls of Shanghai were replete with translations from Pirandello, Yiddish short stories, and Esperanto renditions of *Chips with Everything*.[22]

The spirit of May Fourth cosmopolitanism was kept alive on the fringes of Chinese political life. The fringe, however marginal, had a central political function: it burst open the doors of the Chinese intellectual world to allow in new currents of thought. The most vigorous wind came from the North, where the Bolshevik revolution heralded national renewal through proletarian uprisings guided by Marxist-Leninist ideas. This gust became a veritable storm in China, sweeping aside the early constellation of May Fourth ideas. Diaspora-minded translators of Ibsen, Wittgenstein, and Pirandello had had their day. By the late 1930s, other revolutionaries claimed center stage. In the words of Joseph Levenson, one of the most insightful, sympathetic scholars of Chinese intellectual life: "It was revolutionary for Chinese intellectuals to be so detached from China. But intellectuals so detached could hardly be hailed by Chinese revolutionaries."[23]

The Communist revolution led by Mao Zedong achieved supremacy on the Chinese mainland in 1949. It had promised—and came close to fulfilling—a renewal that was both modern and native in inspiration. The May Fourth dream of a Chinese renaissance lived on, but in a context that frowned upon critical, comparative rationality. Coming to power on a wave of peasant nationalism, Mao had less and less use for intellectuals like Hu Shi. In fact, mounting a campaign against the "thought of Hu Shi" (the liberal himself had already found refuge in the United States and Taiwan in the 1950s) enabled Mao Zedong to whip into line disciples of May Fourth cosmopolitanism on the mainland.

The 1950s campaigns against "bourgeois" ideas crested in the Red Terror of the Cultural Revolution of 1966–1969. This was not just a campaign against certain ideas or certain intellectuals but a wholesale attack on the educated elite as well as traditional Chinese culture. A perverted version of May Fourth swept over China as bands of Red Guard youths attacked Confucius's birthplace, the palace museum, bearded professors, and foreign books. China became vengefully antiforeign while turning its back on its native past as well.

In the chaos created by vandalism and mass violence, the oldest, most repressed parts of Chinese political culture spilled forth. Long-practiced obedience toward patriarchal authority was skillfully manipulated by those who wanted to foster blind worship of Mao as the infallible helmsman. As the "Red Sun," Mao Zedong came to synchronize the thoughts of millions of followers. He was the author of a text which, in a short time, became more sacred than Confucius's *Analects*: his little red book of quotations.

The ghost of autocracy that had been the object of criticism in the original May Fourth Movement swept across the Chinese mainland almost unchecked in the period 1966–1969. Sun Jingxuan, a poet who has been the target of repeated attacks since 1958, described the predicament of the haunted nation in a 1980 work, "A Spectre Prowls Our Land":

> Oh my brothers! Have you seen
> The spectre prowling our land?

You may not recognize him, though he stands before your eyes
For like a conjurer, a master of never-ending transformation,
One moment a dragon—a robe of gold-brocade
He clasps the dragon-headed scepter,
The next in courtier's gown
He swaggers through the palace halls
And now—behold—a fresh veneer!
The latest fashion! And yet
No mask, no costume, no disguise
Can hide the coiled dragon branded on his naked rump . . .
Our sweat and blood, given from the great Edifice of Socialism
    has built a cathedral of fear . . .
Ah China! My beloved China!
You need fresh blood, air,
Wind, rain, sun;
You need to change your putrid soil!
Ah China! do not fear jeans, long hair, Taiwanese love-songs,
    Indian love-songs;
Fear the spectre from within the ancient fortress,
Prowling our land.[24]

Sun Jingxuan, like the May Fourth intellectuals before him, was attacked for pointing such a naked finger at the shortcomings of the native past. Sun had attacked what was commonly disparaged as "feudalism" in the new age of Deng Xiaoping's reforms. But he had spoken too plainly. He had held the mirror too close to the present and thus became the target of a campaign against "bourgeois liberalism."

Sun Jingxuan was forced to write an ignominious self-criticism in May 1982. But by the spring of 1989 the ideas and ideals of the original May Fourth Movement were once again alive on the streets of Beijing. Students sporting T-shirts inscribed with "Science and Democracy" congregated in Tiananmen Square as their predecessors had seventy years earlier. Historical memory came alive in China as so often before. The past was literally being born anew in 1989 as a million students chanted the slogans mouthed so tremulously by hundreds in 1919.

HISTORY—THE TIE THAT BINDS

In traditional China, history took the place of religion.[25] To be more precise, historical mindedness—a scrupulous, textually anchored attachment to the communal past—became a sacred commitment over time. References to history were, and continue to be, a fertile source of moral value, literary allusion, and guidelines for self-cultivation. In spite of political repression, foreign conquest, and individual despondency, historical memory nourished the spirit of traditional Chinese literati much as it did the idealism of students in Tiananmen Square.

The rebirth—the flood really—of the May Fourth ideals of "science" and "democracy" in 1989 marks the triumph of unofficial remembrance over politically enforced amnesia. In the decades after the event of 1919, political authorities, both on the Right and on the Left, used and usurped the meanings of the original enlightenment movement. Both the Communist party and the Guomindang sought to take the event of 1919 away from its constituency: the intellectuals. In the long run both parties failed to defeat the intellectuals' commitment to historical remembrance.

From the perspective of the Nationalist party, patriotic students of the May Fourth era had been deflected into dangerous iconoclasm by Communist agitators. In the eyes of Chinese Communist historians, the student demonstrations of 1919 were nothing more, or less, than a "necessary" prerequisite for the social revolution that led to the founding of the Chinese Communist party in 1921. Selective forgetting was the soil that nurtured both of these didactic, teleological versions of the event of 1919. These party-sponsored histories ran against the grain of remembered history, against the participants' own recollections of the original May Fourth Movement. The survivors of the event of 1919 knew only too well that the graciously titled "Chinese Renaissance" had been an eclectic jumble of Marx, Ibsen, Freud, Dewey, Russell—even Confucius. The ideas, the organizations that prevailed in the late 1910s and early 1920s, did so *not* because of historical "necessity." Rather, they were the outcome of unpredictable events, old friendships, and the accidental confluence of certain readings with a rapidly changing world.

The victory of communism on the Chinese mainland in 1949 gave the Party the power to demand and to codify a selective forgetting of May Fourth. The event of 1919 went on being loudly commemorated year after year. Its surviving participants were forced to produce made-to-order memoirs. They used bits of the remembered past to buttress a distorted version of history which claimed Chinese communism (or more precisely Marxism-Leninism-Mao Zedong thought) to be the one and only "true" outcome of the May Fourth Movement of 1919.

The suppression of genuine historical recollection was more venge-

ful after 1949 than it had been even during the bitterest conservative
attacks of the May Fourth period. Radical young intellectuals in the
1910s had turned their back on the native past while being free to explore the very Confucian teachings which they had sought to critique.
They had been free to laugh at, to argue with, even to read with reverence Gu Hongming's diatribe in the *Millard's Review*. In sum, they had
been free to quarrel with the past while remaining offsprings of history.
Official Communist historiography, by contrast, demanded that May
Fourth survivors pretend that they had left behind the "bourgeois"
ideals which they in fact had cherished and explored so briefly in the
late 1910s and early 1920s.

Intellectuals in particular, and China as a whole, paid an exorbitant
price for the distortion of memory enforced after 1949. Unremembered,
the original enlightenment movement simmered beneath the surface of
boisterously proletarian politics. It was powerless to arrest the rebirth
of traditional autocratic practices during the Cultural Revolution of
the 1960s. No wonder then that Sun Jingxuan's epigram for his 1980
poem "A Spectre Prowls Our Land" was George Santayana's warning:
"Those who do not remember the past are condemned to repeat it." [26]

Politically enforced amnesia, however, held incomplete dominion
on the Chinese mainland. As in Eastern Europe—where we just witnessed the renaissance of democratic commitments, of Mazaryk's ideals
in Havel's presidency—China, too, kept its alternative history alive
during the long decades of totalitarian control. Even as the event of
1919 was being domesticated in the pages of official Communist historiography, the iconoclastic spirit of May Fourth kept on erupting over
and over again. Appropriated by young intellectuals in Taiwan and on
the mainland, the original new thought movement became a torch with
which to light up the shortcomings of contemporary political authority.

Cut off from its roots in public history, May Fourth became an inspirational allegory through unofficial recollections of the event of 1919.
It became an unseen yet powerful bond between critical-minded young
intellectuals and survivors of the generation of 1919. In Taiwan, the
allegory of May Fourth broke out of the confines of publicly sanctioned
commemoration in a 1957 editorial in the journal *Free China*. This
magazine provided concrete contact between older May Fourth lumi-
naries such as Hu Shi and a new generation of cultural rebels. Entitled
"Rekindle the Spirit of May Fourth," the 1957 editorial proclaimed:

Thirty-eight years ago, on May Fourth, China experienced its most meaningful, most precious day. What this day shows is the ability of awakened intellectuals to set in motion a genuine enlightenment movement in China. This day of May Fourth belongs to those progressive intellectuals who want a renewed China. . . . Most young people don't even know what occasion this is. A few scholars who understand bury it deep within their hearts and wish that May Fourth was a day of commemoration that would pass into oblivion.[27]

The same month, on the Chinese mainland, students at Beijing University began their own unofficial commemoration of May Fourth. Taking full advantage of Mao's call for more outspoken criticism of the Communist party's shortcomings, they too appealed to the "spirit of May Fourth" to justify dissatisfaction with authoritarian politics. Like their fellow travelers in Taiwan, students at Beijing University in 1957 refused to give over the event of 1919 to those who would commemorate only its patriotic, nationalist significance. Instead, these young intellectuals insisted on the enduring significance of critical thought. In the words of a young physics instructor, Liu Jisheng, May Fourth was a "torch" that could illuminate the darkest corners of contemporary life:

> My praise
> Is dedicated to the torch,
> My passion
> Is dedicated to the torch-bearing madman.
> Ah, flame of May Fourth
> Though you have been dimmed for years
> The time has come
> To burn again
> As fiercely as thirty-eight years ago . . .
> Today you are needed to burn down wall-less walls,
> The chains of ideology
> The hypocritical masks
> Hearts stilled by fear . . .
> So what if cowards blame you for being extreme!
> Let all those too comfortable with winter sleep
> Mock you for stirring up trouble.[28]

Liu Jisheng was dismissed from the university and accused of being a "rightist" shortly after he posted this poem on the Democracy wall at Beijing University in May, 1957. His fellow May Fourth admirer in Taiwan, Lei Zhen—the young editor of *Free China*—was also attacked:

Lei's journal was closed down in spite of Hu Shi's efforts to protect it with his own prestige and Lei himself was arrested for subversion and jailed.

In spite of the tragic fate that befell guardians of the spirit of May Fourth in the 1950s, the torch in fact did burn on. Just as Liu Jisheng had intuited, China's own problems, the unassuaged ghosts of autocracy ensured the repeated renaissance of critical thought. The history of May Fourth could never be forgotten as long as China still lacked science and democracy, and as long as some survivors of the May Fourth era were willing and able to sanction the efforts of a new generation of intellectual rebels.

In 1979, after the death of Mao Zedong on the mainland and Chiang Kai-shek in Taiwan, a new mood of openness, of acceptance of history—including the ambiguous, promise-filled legacy of May Fourth—swept over both sides of the Taiwan Straits. In Beijing long-silenced intellectuals like Zhang Shenfu reentered public life with personal recollections of the iconoclastic event of 1919. Far from being apologetic about the harsh, critical edge of the original enlightenment, Zhang Shenfu's essay commemorating the sixtieth anniversary of May Fourth restated the enduring goals of "science and democracy," especially in a country as addicted to ideology as China had been under Mao.[29]

Zhang Shenfu's fellow *New Tide* member at Beijing University in 1919, the literary critic Yu Pingbo (who was repeatedly attacked in the 1950s and finally silenced during the Cultural Revolution), also joined commemorations of May Fourth with a markedly personal recollection of the event of 1919. Yu also resisted the pressure to augment the significance of the original student movement by linking it with the "glorious" rise of the Chinese Communist party. Instead, he dwelt on his own classmates, on unsung pioneers in a small circle of cultural rebels, on his own naïveté during a moment endowed with too much heroism, too much certainty by official historians of the Chinese revolution.[30]

In Taiwan another *New Tide* member, the historian Mao Zishui—who had pioneered critical studies of ancient texts—also broke his long silence about the event of 1919. Mao Zishui, too, had been a participant in the new thought movement, in student demonstrations sixty years earlier. He also refused to mythify the movement retrospectively. He turned down the opportunity for retrospective heroism by dwelling on his own fears: "On the day of May Fourth, I stayed with the demon-

stration until the fire at Cao Rulin's house. Then I got scared, I lost
interest and went back to the dormitory. That night, when there was a
sudden meeting to decide on a strike, I felt torn. Although I didn't like
going to classes. I also disapproved of the strike. But I said nothing."[31]

Torn, shy, even cowardly—the participants of the event of 1919 now
presented themselves in public full of the foibles long denied in the
public myth of May Fourth. These survivors had been architects of the
original enlightenment movement. They had paid dearly for their initial
quarrel with China's inherited tradition, and then again for their un-
willingness to reduce May Fourth to a politically useful patriotic movement. In 1979 they rescued historical memory, and with it the possibility
that a new generation might reinherit May Fourth unencumbered by
the polemics of the Communist party and of the Guomindang.

The hope of 1979 burst into full bloom with the student demonstration of 1989. The seventieth anniversary of May Fourth was shown
on television in China and around the world; hundreds of thousands
of young Chinese marched in Beijing chanting "science and democracy," honoring and reappropriating the event of 1919. The Communist
party's plans to host a more modest, more controlled commemoration—that was to include newly sanctioned dancing parties as well as
scholarly meetings—was upstaged by the students who took to the
streets and insisted that the past had a direct, questioning relevance to
the present. Locked in struggle over the Party's corruption, over the
slow pace of political as opposed to economic reforms, students taunted
Party elders to come and join them in living up to the spirit of May
Fourth.

On the actual day of May 4, 1989, Chinese scholars from Taiwan,
Hong Kong, Singapore, and the United States joined student demonstrators in Tiananmen Square. The diaspora that began spiritually in the
May Fourth period and firmed up with barbed wire in 1949 appeared
to be over, as Chinese intellectuals of different generations, different
homelands gathered to celebrate their common point of historical origin. One older scholar, Professor Chow Tse-tsung—who began writing
about May Fourth on the mainland and then made his career in Taiwan and in the United States—was literally carried on the shoulders of
Beijing students as they heard and recognized the name of the author
of the most famous book on the original student movement of 1919.[32]

In the bright sunshine of May 4, 1989, the tanks that would quell student optimism were nowhere in sight, yet. An exuberant homecoming to history was celebrated in Tiananmen, a homecoming to 1919 and a moving forth to the democratic China dreamt about seventy years earlier. For a brief moment, China appeared to be fully mobilized around its intellectual youth, ready to follow its lead.

In the heat of this excitement, there was little time to recall May Fourth warnings about the limitations of intellectuals. In 1989 China and the world wanted a totally positive, lovable (*keai* was the most frequent Chinese expression used to describe students) view of idealistic youth and could not be bothered to recall—at least not in public—the many ways in which the educated elite was and remains part of the very culture they criticize with such passion. Made-for-media proclamations about the past and future glories of May Fourth replaced the self-critical musings of 1979.

During the May Fourth Movement of 1919, champions of enlightenment knew themselves to be deeply stained by the very prejudices and myths they sought to uproot with the aid of Western-inspired rationality. Lu Xun, China's foremost writer, voiced this sense of culpability most acutely in his path-breaking short story "Diary of a Madman." In this work Lu Xun equated Confucianism with cannibalism, and yet also called himself an eater of human flesh. His only hope at the end of the story was: "Perhaps there are children who haven't eaten men? Save the children."[33]

Contaminated by his own sister's "flesh"—the knowledge that he was deeply rooted in the patriarchal, authoritarian society he was seeking to overthrow—Lu Xun never arrogated to himself more than the role of critic-accomplice. His sense of the limited yet vital utility of intellectual dissent did not flourish in the decades after 1919. Nationalist leaders of the Chinese revolution had less tolerance for critical-minded cosmopolitans. The intellectuals who could not or would not tow the various party lines were cast to the margins of history or exterminated as "enemies of the people." Injured and besmirched, Chinese intellectuals nonetheless survived the Maoist era long enough to bequeath the next generation the unfinished legacy of May Fourth.

INTELLECTUALS—THE FRACTURED VESSEL

Confucius once said "the gentleman is not a utensil," not someone who can be used or discarded at the whim of political authorities. Teaching in the fifth century B.C., however, Confucius could not have imagined the terrors inflicted on his own kind in the age of Mao Zedong. Not only were intellectuals used and abused, beaten and incarcerated in "cow pens," they were robbed of silence as well. Confucius has taught the gentleman to maintain his inner autonomy through self-cultivation. Even if his point of view, his values did not prevail in the world, they were safe in the gentleman's heart-mind. This spiritual practice was increasingly difficult to maintain in Mao's China, where intellectuals were repeatedly required to castigate themselves, to incriminate themselves and their colleagues.

If Confucius stands at the headwaters of a long, glorious tradition of intellectual accomplishment in China, survivors of the Cultural Revolution mark its tragic diminution. But herein lies their unique historical opportunity, indeed obligation, some would say. Unable to pass down with confidence the accumulated wisdom of the past, unwilling to serve as bureaucratic managers of a somewhat virtuous ruler (as their predecessors had in imperial times and they themselves had been tempted to do in the 1950s), contemporary Chinese intellectuals have become fractured vessels—broken-hearted witnesses to their own and their countrymen's suffering.

In their internal fragmentation lies China's best hope for recovery, for a new kind of spiritual wholeness. If the survivors of the Cultural Revolution can bear witness to the abuses of the past, China's future might be spared painful repetitions. Fidelity to historical memory, however, is a complicated, difficult undertaking. It requires intellectuals to acknowledge their own complicity in China's long-standing autocracy. This is an important and also a rather bleak responsibility.

The cultural capital of intellectual survivors is not immediately apparent or appreciated in the post-Mao era. Official reformers require (and impose) optimism about the future and amnesia about the details of the Cultural Revolution. Younger intellectuals, who were themselves Red Guards in the 1960s, prefer to dwell on their wounds, on their disillusionment with Mao as the "Great Helmsman" and to ignore their own culpability in the frenzy that swept over China. Thus, it is the older, historically seasoned intellectuals of the May Fourth era who are left with the lonely task of the reminder: to bring to mind both the courage and the cowardice of China as a whole.

The octogenarian writer Ba Jin addressed this need for reminders when he called for the establishment of a Cultural Revolution Museum.

A fifteen-year-old boy during the May Fourth Movement, Ba Jin went on to describe its passions and eventual unraveling in a series of novels beginning with *Family*. Much persecuted during the Cultural Revolution (his wife died in its throes in 1973), Ba Jin refused to forget what he saw and endured. His was not simply a personal gesture—although he described his last collection of essays as a personal sort of "Cultural Revolution Museum."[34] Rather, what Ba Jin wanted was for his countrymen to have a place, a way to see their nightmares remembered. Using the analogy of the Holocaust, he wrote in 1986:

Everything that happened twenty years ago is still clearly before my mind's eye. Those endlessly long and painful days, the degradation and torture. You cannot tell me we should forget all about it, or forbid people to talk about it. That would only make it possible for another Cultural Revolution to take place in twenty years' time. By then people would think it was something new. . . .

It's not that I don't want to forget; it's simply that the gray specter of the past has me in its grip and won't let me go. How I let myself be disarmed, how the disaster crept up on me, just how that tragedy unfolded, and the hateful role that I played in it all, walking step by step toward the abyss. . . .

The building of a Cultural Revolution Museum is not the responsibility of one person. Everyone owes it to their children and the future to leave a monument to the harrowing lessons of the past. Don't let history repeat itself should not be an empty statement. Everyone should be able to see clearly, remember fully.[35]

There is no Cultural Revolution Museum in China today. But Ba Jin's words echo on after his death—"everyone should see clearly, remember fully." Witness the rush among Chinese students abroad to set up a memorial to the Tiananmen events of 1989. If not within China (though there is an extraordinary amount of underground remembering going on there as well), at least abroad, in the ongoing Chinese diaspora, Chinese history is being recorded and scrutinized with care. A call from modern Jewish experience—"never again"—has been picked up by Chinese intellectuals who have an increasingly large repository of pain-filled, shame-laden experiences which they cannot, must not, forget.

The modernity quested for imaginatively in the May Fourth era has now been bestowed, *faute de mieux*, by Chinese history itself. In the 1910s, a new China, a new individual was only dreamt about by critical-minded thinkers who used Western ideas to question inherited culture. Today, in exile (whether spiritual or geographic), identities are refashioned constantly. Displaced, dispossessed, Chinese intellectuals no longer take solace from grand notions such as "the people"—*ren-min*—an idea that became a club with which Mao Zedong beat cosmopolitans into submission. Today's intellectuals are also less beholden to heroic images of individualism on the model of Ibsen's Nora, who walked away from family and community in the name of a higher duty, "the duty to Myself."[36]

On the La MaMa stage in New York a Chinese dancer struggles to get into, to stay in the privy. The voice above him declares: "I love the toilet. . . . It is the only place to be private. I love the toilet, especially when there is no toilet paper, then you can use anything at hand, old history books are best."[37] The old May Fourth dream of escape from history, of liberation of the individual is now enacted in a cramped bathroom. A near nightmare, the dream goes on.

At the Iowa International Writers program, a veteran May Fourth writer explains his reasons for taking up the pen after the death of Mao through a parable—an old Chinese story about a village filled with wife-fearing men. Wu Zuguang, a writer who has survived many humiliations in Mao's China, continues to write, to be contentious in his own way. Wu was not ashamed to conclude in Iowa: "I suppose I'm like that fellow, I'm terrified of my wife and scared of crowds too. All of us men are like that, where I come from. So I thirst for freedom. Why exactly are we scared? Because they won't leave us alone. So I long for an environment where I can be left alone. That for me is freedom."[38]

A village of scared men longing to be left alone—that is the ironic, bitter posture into which Chinese intellectuals have been forced by modern history. They are far from being alone in this predicament. Intellectuals in recently emancipated Eastern Europe are also discovering how compromised, how fear-ridden their voices have become. Their longing for freedom is also colored by an awareness of their prolonged acquiescence to totalitarianism. As Václav Havel put it in his 1990 presidential address on the occasion of the New Year: "All of us have become accustomed to the totalitarian system, accepted it as an unalterable fact and therefore kept it running. . . . None of us is merely a victim of it, because all of us helped to create it together."[39]

Long before Havel became president, his compatriot Franz Kafka began to dissect this predicament of complicity, terror, and a longing for exilic knowledge. In one of his short stories, "The Great Wall of China," Kafka took on the time-worn voice of a builder of the Great Wall to raise questions about historical knowledge and its relationship to political authority. Written in 1917—the year of the Russian Revolution and also of Kafka's diagnosis which showed him to have tuberculosis—the story centers on the connections between memory, power, and an ongoing sense of cultural identity.

Kafka's builder confesses that he is but a small brick in the edifice of what will become the hallmark of China's greatness. Kept willfully ignorant of the nature and the plan of the huge imperial project, each mason works for a limited time on a fragment of the whole. And yet the urge to know, the urge to question imperial intentions, the urge to place the Wall in some comparative context alongside the Tower of Babel, wins out. Almost shamefaced the builder tells us: "During the building of the wall and ever since to this very day I have occupied myself with the comparative history of the races—there are certain questions which one can probe to the marrow, as it were, only by this means—and I have discovered that we Chinese possess certain folk and political institutions that are unique in their clarity, others unique in their obscurity. The desire to trace these phenomena, especially the latter, has always teased me and teases me still."[40]

In 1917 Kafka wrote about "we Chinese." A tortured modern Jew in Prague took the imaginative leap toward China for much the same reason that Chinese intellectuals took their leap toward the West: to gain some distance from the "unique obscurities" of his native inheritance. Kafka's builder knows that he risks death by pressing his questions about the Great Wall too far. After all, mystery, uncertainty, fragmentary knowledge is what keeps imperial authority in place.

Chinese thinkers who tried to see through, to look past the greatness of the Great Wall also ran a great risk. Their conservative contemporaries and revolutionary successors damned them for being "unChinese," for betraying something that was precious, noble, the very essence of what Gu Hongming described as "the greatness of the moral and spiritual inheritance of the Chinese Civilization." And yet, despite virulent accusations and tremendous self-doubt, Chinese intellectuals continued to question the greatness of Chinese civilization. They continued to quarrel with the Great Wall. They came to see it more and more as a self-created obstacle to freedom and to contact with other civilizations.

Today, with the collapse of the Berlin Wall, the whole world is discovering what Kafka and Chinese intellectuals intuited decades earlier: that walls of the mind are far more entrenched, far more dangerous than those rising out of the soil. Ethnic chauvinism and anti-Semitism in Europe and xenophobia in China remained alive and well during the long period of Communist revolution. It is not enough to dismantle external barriers to freedom; inner ramparts must be scaled as well. In the words of Lu Xun, Kafka's spiritual kin in China, it is not enough to take apart the wall, brick by brick. One must come to terms with its curse as well. This is what historical memory is for, this is what makes being Chinese (or more literally, "doing Chineseness," *zuo Zhongguo ren*) in the twentieth century so difficult and yet so challenging:

"I am always conscious of being surrounded by a Great Wall. The stone works consist of old bricks reinforced by new bricks. They combine to make a wall that hems us in. When will we stop reinforcing the Great Wall with new bricks?"[41]

This question is still unanswered. Not only in China but in the contemporary West as well.

4

Being Chinese: The Peripheralization of Traditional Identity

Myron L. Cohen

Embedded in China's late traditional culture was a representation of that country's social and political arrangements so strongly developed as to convey to the Chinese people a quite firm sense of their involvement in them.[1] Indeed, China's society and polity were represented as dimensions of the cosmos itself. Being civilized, that is being Chinese, was nothing less than proper human behavior in accordance with cosmic principles. It therefore is ironic, and for much of the Chinese people most problematic, that the modern Chinese nationalism articulated since the beginning of this century by China's new elite has involved a forceful and near-total rejection of the earlier traditional and culturally elaborated sense of nationhood. Those who today identify themselves as Chinese do so without the cultural support provided by tradition. Some, having rejected that tradition, are unable to replace it with an alternative cultural arrangement for a nationalism that provides a satisfactory form of identification. The vast majority of China's population neither rejected tradition nor saw it as incompatible either with modern nationalism or with national modernization. Yet this majority has seen its traditional forms of identification with the nation derided as backward and actively suppressed by China's modern political and intellectual elites, whose views on other matters range across the political spectrum from extremes of Left and Right. China's traditional elites were cultural brokers, for their high status in society was based upon nationally accepted standards that were also validated by local culture. In contrast, the pronounced cultural antagonism separating the new elite from the masses represents a barrier between state and society, one hardly conducive to the construction of a form of modern nationalism that would engage, reinterpret, and derive support from the traditional consciousness of national identity.

COMMON CULTURE AND NATIONAL IDENTITY

In late traditional times there was in China a common culture in the sense of shared behavior, institutions, and beliefs. Common culture need only be a matter of the geographic distribution of such traits in a way that defines what anthropologists call a "culture area," but China's common culture was also a unified culture in the sense that it provided standards according to which people identified themselves as Chinese. Taking this Han or ethnic Chinese culture as a whole, there can be no doubt that the historical trend in premodern times was toward increasing uniformity. By the end of the traditional period the Han Chinese had hardly attained a state of total homogeneity, but the extent to which the Han Chinese shared a common culture was considerable in comparison with many traditional empires or states, and all the more impressive given the size of the Chinese empire and the very small proportion of non-Han within it.

Diffusion and acculturation account for much of the replication of many aspects of social organization, economic behavior, and religious ritual and belief throughout the Han population. Some of this diffusion was brought about simply by migrations, there being some very large-scale population movements even as late as the Ming and Qing dynasties. In many cases Han Chinese immigrants simply swamped earlier settlements, while in others Han Chinese of varying social backgrounds gained the upper hand when interacting with natives. Their agriculture was far more productive than the slash-and-burn cultivation often encountered in the south, for example. Again, the entrepreneurial orientation built into traditional Chinese family organization could facilitate Han economic dominance and thereby form the basis for the emergence of a Han local elite that would transform local culture. The Chinese imperial state played a paradoxical role in these migrations. When it was strong it controlled regions extending far beyond areas where large Han populations already were in place, and therefore provided a security umbrella for Han movement toward the frontiers. When the state was weak or divided, the resulting wars and chaos also drove large numbers of refugees to seek new homes in distant regions.

While China's unity is often described as having been achieved despite its pronounced linguistic diversity, I am more impressed by the fact that in late imperial times perhaps two-thirds or more of the Han Chinese had as their native tongue a variant of Mandarin. Among the Han, extreme linguistic heterogeneity was mainly characteristic of the southeastern coastal provinces in an arc extending roughly from Shanghai through Guangdong and into Guangxi. Furthermore, the "Mandarin" that was the "official language" (*guanhua*) was in fact the basis of a nationwide *written* vernacular used in novels, some operas, and in certain ritual texts recited during rural and urban ceremonies of popular religion. This was linguistic unity at a high level, facilitated by the descent of later forms of spoken Chinese from a common earlier language; by the educated elite's use of a common script and an elaborated style of classical writing, which in a simpler version was widely employed in business contracts and other everyday documents; and by the widespread circulation of printed texts representing all prevalent writing styles. Printed texts conveyed much information that was absorbed into popular lore; they also served as vehicles for the transmission of opera and other performances that portrayed a history of China which also described its current polity and society.[2]

On the basis of my own field research in four widely separated Chinese villages, I can confirm that even where differences in spoken language were most obvious, the Han Chinese shared traits so numerous as to readily place them in a culture area easily distinguished from those of nearby state civilizations in Asia. My earliest fieldwork, in the 1960s, was in the southern part of subtropical Taiwan. During 1986 and 1987 I carried out field research in the northern province of Hebei, notable for its long, cold winters. Most recently, I divided the first half of 1990 between fieldwork in villages in east and west China—one near Shanghai, the other on the Chengdu Plain of Sichuan Province. These villages are thus found in what were the northern, southern, eastern, and western regions of agrarian China during late traditional times. If considered as they were before the changes they have undergone in the past fifty years or so, they provide evidence in the form of near-total identity that key features of family organization were common to Han society throughout China. These include a patrilineally oriented and male-centered arrangement of marriage and authority, and social and economic roles that reflected the family's character as being as much an enterprise as a domestic group. Among the characteristic roles were those of the family head (*jiazhang*)—the senior male and the family's formal representative to the outside world—and the family manager (*dangjia*), who was in charge of family work and earnings. Although there was a clear social distinction between these two roles, in small families the father would have both; with his advancing age and increasing family size, the position of family manager was frequently taken over by one of his sons. Brothers had equal rights to family property, the dominant form of ownership, but were also obligated to pool their earnings as long as the family remained intact. The distribution of family property among them was a key element in family division (*fenjia*), which also involved the setting up of separate kitchens for each of the new and now economically independent families. The four villages also amply confirm that other features already generally noted as having been characteristic of late traditional China were indeed embedded in village life: I have in mind a high degree of premodern commercialization and commoditization, where land was commonly bought, sold, and mortgaged, and where contracts, written and oral, played an important role in village life. It was in this context that families and the family farm were distinctly entrepreneurial and market-oriented to the extent permitted by their resources. Contracts even entered into the intimacies of family relationships and conflicts, as in the businesslike partition documents that were signed by brothers about to form separate households.

Among the more obvious of the other factors behind the spread and reproduction of Han culture across China was the state's ability to define a national elite through an examination system requiring the mastery of a standard curriculum. These examinations both generated candidates for the bureaucracy and created an even larger class of degree holders whose status gave them positions of influence in their home communities at the same time that it confirmed their social equality with the bureaucrats. Cultural integration was also fostered by China's well-developed traditional economy, which linked large regions in marketing arrangements, supported a high degree of urbanization, and involved large-scale circulation of merchants and commodities. Like the examination system, the economy provided a means to validate local elite status through participation in wide-ranging extralocal relationships.

How did the participation of elites in a national culture lead to this culture's deep penetration into local society? It has been suggested by James L. Watson that a key element in China's unified culture was acceptance of particular standardized rituals.[3] Through participation in such rituals one was Chinese, and one was civilized. The use of ritual to validate cultural status is indicative of the Chinese focus on proper behavior rather than on proper ideas, on orthopraxy rather than orthodoxy. While correct ideology was hardly insignificant for the state or for the scholarly elite,[4] there can be no doubt that ritual or *li* loomed very large in Confucian thinking and was a major concern of the Master himself. From the elite Confucian (or later neo-Confucian) perspective, *li* was indeed a civilizing force. The term referred both to ritual and to proper behavior, and in the latter sense it can most appropriately be translated as "etiquette." By late traditional times, as Watson emphasizes, both the term and its different referents had been fully absorbed into the vocabulary and thinking of ordinary people throughout China.

Ritual and etiquette are very different kinds of behavior. Ritual behavior is distinct from that of daily life and involves actions held to be instrumental either on the basis of the particular theory, goals, or beliefs linked to the ritual itself or simply as confirmation that the ritual is being properly performed. Etiquette, on the other hand, is precisely the regulation of everyday behavior according to standards accepted as proper. From the point of view of state Confucianism there was a strong emphasis on etiquette as well as ritual, for in the final analysis both were held to be based upon ethics and also to be means of inculcating ethics, while such ethics were themselves validated as being elements of a total, morally good cosmic order. It was as important for filial piety, for example, to receive proper expression during a funeral as it did in the respect children accorded their living parents. Indeed, the Chinese term *xiao* means both "filiality" and "mourning." Thus proper morality meant full adherence to *li* in all senses of the term. Moreover, it was understood that not everyone could live fully in accordance with these standards, and that those most able to do so would serve as exemplars for the rest of society.

It may be difficult to judge the extent to which China's scholarly elite, who understood the state Confucian theory of *li*, related it to their style of life. Nevertheless, there is little doubt that in late traditional China there was an impressively homogeneous elite life style involving, among many other things, classical learning, avoidance of physical labor, styles of dress and home furnishings, decorous behavior, and full adherence to *li* as ritual. The elite population spanned the divides between commercial wealth, landholding, and status based on the possession of an examination degree, and it was distributed throughout China. This elite has long since passed from the scene, which may be why, in much of the anthropological literature, its local impact on culture and society tends to be underestimated and in some cases ignored altogether. To the extent that late traditional Chinese culture has survived to come under the scrutiny of fieldworkers, it is a culture stripped of its elite component, one that tells only part of the story. Yet among the now-departed elite, the learned and the wealthy in the cities and in the countryside alike, the *li* of etiquette and the *li* of ritual were as one.

Ordinary people, however, had neither the leisure nor the financial wherewithal to live in full accordance with the standards of *li* as etiquette. But for most of them *li* as ritual certainly was in their grasp. Ritual has a beginning and an end, and the most important life-cycle rituals did not occur with great frequency in any one family. They were indeed expensive, but it appears that in any region a particular ritual was available in packages of varying cost, such as one-day, two-day or three-day funerals, or—in Hebei—one-palanquin or two-palanquin weddings. Again, throughout China guests invited to the feasts invariably accompanying such rituals would make cash contributions that often helped subsidize these events. In any case, differences between rituals related more to their scale than to the presence or absence of key elements, such as those described by Watson for funerals. As Evelyn Rawski has shown,[5] the same basic ritual ingredients were present in the funerals of emperors and ordinary farmers. Furthermore, such rituals were expensive for villagers precisely because they represented the closest approximation to elite standards of *li* such people could manage. Thus in much of China the use of palanquins by bride and groom was common to both elite and ordinary weddings. For most people this was purely a ritual vehicle, while for the elite its use was merely one element in the etiquette that generally governed their lives. Again, even among farmers the formal wedding attire of bride and groom was based upon elite versions; the groom, especially, wore a formal gown of the kind a member of the elite might wear under a great variety of circumstances. The food consumed by ordinary villagers during the banquets associated with weddings, funerals, and festivals was a far cry from their usual fare and to varying degrees approximated ritual and nonritual elite culinary standards.

Rituals firmly linked China's common people to a national culture through their emulation of *local* elites. This process was facilitated by the local-level social mobility that by late traditional times was institutionalized in many different ways: through partible inheritance, the pronounced commoditization of land and other valued goods, the examination system, and the strong deemphasis of hereditary status discriminations implied by all of these. As to the elites, even those living in rural communities were immersed in much larger social networks based on marriage, commercial ties, the examination system, and many other elements. The social universe of the elite was united by a culture largely colored by both etiquette and ritual precisely because involvement in that culture had to be based primarily on norms recognized and accepted in China as a whole.

Despite the operation in China of strong forces making for cultural unity, there remained readily apparent differences in language and custom. Most recently among anthropologists there has been a strong reawakening of interest in such regional differences in Chinese culture, or, indeed, in Chinese regional cultures. One source of variation pointed to with increasing frequency is the absorption of elements from earlier native cultures.[6] There can be no doubt that aboriginal traits have entered into Chinese culture, and that at one time or another this has occurred everywhere in the country, with the Han Chinese being the product of a fusion of cultural elements. Variations, however, are not explained by asserting or even demonstrating their aboriginal roots, for this begs the question of why some such traits made it into the Han mainstream (or even into Han tributaries) while others fell by the wayside. Another problem is that not all variation can be attributed to particular aboriginal influences. Under circumstances of premodern communications it is almost inevitable that variations will develop, given that rural populations generally remain rooted in their locales for long periods of time. In his original study of marketing in rural China,

G. William Skinner proposed that the "standard marketing community" was a kind of semiencapsulated catchment area within which a particular localism might emerge and differentiate the marketing community even from the one next door.[7] Certainly villagers I spoke with in Hebei in 1986 and 1987 could readily note how their marriage customs differed from those of nearby communities, with which they in fact had marriage ties; they seemed to thoroughly enjoy describing how these differences had to be reconciled when marriages were negotiated. Earlier, I encountered precisely the same situation in Taiwan, where the residents of the southernmost Hakka villages on the Pingtung Plain married in ways somewhat different from people in Hakka villages less than 20 miles to the north, so that compromises had to be made to allow the frequent marriages between these two areas to go forward.

Whatever their origins, there were many regional variations in Chinese culture far more pronounced than those just noted, and these were reflected in the four villages where I have worked. The south Taiwan village was a Hakka-speaking community and, as among the Hakka generally, female footbinding had never been practiced. In each of the other villages, by contrast, footbinding had been almost universal, so that these villages were fully representative of what had been the dominant Han pattern in late traditional times. While the practice and especially the distribution of footbinding have yet to be given the full scholarly attention they merit, this custom would appear to have been firmly established throughout much of urban and rural China during the Qing dynasty.[8] Major exceptions were among the Hakka, who entirely avoided it, and the Cantonese, among whom it seems to have been restricted to the elite. The Cantonese therefore lend credence to the otherwise erroneous but widespread Western notion that this was an upper-class custom only. In much of China only socially marginal women such as unmarried servants had natural feet, and if for no other reason mothers would bind their daughters' feet to ensure their eligibility for marriage. In most areas where footbinding was practiced, it was forced upon women as being as essential a manifestation of "proper" or "civilized" status as a ritually correct marriage or funeral. In these areas, in other words, a woman's being Chinese required that she have bound feet. Thus if some of the rituals and practices associated with being Chinese were in fact found throughout the Han population, others may have had a more limited distribution. The consciousness of being Chinese, therefore, can be distinguished from specific attributes associated with that state of being in any particular region.

Following the lines suggested by Skinner, we might usefully consider the extent to which the generation or preservation of differences was the flip side of the creation of uniformities in late traditional Chinese culture. Anthropologists, after all, have long been interested in how particular groups actively construct (or at least manipulate) their cultural milieu in order in some cases to assert their unique identity and in others to create claims for acceptance within a larger group. That differentiation and integration may occur concurrently, especially in complex societies, should hardly come as a surprise. This of course is what the "ethnic" factor in American politics is all about. In China, differentiation was encouraged by the fact that local communities (however defined and at whatever scale of organization) had their own parochial interests to consider. Such interests could be protected or advanced by local elites, community defense organizations, and by many other means, while a major focus of community religion was the enhancement of local welfare.

Place of origin was one of the major ascribed statuses in Chinese society.[9] A common place of origin served as the basis of organization for merchants and others away from home, and such people were expected to contribute to the welfare of their native communities should they succeed on the outside. In general there was, among the Chinese, a deep and very sentimental attachment to the localisms—be they customs, food, or "local products"—of their home communities. Furthermore, it was well understood and accepted by the Chinese state that each district had its own "customs," descriptions of which were standard entries in officially authorized local gazetteers. At all levels of society, and among those serving or representing the state, it was considered that one dimension of being Chinese was to have a place of origin somewhere in China. It was therefore as important for a region to have its own personality as it was for it to manifest its Chinese character. Regional differences, whatever their origin, were not as such discouraged by the state's local representatives. While efforts were made to eliminate local behaviors considered uncivilized or heterodox, it was not the aim of the state to impose total conformity, precisely because the only available model for such conformity was the national elite culture that commoners were not expected to be able to emulate.

It is therefore clear that the state's cooptation of localisms or regional practices went much deeper than I have suggested above. Once a community—generally at a scale of local organization well above the village level—had an established local elite conforming to China-wide standards of etiquette and ritual, the stage was set for the reinterpretation of many local practices as Chinese. Almost by definition, this local elite would be involved in the examinations, in the classical education they required, and in commercial, social, and political relationships extending well beyond the community. It would be or would develop into a native elite, with a gradual turnover in membership resulting from the operation of the Chinese institutions that made upward or downward social mobility almost inevitable. Social mobility, as well as the hope for upward mobility, would be factors encouraging cultural interchange between the elite and ordinary people. In conjunction with the development of this elite many local customs would disappear, some deliberately suppressed and others falling by the wayside. There would also be a massive penetration of Han cultural traits, a process which might very well have been under way prior to the appearance of such a local elite and which may have facilitated the latter's development.[10] The area would thus experience the evolution of a syncretic culture to a point that it became acceptably Chinese. One important sign of the local culture's acceptance would be the transformation of some surviving (or invented) local traits into the identifiers used by the local elite to glorify their place of origin within China. Rather than being covered up, acceptable localisms were incorporated by the state and the elite into Chinese cosmopolitanism.

An excellent example of this process is provided by the Bai or Minjia people, who live in the southwestern province of Yunnan.[11] The Bai became anthropologically famous as the subjects of Francis L. K. Hsu's book, *Under the Ancestors' Shadow*, a study of a community portrayed as culturally Chinese. The case of the Bai is especially significant because the cultural absorption of their area into China began only after the Ming conquest late in the fourteenth century, yet by the end of the Qing dynasty the transformation of at least some Bai-speaking communities into Han Chinese was well under way—indeed, for all practical purposes, may even have been completed. In these communities education was based on the same curriculum used elsewhere in late traditional China; the Bai boasted local elites with wide-ranging commercial ties to other parts of the country, and their enthusiastic participation in the examination system receives prominent mention in Hsu's monograph. While much of the aboriginal culture had given way to Han practices, the area was still bilingual, a fact perhaps related to the relatively late arrival of the Han and to the presence of a large settled rural population prior to Han penetration. In any event, what was left of Bai culture had by the end of the Qing dynasty been redefined as Chinese local customs, the practice of which was proof of being Chinese. Thus it is not at all surprising that Bai speakers thought their language was a "Chinese dialect."

A remarkable feature of late traditional Chinese culture was that it linked being Chinese to a firm consciousness of participating in a nationwide system of political, social, religious, and symbolic relationships, with even localisms being transformed into statements of such relationships. The power of the imperial state received direct cultural confirmation in many ways. During the Qing dynasty the subordination of the Chinese people to this state was given blatant expression by near-total compliance with the requirement that all men adopt the Manchu tonsure, shaving their foreheads and arranging what was left of their hair in a queue.[12] Even though rejection of this requirement was thus made an easy symbol of rebellion, by the end of the dynasty this hair style had become a more general signifier of being Chinese, as evidenced by the reluctance of many men to change it after the dynasty fell. Another example of submission to state hegemony is the equally ubiquitous use of imperial reign titles, which served to identify years in the Chinese expression of dates. As they were everywhere else in China, dates were indicated in this fashion in southern Taiwan. I know from copies of old contracts and account books in my possession that in many cases reign years continued to be so used during the first three years or so of the Japanese occupation of Taiwan, which began in 1895, and that it was only after about five years that the transition from the Qing Guangxu to the Japanese Meiji was complete. This Taiwan example also indicates that the use of reign titles was a more general statement of being Chinese.

Few Chinese if any did not know about the examination system, which generated the country's degree-holding local elite and provided candidates for its bureaucracy. Degree holders were ubiquitous in city and countryside alike, and if no degree holder resided in a particular village there certainly would be some nearby. While the examinations hardly presented realistic opportunities for social advancement as far as the mass of China's population was concerned, examination system lore deeply penetrated popular thinking. In many parts of China it was customary for a midwife, having delivered a village woman's son, to express the hope that he would obtain the highest rank (*zhuangyuan*) the system had to offer. China-wide links were embedded in the symbols of the ancestral cult, as in the use of hall names that linked every surname to a place of origin in the old north China heartland of the Han, or in the identification of prominent figures in Chinese history or myth as founding ancestors. Even variations in language could be described in terms pointing to links between regional and national identification. In the rural area of Sichuan where I did my fieldwork, the local form of Sichuanese (itself a Mandarin dialect) was contrasted with that spoken in Chengdu, the provincial seat about 50 miles away, and with the traditional standard Mandarin largely based on the dialect of Beijing, the capital both during Qing times and at present. The speech of Chengdu was known as the "little official language" (*xiao guanhua*), that of Beijing as the "big official language" (*da guanhua*).

The gods of popular religion, in their relationships to one another and to mortals, identified local communities with the organization of the Chinese state and the cosmos. The Jade Emperor, as the supreme ruler of the universe, represented a personified version of the abstract Heaven worshipped by the living emperor, but he was also seen to be the latter's divine equivalent. In the Jade Emperor's court were the major gods and goddesses of the Chinese popular pantheon. In his supernatural bureaucracy the City Gods and other tutelary deities carried out their duties on earth, each with jurisdiction over a particular area. In the underworld, the ten magistrates of hell judged and punished the dead in courts that were images of the offices (*yamen*) where mortal bureaucrats carried out their work. Heaven, earth, and the underworld were united in an arrangement modeled on that of the human imperial order.

Popular images of the Jade Emperor and his bureaucracy on earth and in the underworld appear to have been relatively standardized throughout China. As James L. Watson has suggested, this standardization was encouraged and promoted by the state and represented one aspect of its deep involvement in popular religion. City God temples, for example, were focal points of popular religion; yet they also were official, and it was required that at each administrative seat such a temple be constructed, together with those dedicated to Confucius and Guan Yu, the patrons of the civil and military wings of the bureaucracy and the degree-holding class in general. Perceptions of the Jade Emperor's court varied, however, precisely because different communities and regions placed their own particular patron deities and other local gods in positions of prominence, thus linking the religious representation of local society to the larger cosmic system. The court—be it divine or in Beijing—was an arrangement of personal relationships and thus a most appropriate source of protection for the individual or the community. The gods of the divine bureaucracy and court represented a major component of the supernatural entities and forces constituting Chinese popular religion; ordinary people were in constant contact with these gods, so that their religion in fact conveyed an intimate image of the Chinese state, one far closer to home than was the actual government of mortals.[13]

Consciousness of being a full participant in the total political, cultural, and social arrangements of the Chinese state and Chinese civilization was what being Chinese was all about. The symbols, rituals, and lore evoking this consciousness were embedded in local culture, so that being a complete person by local standards was also being Chinese. This late traditional Chinese consciousness was reinforced by a cultural system that both defined the cosmos and monopolized perception of it. The natural, the supernatural, the family, society, the state, and the universe were subsumed within a total cosmic plan that left little if anything unaccounted for. It is no wonder that those who because of poverty or for other reasons were unable to live or to succeed in accordance with local standards could be attracted to various "heterodox" beliefs, and that many of these beliefs implied rejection not only of locally dominant sentiments, but also of the larger cultural design that made proper people Chinese.[14]

ANTICULTURE AND NATIONALISM

The very fact that for elite and ordinary people alike being properly Chinese involved acceptance of an all-encompassing cultural arrangement led to a major crisis in self-identification, first among the bureaucratic and scholarly elite, with the onset of the assault by Western powers in the nineteenth century. For increasing numbers of people Chinese culture simply did not work: as a self-centered definition of the cosmos rooted in its own history, it had little relevance to the unprecedented conditions created by Western domination and the large-scale introduction of new technology, institutions, and ideas. For those most immediately involved in these novel circumstances, such as students in the new schools, treaty port merchants and workers, and many others, the cultural crisis was most acute. Many must have felt that they were living in a cultural vacuum, which could only be filled *both* by the creation of a new cultural design *and*, of necessity, by a redefinition of being Chinese.

These were the conditions leading to the emergence of the cultural realignments and cleavages that have remained characteristic of modern Chinese society. The new definition of being Chinese is firmly rooted in nationalism, in a conception of China as a nation-state with interests that must be protected and advanced in competition with those of other nation-states. Modern Chinese nationalism is hardly an ultimately cosmic orientation, as was the traditional sense of Chinese national identity, for its emergence and growth was prompted by the conviction that China was weak, indeed in many ways inferior to other nation-states. One of the original slogans of this new nationalism, that China must become "prosperous and strong" (*fuqiang*), is still commonly associated with Chinese nationalist sentiment today. The new Chinese nationalism was not at all defined within a larger cultural framework. In this respect it was also very different from the earlier form of Chinese identification, and also unlike many versions of the Western nationalism that precipitated the new Chinese national orientation. This meant that Chinese nationalism could spread across the widening cultural divide between traditionalists—who even at the time of the Communist victory still constituted the large majority of the rural and urban populations—and those involved one way or another in the modernizing sectors of society. Chinese of varying cultural inclinations could identify with the increasingly common anti-imperialist and anti-foreign movements of the early twentieth century. In more recent years, China's successes in science, sports, warfare, and other endeavors are as much a source of pride for ordinary farmers as for nontraditional urban intellectuals.

Among these intellectuals and some other segments of the population, however, there emerged and continues to thrive an important connection precisely between nationalism and, an at times almost ferociously iconoclastic antitraditionalism. Although perhaps anticipated by the mid-nineteenth-century Taiping Rebellion and beginning to develop during the final years of the Qing dynasty, nationalistic antitraditionalism received its first forceful expression during the May Fourth Movement that exploded in 1919. One extreme but nevertheless instructive example of the antitraditionalism of the May Fourth era is Qian Xuantong's letter to Chen Duxiu,[15] who later would be one of the founders of the Chinese Communist Party. The letter reads in part as follows:

Dear Mr. Chen:

In an earlier essay of yours, you strongly advocated the abolition of Confucianism. Concerning this proposal of yours, I think that it is now the only way to save China. But, upon reading it, I have thought of one thing more: If you want to abolish Confucianism, then you must first abolish the Chinese language; if you want to get rid of the average person's childish, uncivilized, obstinate way of thinking, then it is all the more essential that you first abolish the Chinese language.

Qian went on to suggest that the Chinese language had to be replaced by Esperanto in order to save the country. He appears hardly to have been concerned with the extent to which his program might be supported by China's masses, since in his view they were the problem.

Although in recent times nationalistic antitraditionalism received its best-known expression during the severely iconoclastic Cultural Revolution, this orientation has been common to Nationalists, Communists, warlords, intellectuals, and other political groups and movers who have been prominent in modern China and have often fought for control of the country. The Nationalists, for example, began their "Superstition Destruction Movement" in 1928–1929 and sponsored organizations that were to oversee the elimination of the gods and temples of popular religion.[16] Iconoclastic nationalism sees China's tradition to be the source of its weakness. This nationalism provides China's modern political and military elites and its intelligentsia with ideological underpinning for their cultural remoteness from the much larger traditional sector of the population. Other state elites, such as Japan's, have fed their nationalism by embracing their tradition, so as to construct or indeed invent a far more glorious version of it. The Chinese invention, backed by the state and by elites who in many cases may otherwise have been hostile to their government, has been rather different. It is "feudalism": traditional culture defined as totally unacceptable. The very logic of this form of Chinese nationalism impels its adherents into a search for a cultural construction that must be totally new but must also work, a search that continues to this day.

One such construction, blending iconoclastic nationalism and Marxism-Leninism and enforced as state ideology, has proved unable, in the People's Republic, to provide an alternative to local, albeit changing, versions of the traditional culture. As anyone who has recently done fieldwork in rural China knows, traditional but sometimes modified religious practices remain very much alive, although their scale and the frequency of their performance are strongly conditioned by the local and national political climate. As noted above, however, nationalism has indeed taken hold. On the basis of my own fieldwork in China, it appears to me that this nationalism involves a single-stranded tie between the individual Chinese and his or her country, and is amazingly devoid of elaborated cultural content. The modern national holidays, for example, have little cultural meaning and elicit no special behavior whatever except for that arranged by local cadres. The contrast with the lunar New Year and other traditional festivals could not be greater.

I see no necessary contradiction between a consciousness of national identification grounded in an elaborate cultural construction and a more recently developed nationalistic consciousness. In many parts of the world, modification of the former and its linkage with the latter have been employed by elites to mold a powerful and deeply penetrating nationalism used to mobilize the population—for better or worse. That such a fusion has not been involved in the creation of modern Chinese nationalism might be viewed with relief in light of the uses to which some variants of state-cultural nationalism have been put in modern times.[17] On the other hand, that in contemporary China rulers interact with those whom they rule in the absence of an elaborated shared cultural framework has had particularly painful consequences. Traditional culture, cast in its entirety as "feudal" and "superstitious," has presented no constraints whatever on the policies that China's rulers have implemented.

Religion has come under the strongest pressure from the state, which at times has resorted to general persecution, as during the now-discredited Cultural Revolution. In more recent times the formidable hostility to religion must be viewed in the context of the official distinction between *zongjiao* and *fengjian mixin* (feudal superstition). The former term is usually translated as "religion," and this is eminently appropriate since *zongjiao* is precisely the Chinese pronunciation of the kanji neologism originally invented by Japanese westernizers to translate the term "religion." However, current Chinese usage, especially in the context of "religious freedom," restricts this term to officially recognized "religions," such as Buddhism, Taoism, Islam, and Christianity. *Zongjiao* now applies to the institutions of these "religions," organized under state control. All else is feudal superstition (*fengjian*, in its modern meaning, and *mixin* are also terms introduced from Japan), and this includes the popular gods of heaven, earth, the underworld, the ancestral cult, the house doorpost, the kitchen stove, and so forth. In other words, what is well known to be the basic traditional religious system of the Chinese people and a major component of the cultural arrangement providing them with national identification is in contemporary China excluded from the domain of officially tolerated religion.

Contemporary state hostility toward Chinese popular religion has been fed by the earlier intellectual antitraditionalism associated with the May Fourth Movement and by Marxism-Leninism. Hostility toward so-called feudal superstitions is hardly confined to ideologically sophisticated and committed Communist Party members, but is also characteristic of urbane intellectuals of varying political persuasions living at home or abroad; a similar hostility was also displayed by the Chinese Nationalists when they controlled the mainland and for much of the period following their retreat to Taiwan. The obviously outstanding feature of the religious beliefs and practices attacked as "superstitious" is their embeddedness in the very structure of social life, such as in the family, lineage, or village community. Attacks on "superstitions" represent efforts by those who are cultural outsiders (by birth, self-definition, or both) to control and remake society. These efforts on the part of Communists and non-Communists alike have been undertaken in the context of a hostility so pronounced as to warrant consideration of the entire historical process as cultural warfare. The war of the elite and the Chinese state against popular religion has resulted in the stripping from China's cities and countryside of most of the colorful physical manifestations of traditional culture. This assault, involving the destruction or conversion of temples, shrines, ancestral halls, and a wide variety of other structures and monuments having important local cultural significance, began during the final years of the old dynasty and was well under way when China was under Nationalist and warlord rule, but under the Communists it has been carried out with unprecedented intensity and thoroughness.[18]

Because political relationships in modern China have no shared cultural framework they are largely expressed in the form of naked commands, obeyed because of the formidable state power they represent and irrespective of their consequences, cultural or otherwise. Hegemony in modern China receives no commonly accepted legitimization through culture; rather, it represents the culture of the barracks, a culture of compliance, slogans, posters, and mobilizations conveying messages and commands rather than meaning. This form of flat, cultureless culture was most emphasized during the various movements or campaigns (*yundong*) that were especially characteristic of the first three decades of the Communist era, and perhaps achieved its strongest expression during the Great Leap Forward, in the form of the mess halls that were meant to eliminate family commensalism. Yet the culture of the barracks consistently has been a major theme in the Communist reorganization of economic and social life: factories, stores, and other organizations are often given numbers rather than names; the basic designation for almost any kind of organization is *danwei*, or "unit," another term derived from Japan and originally used in a military context. The past decade, marked by reforms that have seen the retreat of the state from many areas of social and economic life, has been characterized by the reappearance of cultural diversity. However, much of this diversity takes the form of a new popular culture derived from the West, Taiwan, Hong Kong, and Japan; it is expressed in styles of clothing, music, and other elements having little relevance either to state ideology or to a cultural redefinition of Chinese identity.

The state has achieved impressive physical compliance with its directives. However, the absence of cultural links between China's population and its political elites at all levels of government and party organization has led to the ironic consequence that the state has had little or no success in realizing its ideological or cultural goals. After four decades of attacks on popular religion, the result of a lessening of state surveillance in this area has been its widespread reappearance.[19]

The inability of the state to implement deep cultural change has as its cause the totally alien quality of the new elements it seeks to impose on China's masses. Furthermore, the period the Communist Party has been in power has been marked by so many major policy changes and reversals that there has been no consistency in what the government has tried to have people do or believe. No effort whatever has been made to introduce or negotiate culture change within a framework of common understandings. Perhaps such negotiation is now impossible, even in the unlikely event that the state would want to participate in it, given the formidable cultural gap that is now apparent to all.

The possibility that traditional Chinese culture might positively be involved in the creation of a modern national consciousness is more than hypothetical, for Taiwan provides an ironic example of just such a process. On that island the forceful expression of antitraditionalism occurred under circumstances rather different from those of the China mainland. Until seized by Japan, Taiwan had long been part of the Qing state, and its overwhelmingly Han Chinese population largely comprised immigrants from nearby mainland provinces and their descendants. During the period of their colonial rule (1895–1945), the Japanese understood all too well that incorporated into the culture and religion of their subjects was a strong identification with the totality of Chinese society. As World War II drew to a close, the Japanese authorities, increasingly fearful of the form Taiwanese loyalties might assume, launched an assimilation campaign aimed at ensuring that the island's people stayed on their side. One important component was an assault on popular religion: the destruction of temples, shrines, gods, and other physical manifestations of this religion was on a scale perhaps to be surpassed only during the Cultural Revolution on the mainland two decades later. In Taiwan, however, such religious structures were quickly rebuilt after Japan's surrender, when there was a strong revival of popular religious practices. These practices, together with many other traditional elements, increasingly were redefined as identifiers of "being Taiwanese" in the context of the growing hostility between the local population and the mainlander-dominated Nationalist government that had fled to the island by the time of the Communist victory.

It is not surprising that the Nationalist political and intellectual elites who came to Taiwan brought with them an antitraditionalism quite similar to that of their mainland enemies, for they all shared the May Fourth heritage. By the time they reached the island, however, the Nationalists' hostility toward traditional popular religion and culture had assumed more muted forms of expression: restrictions were placed on the frequency and costs of religious celebrations, and these were indeed denounced as superstitious, but there was no repetition of the temple-busting they had carried out on the mainland. More important was the fact that on Taiwan the lines were drawn differently. With traditionalism transformed into being Taiwanese, the Nationalists lost ideological control; attacks against tradition justified in the May Fourth spirit of "progress" were invariably reinterpreted by those adhering to such traditions as assaults of mainlanders against Taiwanese. In turn, politically active Taiwanese intellectuals became increasingly, and conspicuously, involved in popular religion, even though many had originally been as alienated from traditional beliefs and practices as the mainlanders of similar background. In contrast to its fate on the mainland, traditional Chinese culture on Taiwan was transformed into a modern assertion of national identity, but in this case the identity was Taiwanese and the nationalism was linked to the movement for Taiwan independence. Against this background there has been in recent years a transformation of the Taiwan government's attitude toward popular religion. This was dramatized in 1980 when President Chiang Ching-kuo, the government's leader, presented an image of Mazu, one of Taiwan's most important deities, to her major temple on the island.[20] In Taiwan, at least, one legacy of the May Fourth era has finally come to an end. It remains to be seen, however, what effect the legitimization of popular religion will have on the continuing tension between competing Taiwanese and Chinese identities.

On Taiwan and on the mainland, the nationalism which is the common framework for the expression of Chinese identity remains culturally incomplete. For a large proportion of the population in the People's Republic, especially in the countryside, nationalism coexists with a sense of being Chinese still conditioned to varying degrees by traditional orientations. However, because these people are told by the state that their traditional outlook is objectionable, the cultural content of their nationalism is sparse indeed. Ironically, it is precisely this culturally impoverished nationalism that facilitates its providing a thin veneer of common identification for traditionalists, nontraditionalists, and antitraditionalists alike. Especially among many of the last, on the mainland, in Taiwan, and abroad, there is the further problem that *being Chinese* no longer is buttressed by a firm sense of cultural participation in *something Chinese*. Hence the ongoing crisis of "identification" which has so deeply colored intellectual discourse in China during the twentieth century, and which, to this very day, is expressed with an intensity no less than that of the May Fourth era more than seventy years ago. In sum, for much of China's population being Chinese is culturally much easier today than it ever was in the past, for this identification no longer involves commonly accepted standards of behavior or belief. Existentially, however, being Chinese is far more problematic, for now it is as much a quest as it is a condition.

5

Kuan-hsi and Network Building: A Sociological Interpretation

Ambrose Yeo-chi King

No one who has had firsthand experience with Chinese society could fail to note that Chinese people are extremely sensitive to *mien-tzŭ* (face) and *jên-ch'ing* (human obligation) in their interpersonal relationships.[1] Likewise, no one who has lived in mainland China, Taiwan, Hong Kong, or any other overseas Chinese society could be totally unaware of a social phenomenon called *kuan-hsi* (personal relationship). It is no exaggeration to say that *kuan-hsi*, *jên-ch'ing*, and *mien-tzŭ* are key sociocultural concepts to the understanding of Chinese social structure. Indeed, these sociocultural concepts are part of the essential "stock knowledge," to use Alfred Schutz's terminology, of Chinese adults in their management of everyday life.[2] It is perhaps surprising that, despite the tremendous modernization of social and economic life taking place in mainland China, Taiwan, and Hong Kong in the past decades, these sociocultural concepts still play significant roles in shaping and influencing the social behavior of the Chinese. It is striking to note that although the Chinese Communists in mainland China have repeatedly launched vigorous campaigns—including the Great Proletariat Cultural Revolution—to attempt to uproot "feudal" elements of the Chinese culture, these concepts, *kuan-hsi* in particular, remain strong; they even threaten the formal and official ideological system of Marxism-Leninism. Liu Pin-yen, a former senior reporter of the *People's Daily*, writes:

In Ping county, you simply cannot clearly figure out the *kuan-hsi* [personal relations] among people. It seems that in everyone's body there is a particular switch. If you touch a person, it will unexpectedly affect a large number of persons. . . . There are complicated and overlapping relations between and among people, weaving a thick and tight social web. Whatever "isms" or principles, whatever policies or program guidances, as soon as they touch this social web, they lose their function immediately, just like being suddenly electrocuted.[3]

Fox Butterfield, a former foreign correspondent for the *New York Times*, has the following observations:

I began to appreciate how differently Chinese order their mental universe than do Westerners. We tend to see people as individuals; we make some distinctions, of course, between those we know and those we don't. But basically we have one code of manners for all. . . . Chinese, on the other hand, instinctively divide people into those with whom they already have a fixed relationship, a connection, what the Chinese call *guan-xi* [*kuan-hsi*], and those they don't. These connections operate like a series of invisible threads, tying Chinese to each other with far greater tensile strength than mere friendship in the West would do. *Guan-xi* have created a social magnetic field in which all Chinese move, keenly aware of those people with whom they have connections and those they don't. They explain why the Communist leadership, which was so grateful to Richard Nixon for helping make the breakthrough in Sino-American relations, could never understand Watergate and why Peking even sent a special plane to bring Nixon back to China for a visit after his disgrace. In a broader sense, *guan-xi* also help explain how a nation of one billion people coheres.[4]

The ever-present social phenomenon of *kuan-hsi* is not confined to mainland China. Various field workers convincingly testify to the prevalence of *kuan-hsi* in other Chinese societies.[5]

I attempt here to give a sociological interpretation of *kuan-hsi* and network building, first, to see how *kuan-hsi* is conceived in Confucian social theory; second, to analyze the ingredients of *kuan-hsi* construction and the social skills needed in the establishment and maintenance of personal networks; third, to analyze the function of *jên-ch'ing* in network building; and fourth, to describe strategies of *kuan-hsi* avoidance and *kuan-hsi* disengagement, which are built-in cultural mechanisms to ensure universalistic rationality for the management of economic and bureaucratic life.

KUAN-HSI IN CONFUCIAN SOCIAL THEORY

Confucian social theory is concerned with the question of how to establish a harmonious secular order in the man-centered world. According to Confucianist philosophy, the individual is never an isolated, separate entity; man is defined as a social or interactive being.[6] It is no accident that the Chinese character *jên* (benevolence) means two men. Indeed, there is no concept of man as separate from men. Hu Shih states: "In the Confucian human-centered philosophy man cannot exist alone; all action must be in a form of interaction between man and man."[7] *Jên,* the highest attainment of moral cultivation, would be nothing if it were not placed in the context of the social relationships among men. Tu Wei-ming writes that "the original Confucian intention . . . is the moralization of the person in human relationships."[8] Francis Hsu notes:

The Chinese conception of man (also shared by the Japanese but pronounced *jin* as opposed to the Chinese term *jên*) is based on the individual's transactions with his fellow human beings. When the Chinese say of so and so, *"t'a pu shih jên"* (he is not *jên*), they do not mean that this person is not a human animal. Instead, they mean that his behavior in relation to other human beings is not acceptable. . . .

But the concept of *jên* puts the emphasis on interpersonal transactions. It does not consider the individual psyche's deep cores of complexes and anxieties. Instead it sees the nature of the individual's external behavior in terms of how it fits or fails to fit the interpersonal standards of society and culture.[9]

What constitutes proper human relationships is the central problem in the Confucian project. Liang Sou-ming, comparing the Chinese social system with Western ones, asserts that Chinese society is neither *ko-jên pen-wei* (individual-based) nor *she-hui pen-wei* (society-based), but *kuan-hsi pen-wei* (relation-based). In a relation-based social system, Liang writes:

The focus is not fixed on any particular individual, but on the particular nature of the relations between individuals who interact with each other. The focus is placed upon the relationship.[10]

In a nutshell, man is a relational being in the Confucian system.[11] True, the word *kuan-hsi*, which is a relatively modern expression, is not found in the Confucian classics; instead, the word *lun* is used. *Lun* means order[12] or, more specifically, "differentiated order" among individuals. Pan Kuang-tan points out that the Confucian concept of *lun* is basically concerned with two problems: the kind of differentiation to be made between individuals, and the kind of relations to be established between individuals.[13] Confucian social order is constructed upon the concept of *lun*, which is primarily concerned with the problem of *pieh*, or differentiation among role relations.

The phrase *pu shih ch'i lun* means that every role relation is properly in order. To be more specific, it means that role relations are properly differentiated according to the nature of relations between particular individuals. Social order and stability rest on differentiation rather than homogeneity.[14] Furthermore, Fei Hsiao-t'ung sees *lun* as *ts'u-hsu*, which refers to differentiated and graded relations according to the degree of intimacy attaching to the individual concerned.[15] The closer the other is to the individual, the more intimate their relations will be. It is true also in the reverse situation. Here, it should be mentioned, according to Confucians, there are many kinds of relations between individuals of which the well-known five cardinal relations are the most fundamental. These five relationships and their appropriate tenor are *ch'in* (affection) between parent and child; *i* (righteousness) between ruler and subject; *pieh* (distinction) between husband and wife; *hsu* (order) between older brothers and younger brothers; and *hsin* (sincerity) between friends. Among the relations, "some of them are preordained givens, while others are voluntarily constructed; the father-son and brother-brother relations belong to the former type, husband-wife and friend-friend relations belong to the latter type."[16]

It is here that we touch on the very nature of the individual in the Confucian social theory. The question is: What is the role of the individual in the process of relation construction? In particular, what is the role that the individual plays in those relations which are voluntarily constructed? Apart from the preordained relation, for example, the father-son *lun*, in which individual behavior is more or less prescribed by fixed status as well as fixed responsibilities, an individual has considerable freedom in deciding whether to enter into voluntarily constructed relationships with others. Most of the literature, sociological or not, depicts Confucianism as a social theory that tends to mold the Chinese into group-oriented or, more specifically, family-oriented and socially dependent beings.[17] Without question this view has a good deal of sociological truth. Nevertheless, this typical presentation grasps only a part of the total complexity.[18]

Confucianism attaches a good deal of autonomy to the individual. The expression *wei jên yu chi* testifies that achieving the highest virtue (*jen*) is, in the final analysis, in the hands of *chi* (self). Admittedly, in the Confucian relation-based social system, the focus is not fixed on any particular individual but on the particular nature of the relation between individuals. However, as de Bary correctly notes, "the relations alone . . . do not define a man totally. His interior self exists at the center of this web and there enjoys its own freedom."[19] It is important to bear in mind that the Confucian individual is more than a role player mechanically performing the role-related behavior prescribed by the social structure. To use Meadian terminology, the Confucian individual consists of a self (*chi*) that is both an active and a reflexive entity. In relation construction it is the individual who is capable of defining roles for himself and others, and is always at the center.[20] Precisely because of the voluntaristic nature of the self, the Confucian individual is the initiator of social communication in the nonpreordained, *lun* relation with others outside the family structure. Indeed, he is the architect in relation construction.

It is necessary to examine the relation between *chi* (self) and *ch'ün* (group) if the dynamic relation construction of Chinese behavior is to be more fully appreciated. In Confucianism, as was mentioned, the voluntaristic nature of the self is fully recognized, while the conception of group (*ch'ün*) is the least articulated. Fei Hsiao-t'ung convincingly argues that the boundary between self (*chi*) and group (*ch'ün*) is relative and elastic.[21] In the Confucian mind, there is no group boundary as such.[22] The term *chia* (family), which is the basic social unit, is an elastic entity; it sometimes includes only members of a nuclear family, but it may also include all members of a lineage or a clan. The common expression *tzŭ chia jên* (our family people) can refer to any person one wants to include; it is entirely up to the individual to contract or expand the boundary of the concept of *chia*. It can theoretically be extended to an unlimited number of people and thereby becomes what is called *t'ien-hsia i-chia* (all the world belongs to one family). The elasticity of the boundary of the group (the family or other collectives) gives the individual enough social and psychological space to construct his *kuan-hsi* with an unlimited number of other individuals on kinship or fictive kinship bases.

At this juncture the definition or an English translation of *kuan-hsi* is in order. *Kuan-hsi*, which J. Bruce Jacobs defines as "particularistic tie," is basically a kind of personal connection. In recent years a new interdisciplinary field of personal relationships has emerged.[23] J. Clyde Mitchell, in one of the pioneer works on the social network, writes:

The point of anchorage of a network is usually taken to be some specified individual whose behaviour the observer wishes to interpret. Which individual is taken will turn on the particular problem that the observer is interested in. . . . This has led to the specification of this type of network as ego-centred though the term "personal network" may be more acceptable.[24]

It seems to me that either "particularistic tie" or "personal network" does carry the meaning of *kuan-hsi*, but neither fully grasps the complicated and rich meaning of the word. A Chinese anthropologist argues well that the concept of *kuan-hsi* should be kept and incorporated into modern social science literature.[25] Indeed, if a new science of relationships is going to be developed, *kuan-hsi* is a concept that can hardly be excluded.

THE INDIVIDUAL, ATTRIBUTE, AND NETWORK BUILDING

I hope I have made it clear that Confucian social theory has the theoretical thrust of developing a person into a *kuan-hsi*-oriented individual. The Chinese preoccupation with *kuan-hsi* (relationship) building has indeed a built-in cultural imperative behind it. It is not surprising, therefore, that the Chinese in their everyday life have demonstrated impressive and sophisticated skills in network building. La Barre, an anthropologist, notes: "Chinese culture has developed inter-personal relationships to the level of an exquisite and superb art."[26]

Let us take the way in which the Chinese construct their personal networks a step further. Chie Nakane, a Japanese anthropologist, has provided us with some very useful analytical tools. She uses two terms, *attribute* and *frame*, as contrasting criteria of group formation. According to Nakane, "Groups may be identified by applying the two criteria: one is based on the individual's common attribute, the other on situational position in a given frame. . . . Frame may be a locality, an institution . . . [it] indicates a criterion which sets a boundary and gives a common basis to a set of individuals who are located or involved in it." On the other hand, "attribute may mean, for instance, being a member of a definite descent group or caste." And "attribute may be acquired not only by birth but by achievement."[27] In making her point, Nakane illustrates the contrasting principles of family formation in Japan and China:

The Japanese family system differs from that of the Chinese, where family ethics are always based on relationships between particular individuals such as father and son, brothers and sisters, parent and child, husband and wife, while in Japan they are always based on the collective group, i.e., members of a household, not on the relationship between individuals.[28]

Nakane asserts that the formation of social groups on the basis of fixed frames is characteristic of Japanese social structure. As for the Chinese system, the principle of attribute is indeed much more applicable; in fact, a few Chinese anthropologists have found that the concept of *fēn lei* (similar to the concept of attribute) is the constitutive rule of Chinese social structure.[29] That is to say, Chinese group consciousness is formed on a set of criteria—such as kinship, native place, dialect, religious belief—as a base for group identification. Wang Sung-hsing argues that, unlike the Japanese, the Chinese have "pluralistic" identifications with other individuals or social groups according to the "attributes" the individual has in common with other particular individuals or social groups. The more attributes the individual has, the more *kuan-hsi* he is able to establish. The more *kuan-hsi* he has, the more advantageous his position in mobilizing resources in order to achieve his goals in a competitive world.[30] *Kuan-hsi* is established through social interaction between two or more individuals. *Kuan-hsi* building is a work of social engineering through which the individual establishes his personal network. The existence of *kuan-hsi* depends on the existence of the attributes shared by the individuals concerned. The shared attributes are what Jacobs calls "a base of *kuan-hsi*." He writes, "In Chinese culture (and perhaps cross-culturally), a base for a *kuan-hsi* depends upon two or more persons having a commonality of shared identification."[31] In Chinese societies the most common shared attributes for building networks are locality (native place), kinship, coworker, classmate, sworn brotherhood, surname, and teacher-student.[32] It should be remembered that as the base of group identification, the shared attributes are not constant or unchanging; people can form a group on the shared attribute of kinship at one time and on the shared attribute of dialect at another time. Moreover, the nature of shared attributes is quite elastic in the sense that they can be contracted and expanded; for example, locality can refer to a natural village, a county, a city, or a province. It can even be stretched to mean a regional grouping of provinces (such as *Ho-peh Shan-tung tung hsiang hui*).

In network building, *la* (pulling) *kuan-hsi* is the social phenomenon Chinese are most familiar with. "Pulling *kuan-hsi*" means to establish or strengthen relations with others when no preestablished relation exists between them, or where a preestablished relation is remote. Ways of pulling *kuan-hsi* are varied and have developed in mainland China into such a subtle and complicated "science" of the management of human relations as to be called *kuan-hsi hsüeh* ("relationology").[33] "Walking through the back door" (*tsou hou mên*) is widely known to be the most effective and necessary way to get things done through personal networks (*kuan-hsi*) in today's Communist China. Butterfield observed the following:

Ling's tickets to these films were classic back-door deals. As Chinese friends described the workings of the back door, these exchanges usually do not involve money. That would be considered bribery and therefore illegal. Instead they are based on the traditional use of *guan-xi* [*kuan-hsi*], the cultivation of contacts and connections among friends, relatives, and colleagues. The longer I stayed in Peking, the more I sensed that almost anything that got done went through the back door.[34]

Chu and Ju's important and comprehensive survey, which was carried out in Shanghai and Qingpu (a rural county outside Shanghai) in 1988,[35] clearly shows that people perceive *kuan-hsi* to be essential to social-economic life. When asked to rate the importance of network connections in Chinese society, an overwhelming majority of the respondents said that network connections are: very important (42.7 percent); important (26.9 percent); or somewhat important (22.8 percent). Only a few (4.9 percent) said that they are not very important, and still fewer (2.6 percent) said that they are not important at all. Furthermore, when asked to respond to the following: "Suppose you have a problem. If you follow the normal channels, it will take a long time, and the result may not be satisfactory. Do you think you should try to go through some connection?", over two-thirds of the respondents (71.7 percent) said they "should first try some connections." Only one in five (19.6 percent) would rather follow normal channels, saying they "should not try connections"; the remaining 8.8 percent were not sure.[36] The findings confirm the prevalence of the practice of *kuan-hsi* in mainland Chinese society today. The same survey also shows an interesting phenomenon: younger people seemed to attach greater importance to *kuan-hsi* than older people. Almost half of the young people (46.0 percent) said it was very important, as compared to 35.1 percent of the older people. Only 5.0 percent of the young people said it was either not very important or not important at all, as compared to 13.6 percent of the older people.[37] Indeed, as Chu and Ju pointed out, the practice of using *kuan-hsi* to get something done in a hurry has always existed in Chinese society, but it has now reached almost epidemic proportions.[38]

At this point it might be appropriate to discuss, in brief, how the practice of *kuan-hsi* has evolved in Communist China over the last four decades. The Chinese Communist party, as soon as it gained control over the mainland in 1949, launched a series of campaigns and movements with the purpose of transforming the traditional norms of personal relations in China from what Vogel calls "friendship" to "comradeship."[39] Friendship in Vogel's ideal construction is a particularistic or private morality, while comradeship is a universalistic ethic. Comradeship was taken to mean the embodiment of a citizen's public spirit in the socialist state. In a sense, comradeship is an ideal based on universalistic socialist values, which were supposed to transcend those particularisms based on kinship, locality, and so on. In short, the Chinese Communists intended to create the new Socialist man for the new Socialist society. Among the many Confucian-feudal elements they were determined to eradicate, *kuan-hsi* was on the priority list. According to Vogel, the Communists' gigantic project of value transformation was achieved largely through fear. It is worth mentioning that the Chinese Communist party had struggled to effect a revolutionary change in the 1950s and 1960s by using "organization" to destroy and replace the institutional structure of the Chinese traditional social system. By the end of the 1960s, Communist China had become, to use Franz Schurmann's perceptive (though somewhat exaggerated) expression, "a China of organization."[40]

The party-state structured the society into an all-inclusive, functional collectivity called *tanwei*. In mainland China, almost every working adult belongs to a *tanwei*, which provides its members with extensive goods and services.[41] The relation between the individual and *tanwei* is near total and the high degree of individual dependency on the *tanwei* has created a "culture of organized dependency," as Walder demonstrated.[42] During the Cultural Revolution of 1966–1976, the Party's domination over society reached its highest point. It attempted to bring all aspects of social life under its control through the concept of the "all-round dictatorship over the bourgeoisie." The Party not only tried to monopolize activities in the public sphere, it even tried to eliminate the private sector. The Cultural Revolution marked the culmination of the totalitarian tendency at the brink of "revolutionary feudal totalitarianism."[43] During this period, despite the unabashed ideological rhetoric on public or proletarian morality, the social order and public civility were seriously eroded. Distrust existed in all relationships, and a pervasive amorality and cynicism prevailed. An extreme form of instrumentalism colored norms of behavior in personal relations.

In the aftermath of the Cultural Revolution, under the new slogan of the Four Modernizations (particularly with the advent of economic reform advocated by Deng Xiaoping), a drastic change in social-political life took place, accompanied by a retreat of political power from its increasingly deeper penetration into civil society and the economy. The operation of the market was accepted as a supplement to a planned economy. Tang Tsou writes, "In short, civil society is being revived and the relationship between political power and society has changed."[44] With the resurgence of market and civil society and the low institutionalization of law and administrative regulation, people who are freed from omnipresent fear for the first time in their lives are eschewing socialist values and ideals and are returning to traditional behavioral patterns now officially sanctioned in the privatized social-economic spheres. Thomas Gold argued in 1985 that at both the micro and the macro levels, "instrumentalism and commoditization had supplanted both friendship and comradeship as primary characteristics of personal relations. It located the causes of this situation in certain aspects of the Cultural Revolution and current development-oriented reforms."[45] In present-day China, both traditional and socialist moral values are cast in doubt, practical utilitarian concerns have gained an upper hand.

Starting in 1977 the socialist modernists in China were anxious to reestablish universal standards and universalistic ethics, and they did make some progress. For example, examinations were instituted as the basic criterion for admission to universities and schools. The appointment of friends and relatives was widely attacked in the media and some officials became more cautious about this practice. However, "It was not uncommon, for example, for official A to appoint a relative of official B and for official B in return to arrange an appointment for a relative or friend of official A. Or official C, believing their connection would be useful, sometimes hired a relative of high official D without any intervention by official D."[46] Vogel, in writing about Canton in 1989, observed that "the cultivation of personal connections, long a prominent feature of Chinese society, was moderated beginning in the late 1970s by the new concern for universal standards, but at the same time *guanxi* [*kuan-hsi*] blossomed to play a new instrumental role for entrepreneurs taking advantage of market opportunities."[47] However, "in Guangdong in this early but dynamic stage of commodity society, when markets were not yet fully opened, the new desire to make things happen led many entrepreneurs to use *guanxi* [*kuan-hsi*] to achieve what was otherwise impossible."[48]

JÊN-CH'ING AND NETWORK BUILDING

As discussed above, in the Confucian social theory the individual self, as a dynamic and reflexive entity, is at the center of relation construction. Apart from natural relations (that is, father-son, brother-brother relations), nonnatural relations are voluntarily constructed with the individual self as the initiator. Indeed, Chinese *kuan-hsi* building can be characterized as an ego-centered social engineering of relation building. We have shown that one's *kuan-hsi* or personal network is based on the attributes shared by people. However, if there is no interaction between individual A and individual B, and if A wants to establish *kuan-hsi* with B, whether or not B has common attributes with A, B is a "stranger" to A. Under such circumstances, an intermediary (*chung chien jên*) is often used as a cultural mechanism in *kuan-hsi* building. Through the intermediary the individual is able to associate with the "stranger" on relational terms. In the Chinese art of relation management, that is, the establishment and maintenance of *kuan-hsi*, *jên-ch'ing* plays an important role.[49] It should be pointed out that *jên-ch'ing* is different from *kan-ch'ing* which is merely sentiment, or an affective component of all human relations. *Kan-ch'ing* is personal, while *jên-ch'ing* is social. Yang Lien-sheng renders *jên-ch'ing* as "human feelings," which, he writes, "covers not only sentiment but also its social expressions such as the offering of congratulations or condolences or the making of gifts on appropriate occasions."[50] Robert Silin's translation "human obligations" is probably closer to the meaning of the word *jên-ch'ing*.[51] *Jên-ch'ing* can be interpreted as the norms of Chinese interpersonal relationships. The Confucian norms of interpersonal relationships are fundamentally based upon the concept of *shu*, or reciprocity, which Max Weber takes as the foundation of Confucian social ethics.[52] J. H. Weakland writes:

The system of reciprocal aid in Chinese life—except within the circle of the family and very close friends where mutual help is at least assumed to occur with no question of exchange at all—is centered around the concept of *jên-ch'ing*.[53]

True, "in part *jên-ch'ing* can be equated with the content of the Confucian *li* (propriety). The emphasis in the concept of *li* is on the individual's responsibility to know and act on certain prescribed rules of behavior."[54] If a Chinese is accused of "knowing no *jên-ch'ing*," it means that he is lacking *li* and is incapable of managing interpersonal relationships. The Shanghai and Qingpu survey shows that *jên-ch'ing* is still playing an important role in Communist China. When people were asked: "Suppose a relative wants your help to ask someone to do something. You are able to do it, but it will give you some inconvenience. What will you do?" Over two-thirds of the sample (70.9 percent) would offer to help; very few (8.0 percent) would decline. Some others (5.1 percent) said they would help if the request was for a good cause. When a similar question regarding *jên-ch'ing* for friends was asked, 64.3 percent of the sample would offer to help. Quite a few (24.3 percent) said it would depend, and 11.4 percent said no.[55] It is not surprising that kinship is a more weighty factor than friendship in people's interpersonal relationships.

It is worth mentioning that there are two basic types of interpersonal relationships or *kuan-hsi*. One is economic exchange (economic *kuan-hsi*), the other is social exchange (social *kuan-hsi*). In a strict sense *jên-ch'ing* hardly enters into economic *kuan-hsi* since economic exchange is dictated by impersonal market rationality. On the other hand, in social *kuan-hsi*—which is diffuse, unspecific, and is ruled by the principle of reciprocity—*jên-ch'ing* plays a central role. In social exchanges among Chinese, *jên-ch'ing* serves as a medium. The common expressions "to give you a *jên-ch'ing*" (*sung ko jên-ch'ing*), "to give me a *jên-ch'ing*" (*t'a chi wo i ko jên-ch'ing*), "he owes me a *jên-ch'ing*" (*t'a ch'ien wo i ko jên-ch'ing*), or "I owe him a *jên-ch'ing*" (*wo ch'ien t'a i ko jên-ch'ing*) show clearly that *jên-ch'ing* is a kind of resource or social capital in interpersonal transactions. Because of the intricate relation between *jên-ch'ing* and *kuan-hsi*, the two sometimes become interchangeable; for example, the saying "there is no *jên-ch'ing* between us" is equivalent to saying "there is no *kuan-hsi* between us." Cultivating *jên-ch'ing* is a prerequisite to establishing or sustaining *kuan-hsi*. The degree of *jên-ch'ing* between two persons is usually a good indication of the "closeness" or "distance" of *kuan-hsi* between them. A Chinese typically feels that he is locked into *jên-ch'ing wang* (web of human obligations) or *kuan-hsi wang* (web of personal networks).

KUAN-HSI AVOIDANCE AND UNIVERSALISTIC RATIONALITY

We have discussed at length the social phenomena of *jên-ch'ing* and *kuan-hsi*. Indeed, they are important tissues in the Chinese social structure. There is a general impression, correct or not, as observed by Liu Pin-yen, Butterfield, and others, that the Chinese are hopelessly interlocked in *jên-ch'ing wang* or *kuan-hsi wang*. True enough, Chinese individuals have commonly utilized this kind of highly personal relation construction as a cultural strategy for securing social resources toward goal attainment. However, we must be reminded that this is only a partial picture of the Chinese cultural dynamic of network building. In the Chinese cultural system, there are also cultural mechanisms to neutralize or to freeze the practice of *jên-ch'ing* or *kuan-hsi* in order to carve out room for instrumental rationality, which is necessary to maintain economic and bureaucratic (in the Weberian sense) life. To engage in *jên-ch'ing* or to establish *kuan-hsi* with others usually means a heavy social investment. Once one is inside the *jên-ch'ing wang* or *kuan-hsi wang*, he is locked into an intricate relationship of interdependence with others. He is, in this case, socially obliged to respond to any request for help from others. As such, the individual will lose autonomy and freedom. Therefore, it is not surprising that some Chinese have consciously tried to avoid relating themselves too intimately with others in order to avoid this dependence.[56] A student of Chinese society, describing the quality of interpersonal relationships in a town called Lukang in Taiwan, points out the importance of social distance:

The aim seems to be a lot of amiable, matey, but not intimate ties with as many people as possible. People give the impression of being hesitant about getting too close, too deeply involved with or committed to anyone else. Amiable relationships may break down if too much is expected of them.[57]

The Chinese folk wisdom that one should not allow oneself to be a debtor in *jên-ch'ing* transactions is meant to enable one to preserve some space for autonomy of action. In other words, it will enable individuals to have enough freedom in deciding whether to establish personal networks with others. *Kuan-hsi* is a form of interpersonal relationship which is predominantly based on particularistic criteria. Talcott Parsons, writing on the nature of Confucian ethics, writes:

Its ethical sanction was given to an individual's *personal* relations to particular persons—and with any strong emphasis only to these. The whole Chinese social structure accepted and sanctioned by the Confucian ethic was a predominately "particularistic" structure of relationships.[58]

It became necessary to freeze or to neutralize, if not to eliminate, "particularistic" elements in interpersonal transactions when universalistic rationality was needed, e.g., in the domains of economic and bureaucratic life. In traditional China there was no shortage of cultural mechanisms for preventing the practices of *kuan-hsi* or *jên-ch'ing*. In imperial times there was a system according to which employment of an official in his native place was prohibited and likewise the employment of relatives in the same bailiwick.[59] Max Weber described it as an ingenious "patrimonialist means" of imperial control.[60] We could well argue that the latent, if not explicit, function of this system was to prevent the official from being overly pressured by the particularistic demands of his relatives or friends, thus maintaining bureaucratic rationality. Using similar cultural logic, businessmen in olden times were inclined to leave their hometowns to do business far away. This again was to ensure that business could be conducted according to market principles, freeing the parties from interference by the particularistic pressures of *kuan-hsi*.[61]

Fei Hsiao-t'ung's study of market town behavior is most illuminating. In his study of rural China he observed that within the same village, neighbors usually walked miles to the market town to carry out their transactions there instead of at their front doors. As a result the particularistic role relations between neighbors became impersonal and they could then do business with each other as "strangers." Setting accounts straight is a kind of exchange considered legitimate between strangers without regard to other elements of social relations.[62] De Glopper's findings in contemporary Taiwan are also worth noting:

In ideal terms, people in Lukang describe the sum of their social relations with a set of discrete categories. There are business relations; there are kinship relations; there are neighborly relations; and there are what are usually called "social" relations. Each of these has its own principle and purposes, its own satisfactions and problems.

He continues:

The small businessmen in Lukang desire to maximize their autonomy and freedom of choice, and prefer limited, functionally specific relations to diffuse ties, fused with personal relations.[63]

As a matter of fact, within Chinese society the folk culture, if not the great Confucian tradition, has long developed what may be called a "compartmentalization" strategy to separate the functionally specific economic exchanges from the functionally diffused social exchanges.[64] This compartmentalization strategy is applicable even to the relationships among the most intimate kinsmen (brothers). The folk saying goes, "Among good brothers, neat accounts are a must" (*hao hsiung ti ming suan chang*). According to this folk logic, the functionally specific economic rationality takes precedence over the functionally diffuse particularistic norm in the brother-brother relation, a *lun* in the five cardinal relations. The rationale underlying this logic is, of course, not to damage the cardinal relations; on the contrary, it is intended to protect the cardinal relations from being damaged by the potential conflicts arising from possible muddy economic transactions. In the course of my field study of small factories in Hong Kong, I heard time and again the saying *shu huan shu, lu huan lu* (money is money, *kuan-hsi* is *kuan-hsi*) meaning people are adopting a "business is business" strategy in their economic exchanges.

In this connection it is interesting to note that people in Communist China today, though fully aware of the importance of *kuan-hsi*, tend to condemn those who use it deviously to serve either personal or organizational (*tanwei*) purposes. When asked to identify what constitutes leadership qualification for their *tanwei*, over half the respondents

(59.1 percent) in the Shanghai and Qingpu survey considered having "good outside connections" to be the least important. Why is it that leaders who have good connections (*kuan-hsi*) are rated so negatively? Chu and Ju give the explanation:

We think that the highly negative rating of this qualification was not so much a reflection on the leaders themselves, but rather a condemnation of the wide-spread current practice. While everybody was playing the game, many deplored it.[65]

At normative levels, people seemed to hold a view that devious use of *kuan-hsi* is morally wrong. They are not condemning *kuan-hsi* or *jên-ch'ing* as such; they are condemning it when the practice of it is in conflict with more universalistic ethical concerns. While honoring *jên-ch'ing* in their interpersonal relationships, as mentioned above, people seemed to think that it should be used conditionally. Chu and Ju's study shows that a large majority of respondents (82.2 percent) would refuse to vote for somebody they knew nothing about even if a good friend asked them to do so. Moreover, it is argued that, "despite the widespread use of network connections in society, there is a near universal wish among the Chinese people that the country be ruled by law because they believe that law brings justice to society."[66] I am inclined to think that Chinese in Communist China, like their compatriots in Taiwan and Hong Kong, have felt a need for universalistic rationality in the emerging market and civil society.

CONCLUSION

In the preceding pages I have intended to demonstrate that *kuan-hsi* is part of the "store of knowledge" of Chinese adults in their management of everyday life. To know and to practice *kuan-hsi* is part of learned behavior—of being Chinese. As a sociocultural concept *kuan-hsi* is deeply embedded in Confucian social theory and has its own logic that may be said to form and constitute the social structure of Chinese society. Though Confucian social theory has a tendency to mold the Chinese into group-oriented and socially dependent beings, it must be emphatically argued that Confucianism does attach a good deal of autonomy to the individual. The Confucian individual is the initiator of social communication outside the family structure; he is the architect in *kuan-hsi* building. *Kuan-hsi* building is the Chinese version of network building, which is a phenomenon found in all cultures. Chinese *kuan-hsi* building can be characterized as an ego-centered social engineering of relation building. We have shown that *kuan-hsi* building is based on shared "attributes" such as kinship, locality, surname, and so on, which are the building blocks the individual employs to establish "pluralistic" identifications with multiple individuals and groups. Indeed, network building is used (consciously or unconsciously) by Chinese adults as a cultural strategy in mobilizing social resources for goal attainment in various spheres of social life. To a significant degree the cultural dynamic of *kuan-hsi* building is a source of vitality in Chinese society.

For a long time the social phenomenon of *kuan-hsi*—like that of *mien-tzŭ* (face) and *jên-ch'ing*—has been perceived as undesirable or dysfunctional for China's modernization and development. *Kuan-hsi* is deplored by Chinese modernists, Communist or not, who believe that *kuan-hsi* is a private and particularistic morality, and that what China needs is a universalistic ethic. However, we have pointed out that, within the Chinese cultural system, there are mechanisms to neutralize or to freeze the practice of *jên-ch'ing* or *kuan-hsi* in order to carve out room for the universalistic rationality that is necessary for the management of economic and (in a Weberian sense) bureaucratic conduct. There is no sign that *kuan-hsi* building as an institutionalized mode of behavior is disappearing in modernizing Chinese societies, like Taiwan or Hong Kong. In the modernizing Chinese societies where market rationality and law are becoming the predominant value, the scope of *kuan-hsi* practices has been narrowed and circumscribed and its strategy subtly transformed. The practice of *kuan-hsi* per se is not necessarily incompatible with modernization. What is interesting to note is that the devious practice of *kuan-hsi* for personal or organizational purposes in Communist China today has reached an unprecedented level. The widespread phenomenon of "going through the back door" (to get things done through *kuan-hsi*) has indeed become a social epidemic. It is clear that the gigantic value transformation effort undertaken by the Chinese Communist party—in order to create a new socialist man for the new socialist society—has ended in failure. The Party's efforts—primarily through the use of fear—to eradicate "Confucian-feudal" elements, including the practice of *kuan-hsi*, have not succeeded. During the so-called Second Long March of the Four

Modernizations, which began in 1978, a drastic change has occurred in social-economic life. The market is being partially reinstituted and civil society is being revived. The often criticized traditional behavioral norms are now officially sanctioned in privatized, interpersonal relations. During this rapid transition stage, when the socialist universalistic values are cast into doubt and the market is not yet fully operational, *kuan-hsi* blossoms to play a new instrument which enables people to achieve what is usually denied them through normal channels. There are, however, clear signs that people in mainland China are condemning the devious use of *kuan-hsi* for personal or organizational gains. Nevertheless, the widely cursed phenomenon of "going through the back door" will not go away easily, not until the day when market rationality is fully operational, and law becomes the rule of everyday political life.

6

Among Non-Chinese

Wang Gungwu

Large numbers of Chinese have left mainland China since the end of the Second World War. Until recently, the majority saw themselves as being temporarily abroad rather than as permanent emigrants. Merchants and others joined their families overseas. There were also students, refugees, and exiles. Some were returnees who decided to remigrate, to rejoin their families abroad after an unhappy stay in China. I have written extensively elsewhere about the sojourners (*huaqiao*); about how, since 1945, the idea of the Chinese all being sojourners has been challenged, especially in Southeast Asia.[1] Many more have preferred to see themselves as having settled abroad as foreign nationals; if Chinese at all, they see themselves as descendants of Chinese (*huayi*). I shall not go over the same ground here but will simply note that any study of such Chinese today must take account of the historical experiences of those who left China in the nineteenth and early twentieth centuries, whose descendants form the majority of those abroad who are still identified as Chinese in some ways.[2] Those experiences provide an important background to what it has meant for Chinese to live among different kinds of non-Chinese during the last hundred years or so. They illustrate degrees of self-discovery and rediscovery of Chineseness highly relevant to what the present generation of *huaqiao* or *huayi* are experiencing. They also reflect a growing consciousness that the world outside China is worth knowing and merits critical attention.

Being Chinese in China is in itself a complex problem, but being Chinese outside China has several additional complicating features. It can mean the effort to reproduce what is remembered of Chinese ways and then transmitting them, however imperfectly, to descendants. It can mean straining to keep up with developments in China through relatives at home, or by reading news of the fortunes of the empire or the republic. Many mirrors, some less distorting than others, intervene when a Chinese living abroad constructs his composite image of what it means to be Chinese. Sooner or later, it is impossible to avoid asking what being among foreigners does to one's perception of being Chinese. To look different, to speak differently, to be regarded as Chinese by others, leads naturally to an awareness of what is or what is not Chinese. That awareness may be simple or superficial; it may also be deliberate, even assertive. It can be diminished by distance, by the length of time that one is away from China; it can be enhanced and deepened by regular contact with China and with highly cultivated Chinese. For most Chinese abroad, it is the non-Chinese environment that impinges on their lives most directly. How that helps to define their Chineseness is an important starting-point.[3] I shall concentrate on four themes: the effects of trading, working, studying, and living with non-Chinese.

TRADING WITH NON-CHINESE

Trading in the broadest sense ranges from shopkeeping to financial and industrial investment to the activities of multinational enterprises. In Asia the story began with Chinese merchants in foreign ports or towns. Trading with non-Chinese people required an understanding of foreign languages and the local trading culture—including customs, laws, power relations, and ethical concerns—as well as a technical knowledge of currency, weights and measures, and various transactional norms. Most Chinese merchants and their agents seem to have had no difficulty with their non-Chinese trading partners over centuries, whether in Korea, Japan, or various indigenous kingdoms in Southeast Asia (notably Champa, Cambodia, Siam, and the Malay states including Java).[4] Most Chinese came, traded, and returned home. The few who remained married locally and, unless they became numerous enough to form a community, their descendants were ultimately absorbed into native society. In this context, the Chinese were no different from other foreign traders like the Indians, Persians, and Arabs. There were always a few Chinese who integrated with powerful groups and participated in local politics, but there is no evidence that being Chinese was an issue. As long as local upward social mobility and the ability to return to China were options, trading with non-Chinese did not raise questions of identity or produce cultural tensions.

Between the sixteenth and nineteenth centuries, European naval power in support of trade changed this scenario, but only gradually. Beginning with ports under European control like Malacca, Manila, Batavia, and then Penang and Singapore, the Chinese were encouraged to stay and perform specific trading and artisan roles. By 1800 distinct Chinese communities of mestizos in Manila and other cities of the Philippines and *baba-peranakans* (locally born Chinese) in Malacca, Batavia, and other Malay-Javanese ports had been formed, each dependent on being Chinese in its own way and each sustaining its Chineseness by welcoming newly arrived *totok* or *sinkheh* Chinese. Although the Chinese language was largely lost among those born locally, it remained in use in these communities because of fresh immigration and because trading with China required its continued use. Other Chinese cultural features embodied in birth, marriage, and death practices, major festivals, popular religions, and stories from traditional fiction and opera were passed down for generations. Because of Dutch encouragement, for example, all *baba-peranakans* were proud and conscious that their Chineseness had earned them a key economic place in the eyes of the Dutch. Because there was little possibility of upward mobility into Dutch society, success lay in becoming leaders of the Chinese community whom the Dutch recognized; this required them to remain recognizably Chinese.[5]

During the nineteenth century the flood of Chinese to and from Southeast Asia allowed small Chinese enclaves to become larger ones, and whole towns in the Straits Settlements and the Malay States became predominantly Chinese. The majority of the newcomers were coolie workers and poor young relatives and clansmen of community leaders and wealthy merchants. Owing to the increasing number of children born locally, the Chinese began to establish schools for their children. Teachers were recruited from China, bringing with them new ideas and new books; when newspapers appeared, journalists followed the teachers. When the imperial Qing government realized how wealthy some of the local Chinese merchants had become, they offered official recognition for investments and philanthropy in China. This often led to the award of honorary mandarin titles and occasionally official visitations to confer further honors.

The single most important factor in enhancing Chinese cultural values among the Chinese was the rapid improvement in transportation and communication. Cheaper and easier travel made China and things Chinese increasingly accessible and up-to-date. This included becoming involved with new developments in the politics of China. Being Chinese, therefore, depended on knowing and following China in every possible way. By the beginning of the twentieth century, all Chinese overseas had officially become *huaqiao*, that is, sojourners enjoined to be patriots, even to the extent of supporting a new-found nationalism directed against Manchu rule, later to be focused on national and social revolution.

Except in British Malaya (including Singapore), political conditions did not allow most Chinese to depart from their traditional trading occupations. Trading with non-Chinese, whether at the level of Western agency houses or that of the native village, remained the backbone of every Chinese community. Only in exceptional circumstances, where the Chinese community was itself predominant, were trading activities largely with other Chinese and more directly with China. In these cases trading with non-Chinese became marginal and being Chinese was very easy indeed. Despite the growing numbers of Chinese in Southeast Asia, however, trade with non-Chinese was still the norm. The major difference from earlier periods was that Chineseness had become more conscious and obvious, even more confident and aggressive. This, in turn, roused the anti-Chinese instincts of some colonial governments and many future indigenous nationalist leaders in the region. Economic competition with native trading classes eventually became politicized. Trading with non-Chinese continued to be profitable, but it no longer required the merchant classes and their descendants to behave like traditional Chinese.[6]

Merchants played a much lesser role in trade with non-Chinese outside of China—in the Americas and Australasia in particular. Most Chinese arrived as coolie labor for mines and plantations; many looked for gold and quick fortunes, others worked to build railways and clear land for farming and agriculture.[7] The few who came to trade gradually made their presence felt, but their businesses were marginal compared to those run by people of European origin. Those who learned new ways through trading with these non-Chinese were quick to introduce these new methods to China. The spectacular example of the Kwok and Ma families of Sydney, who built the Wing On and Sincere department stores in Shanghai and Hong Kong, is well known; their success was a source of pride for all Chinese. Trading with non-Chinese not only enhanced their sense of being Chinese, but also encouraged the desire to be modern Chinese.[8] This became true of all Chinese merchants and their families through the first half of the twentieth century.

Since the 1950s several changes have influenced the way the Chinese overseas trade with non-Chinese. In Southeast Asia a new generation of Chinese men, and an increasing number of women, have tried to learn to trade with indigenous businessmen. The Chinese have adapted to their politically disadvantaged position by sharpening their entrepreneurial instincts, by learning modern business, financial, and industrial skills, and by finding partners with cross-national enterprises, especially with Western and Japanese multinational organizations. This, of course, was only possible in countries with open economies. In countries like Burma and Vietnam, those of Chinese descent traded only in very limited areas; in time many were likely to become indistinguishable from other local traders, and would eventually become wholly assimilated. Where international trade had become important to national economies, Chinese participation offered opportunities to settle down and still remain linked to Chinese trading methods and organizations. The ASEAN (Association of Southeast Asian Nations) countries provide the best examples of the Chinese having become increasingly professional in adapting modern Western business and industrial institutions to their use. The key to their success lies in their ability to keep their regional contacts with other businessmen of Chinese descent, with Hong Kong and Taiwan, and through these contacts, with Japan and Korea, as well as with multinationals who value their knowledge of local conditions and their connections with national elites and decision makers.

For most of these merchants and entrepreneurs, being Chinese had nothing to do with becoming closer to China. It was a private and domestic matter only manifested when needed to strengthen a business contact or to follow an approved public convention. Displays of Chineseness were not helpful when trading with non-Chinese. In fact, the pressure to raise their children to study, work, and live among non-Chinese grew stronger. Under these circumstances, being Chinese became increasingly circumscribed in their daily lives. Paradoxically, however, the one legitimate reason to be Chinese in the ASEAN open economies is that it is useful for a wide range of trading purposes. Even nationalistic governments accept that traders and entrepreneurs helping in national development may need to act and think like Chinese in order to maximize their effectiveness in certain Chinese-dominated trading areas. Some Chinese would also argue that such successes depend on their retaining certain Chinese values and organizations.[9] They point to values like industriousness, trustworthiness, risk taking, and family cohesion; there is also the importance of clan and occupational associations, which encourage cooperation and solidarity. They are careful to separate these cultural features from any commitment to—or political link with—either China or Taiwan. Being Chinese, therefore, may be somewhat disembodied or internalized and is confined to activities of economic benefit to business or to the government.

The position still seems to be changeable, dependent on the continued importance of international trade in the region. Singapore's achievements in this area have been vital. They have provided a focus and inspiration for all who are of Chinese descent, but, more than that, they have created new opportunities together with Hong Kong, Taiwan, and with China itself. For millions of Chinese, mostly *huayi*, in the other ASEAN states, trading with non-Chinese within each country could be balanced by the ever-growing foreign trade with non-Chinese overseas. When such outside trading involves links with Chinese and other *huayi*, being Chinese is a legitimate extension of having a profitable—even a locally patriotic—enterprise. The main difference is that trading with non-Chinese is now a global business—owing to new technology and rapid communications—so remaining Chinese has taken on much larger dimensions. These include linkages around the world with non-Chinese as well as with others of Chinese descent who have intensified their trade with a rejuvenated Chinese environment in Hong Kong, Taiwan, and China.[10]

This leads me to the remarkable story of the new *huaqiao* and remigrating *huayi* in the Americas and Australasia. Up to the 1960s that story would have been mainly one of working with and studying with non-Chinese, which I will deal with later. During the past three decades, however, there has been a transformation of the lesser trading groups. Workers and students have been trained in professions;

more Chinese students, both men and women, have chosen professions linked with industry and commerce, and the children of workers have followed them. The exodus from Southeast Asia, Taiwan, and Hong Kong of whole migrant families with modern commercial and technical skills—sophisticated and bilingual as few of their predecessors were— has brightened and rejuvenated Chinatowns in San Francisco, Vancouver, Toronto, New York, Los Angeles, and Sydney.[11] Today, trade with non-Chinese in these cities and dozens of lesser towns is an experience that reinforces Chinese values and institutions in ways unknown anywhere else. It seems not only to have helped the Chinese stay Chinese, but also to have aroused a keen interest in redefining the modern, free, and cosmopolitan Chinese men and women who can confidently trade among non-Chinese as equals. This is such a strikingly new experience that no one yet knows if it is temporary, transitional, or one that their descendants will enjoy for generations to come. Much will depend on the future of international trade in the world economy and the relations between the major trading nations and the Chinese of China, Taiwan, and Hong Kong. Within each of the countries where the new *huaqiao* and *huayi* have chosen to live, much may also depend on how well they are able to adapt to working with non-Chinese.

WORKING WITH NON-CHINESE

During the nineteenth century large numbers of Chinese men were shipped from the China coast to work in mines and later on the plantations of Southeast Asia; others worked in gold fields, on the railways, and on smaller farms, especially in the Americas and Australasia. It was an inauspicious beginning for Chinese workers. For most, there was no question of working with non-Chinese; they worked in all-Chinese teams under non-Chinese foremen for Western employers. There was a great deal of exploitation and cruelty. Many of the Chinese coolies did not survive; many others returned to China embittered by their encounters with non-Chinese, reinforced in their Chinese identity. Those who remained were deeply affected by the experience and became more determined to stand proud as Chinese. These individuals tended to turn to small-scale trading, shopkeeping, laundries, and vegetable gardening; some were able to arrange for their wives and children to join them. They worked for themselves or for other Chinese and limited their relations with non-Chinese to buying and selling and occasional brushes with the law. It would have been rare for them actually to work with non-Chinese. This level of work remained, with little change, until after the Second World War.[12] Confronted with so much discrimination, identifying with China and asserting one's Chineseness became common. These working classes abroad became the backbone of Chinese nationalism and of the anti-Manchu and, later, the anti-imperialist movements. Their children, possibly some of their grandchildren as well, kept up that tradition. Being Chinese to them was strongly imbued with political commitment best expressed by the powerful concept of *huaqiao*, sojourners only temporarily away from China and no less patriotic for being so.

The difference between these workers and the merchants who had to trade with non-Chinese should not be overstated. Traders, too, suffered from discrimination. That discrimination was more marked in the Americas and Australasia, but it was no less true in colonial territories. The main difference lay in the fact that colonial governments often needed the Chinese merchants to help develop the economy and, therefore, gave their entrepreneurship more room to maneuver. The presence of increasingly effective labor unions in predominantly white countries that opposed the importation of Chinese labor not only hurt Chinese labor but also inhibited Chinese trading activities.

Working with non-Chinese was, therefore, limited until well into the second half of the twentieth century. Some signs of change occurred when Chinese workers were able to intermarry easily—as in Thailand in the nineteenth century—and their descendants not only traded but also worked side by side with indigenous workers. Other changes were noticeable in cities where colonial governments and Western agency houses (precursors to multinationals) were large employers of labor and began to train workers of different ethnic origins to work together. This was true to some extent in British territories like the Straits Settlements and Malay states, where sizable groups who could be identified as Chinese proletariat could be found in the cities.[13] Working together in this way was related to new policies toward schools and training centers, which aimed to encourage men and women of different ethnic origins to work together.

Since the 1950s it has become more common for Chinese to work together with non-Chinese at many levels. In Southeast Asia the departure of the colonial powers changed many working relationships. New national elites either nationalized larger foreign enterprises or pressured them to employ more local workers and managerial staff. The governments themselves were localized and, where male and female workers of Chinese descent were concerned, only those who were citizens by birth or naturalization were considered for employment. There was also pressure on Chinese businesses to employ indigenous labor. A great deal of uncertainty accompanied these changes in working conditions for several decades. Chinese workers, long accustomed to working only with other Chinese, were encouraged to accept non-Chinese as coworkers. Many did adapt quickly, especially the women who worked with non-Chinese women, but many others found it difficult because of obvious cultural differences. In Malaysia and Singapore, where the local Chinese proletariat is significant, there exists a strong tradition of Chinese education which has helped to sustain a Chinese cultural identity even after major changes in education policy had shifted the emphasis to the national language, Malay. Workers with such an educational background usually do not feel their Chinese identity is compromised by working with non-Chinese. Elsewhere, however, where those of Chinese descent are less numerous, the pressures to integrate or even to assimilate are stronger. Under these pressures, workers may have only two choices: to go on working with non-Chinese and accept the possibility of ultimate assimilation or to opt not to and become petty traders, joining the majority who had always preferred trading with non-Chinese to any other relationship.[14]

What of the Western migrant nations of America and Australasia? Working with non-Chinese seems quite natural among educated professional men and women, but often requires that these professionals master modern ideas and technologies to enable them to operate fully within Western institutions. Where the working class is concerned, the cultural gap is certainly too big for new migrants to feel comfortable working with non-Chinese, and there is still a tendency for recent arrivals to work in Chinese firms or factories for Chinese employers. There is, however, a growing group of Chinese professionals and others who work comfortably with non-Chinese. This group of Chinese has been influenced by other factors, notably by their having gone to the same schools as non-Chinese.

We may well wonder if working with non-Chinese at the unskilled and semiskilled levels is simply incompatible with being Chinese. Chinese intellectuals and revolutionary leaders have sometimes joined the call for workers of the world to unite, but history has shown that, in practice, this has not led to real unity but at best has merely meant cooperation between states dominated by workers' political parties. Among workers within any particular country, however, the slogan has met with many difficulties. We should not be surprised that Chinese workers at this level meet with resistance and are themselves anxious and suspicious about how much of their Chineseness they would have to give up to be accepted as "one of the boys" (or girls). It would seem that—not unlike the situation in Southeast Asia—the aim is not solidarity with the working class but to choose between educating oneself (or one's sons and daughters) to become skilled workers and turning to trade, gambling on the business route to wealth and cultural autonomy.[15]

STUDYING WITH NON-CHINESE

From an educational point of view, if all children studied in the same schools, some integration or even assimilation should take place. Educational and cultural values imparted in such schools would affect the racially different children in similar ways. However, there seem to be mixed results if we examine the *huayi* boys and girls who joined national school systems in Southeast Asia after independence and compare them with those who studied with non-Chinese elsewhere.

It is first important to distinguish between Chinese in Southeast Asia—both those born in China and those born locally—who sent their children to local schools, and Chinese in China who sent their children to schools in Europe and America. Both these scenarios appeared—rather tentatively—during the second half of the nineteenth century, but they really only became important during the twentieth century; they developed at the same time that Chinese nationalism was on the rise. Indeed, for many Chinese, studying with non-Chinese did not contradict nationalist sentiment, providing one was conscious of being Chinese, identified with the community, and acknowledged the possibility that skills learned could be put to use for China and for the *huaqiao*. Nevertheless, these two ways of studying with non-Chinese have had very different histories and may play contrasting roles in the future.

Indigenous kingdoms in Southeast Asia did little for the education of Chinese sojourners or their children, and Western colonial powers were similarly uninterested. The only early exception was the Spanish regime and the Catholic church, which introduced schools and even universities to bring Christian civilization to the Philippines. Chinese mestizos benefited from this, and the education they received helped their small community gain status, identify with the Filipinos, and still continue their trade with both Chinese and non-Chinese. Studying with the Spanish and with other mestizos brought a high degree of assimilation, but links with Chinese traders remained.[16] In this case, studying with non-Chinese diminished the sense of being Chinese but, as long as they traded with China or other Chinese, did not encourage them to deny their Chineseness.

For the rest of Southeast Asia, colonial and mission schools and Thai national schools grew slowly; some locally born Chinese did study in these schools with non-Chinese of European and Asian origins. The few Chinese children who went to these schools were educated in foreign languages such as Dutch, English, or Spanish. By the beginning of the twentieth century, this picture had changed radically; Chinese nationalism and a shift toward modernism led to the rapid development of primary and secondary schools that taught in Chinese.[17] There were now more children born to recent migrants from China, and there was pressure for locally born Chinese to learn Chinese and to recover their ancestral identity; it became natural to send Chinese children to study with other Chinese children. Serious doubt was raised about the consequences of having their children studying with non-Chinese in colonial or mission schools. This remained true until the beginning of the 1950s, when each new, independent nation-state demanded the unification of each of their national education systems. Education was a means to create and mold citizens for the new nations of Southeast Asia. Tremendous pressure was put on the Chinese communities to close their schools and to send their children to national schools. The Chinese saw this as a threat to their Chinese identity, but in the midst of considerable tension and bitterness, most Chinese were forced to accept the change.[18] Unless they wished to return to China, they had no choice but to conform to the education system of the countries in which they had settled.

In Malaysia a system of national schools was established with Malay as the language of instruction and English as the first foreign language.[19] Chinese students were permitted to learn Chinese or even to attend approved Chinese-language primary schools as long as all courses followed the national curriculum. The requirement to learn the national language, Malay, remained, however, and no access to higher learning was possible without it. The balance achieved was delicate and many issues concerning the cultural identity of Malaysian Chinese remain unresolved to this day. The size of the Chinese population (about 35 percent), however, shows that studying with non-Chinese does not necessarily lead to assimilation. Indeed, even the loss of the use of Chinese languages does not seem to have diminished the wish of many to identify themselves as Chinese, however tenuous that identification may have become.

In short, the issue of studying with non-Chinese is a very complex one in Southeast Asia. It can lead to assimilation, as in Thailand and other mainland Southeast Asian states; it can lead some to religious conversion and intermarriage as steps toward assimilation in countries like the Philippines; on the whole, however, it has not done that. The results depend in part on the number of Chinese in each country, the attitude of the local government toward Chinese minorities, and religious and racial factors. What the Chinese have benefited from is the acquisition of foreign language skills, access to a more modern education that stresses skills and professionalism, and a better understanding of the countries in which they have chosen to settle. It has also allowed for deeper political identification with their adopted country, which has enabled the better educated to work with fellow nationals to pursue trading activities with greater success. However, the need to trade with China, Taiwan, and Hong Kong, or with Chinese elsewhere, continues to reinforce their urge to remain culturally Chinese.[20] It is not clear what this might do to future generations who may also be expected to study with non-Chinese; it is likely to depend on the viability of trading enterprises and the strength of the world economic system.

In contrast to the situation in Southeast Asia, Chinese students in America and Europe have always had a higher status than Chinese who traveled there to trade or to find work. Studying with non-Chinese fellow students was part of an education intended to save China from its own backwardness. Japan was responsive to Chinese students, but the strongest links were those with the American mission universities in China and their sister institutions in the United States.[21] The students who went abroad were among the best educated in China. Most stayed only for a few years and then returned to China; their contributions to China's modernization are well known. They often found themselves explaining China to non-Chinese at school; this led some students to pioneer a new Chinese view of China as seen from afar. What this generation of students learned from outside China eventually served to further define Chineseness for the modern world.[22]

After 1949 there was a small exodus of talented and educated Chinese; all were students or former students in the West. They left China and went primarily to Taiwan and the United States. They were followed by more students from Taiwan during the next three decades. They did not merely study; the majority were offered positions in universities, research institutes, and large enterprises and stayed on to contribute to American knowledge and even to the ever-expanding American economy. Although some decided to settle, many were torn between sojourning abroad and returning home and were really a new kind of *huaqiao*. They were reluctant to admit to being *huaqiao* because they were neither merchants nor the descendants of coolies, usually the ones called *huaqiao*. That term, to the literati and the well bred in China, had, apart from the association with coolies, connotations of rich parvenus who knew little about China and who were only welcomed back to China for their money. These new *huaqiao* were, in fact, modern professionals or a new type of literati and included more and more Chinese who were willing to settle abroad permanently. Whether or not they chose to settle, over the decades they began to develop a collective vision of modern China that is neither the People's Republic nor Taiwan. Since the early 1980s they have been joined by thousands of the brightest students from the mainland, making possible some exciting exchanges among an increasing variety of Chinese now living abroad. The number of Chinese newspapers, magazines, and even television programs serving this growing market shows that a new cultural life has been developing among the Chinese abroad.[23]

The large numbers of literati-like intellectuals, mainly teachers and journalists, who went to Southeast Asia during the first half of this century had a great impact on millions of people of Chinese descent. They brought the message of a proud, reemergent, modernizing China to people whose Chineseness was dubious and ever-diminishing and sought to arrest their descent into a detribalized state. The messengers who went to Southeast Asia were confident and sure of what was Chinese and what was not; they were missionaries out to save the *huaqiao* from foreign cultures.[24] The role of the Chinese sent abroad to study in the West, especially in the United States, was not as clear. Up until the 1950s pride in the greatness of Chinese civilization was the natural and usually unchallenged norm. Since then the focus has widened to a more open attitude toward certain aspects of Western culture, apart from the greatly admired achievements in science and technology. What is intriguing is what the mainland students of the last decade might bring to Chinese communities abroad, which have become increasingly critical of both their cultural heritage and the viability of the type of socialism espoused by the People's Republic of China.

The new literati *huaqiao* now face a generation of *huayi* who have largely confined their interest in things Chinese simply to what is still necessary for their entrepreneurial activities and their trade relations with China and other Chinese. The ongoing debate must take into account the fact that the millions of *huayi* today are not the barely literate sojourners of the past who looked upon the literati from China with awe. They are, for the most part, educated and professional people with their own claims to being a modern kind of cosmopolitan literati. They may have views about their own Chineseness that cannot easily be swept aside by references to an authoritative center in either China or Taiwan.[25] On the contrary, they view with disappointment and exasperation the backwardness and ineffectiveness of modern China. It is not inconceivable that their views, regarded as irrelevant in the past, will have a voice in the debate among the various new groups of *huaqiao* literati who left China and Taiwan during the last four decades. It is also possible that the most talented of the modern *huayi* will leave behind the Chineseness issue and instead will seek to make their mark in the wider world free from the burdens of their ancient heritage. They have, after all, been studying with non-Chinese all their lives and have met that challenge successfully. They are no longer in fear or in awe of these people. They recognize that they have, in their own right, a great deal to offer the world, and if their achievements are seen as Chinese in any way, they are the achievements of Chinese who live outside China.

LIVING WITH NON-CHINESE

This broad discussion of the Chinese abroad trading, working, and studying with non-Chinese presumes that they would be living with non-Chinese. It is common for Chinese to reside in Chinatowns in major cities or in predominantly Chinese neighborhoods near their places of work or institutions of higher learning. This confirms that, for many Chinese, living among non-Chinese poses few problems because they can normally limit the range of their direct personal and domestic contacts to the marketplace, the workplace, and schools and campuses. This was certainly true of the traditional *huaqiao* and is also true, to some extent, of the new postwar *huaqiao*.

The traditional *huaqiao* traveled abroad singly as traders, craftsmen, and coolie workers. They followed practices prevalent among traders and migrants within China itself. Rural Chinese moving into towns brought their family-based culture with them. In a similar way, the core of these same values followed the urbanized traders and artisans when they traveled to foreign parts, even when they were without their families. They felt obligated to send money home to their families in China and to keep in close contact. They established clan and brotherhood organizations as well as trading and guild associations, in part for their work, but also as alternative or substitute family networks. Wherever it was necessary and they were permitted to do so, they would live close together in Chinatowns, which served not only as a marketplace but was also a home near their place of work. What social life there was helped to sustain their heritage and their sense of identity. The various organizations provided shelter for migrants working for low wages, welfare for the sick and elderly who were without family, and, ultimately, defenses against discrimination, intimidation, and the mysteries of alien legal and political systems. Living together in Chinatowns, they rarely shared their daily lives with non-Chinese, but these communities did allow them to share their family values with one another, and it helped to sustain key features of popular Chinese culture.

Since the turn of the century, two major changes have both enriched and perplexed Chinese living abroad. The first change was the arrival of wives to join the men. Having the family live with them also led to the problem of schooling among non-Chinese for their children. The only way to minimize the consequences of this development was to establish Chinese-language schools and to buy homes in predominantly Chinese neighborhoods. This was further encouraged by a more difficult second change. The rise of patriotism and nationalist consciousness brought excitement and new attitudes toward China, but it did not help the Chinese abroad to adapt to the problem of living with non-Chinese. If anything, it either strengthened their defenses against foreign ways or alienated them further from the native or other migrant peoples, many of whom were themselves nationalists who held anti-Chinese views. Apart from some colonial territories, it was not always possible to avoid sending one's children to the national schools by establishing a separate Chinese school network. Educating young Chinese among non-Chinese was therefore inevitable. In this way, their mothers sooner or later met non-Chinese mothers and they learned to appreciate different ways of bringing up children, even different family life-styles. This contradicted the emergent nationalism and often placed more orthodox fathers in difficult social positions.

No less subversive than a foreign education was entrepreneurial success and the possibility of living in middle-class suburbs with equally successful non-Chinese. This, combined with opportunities for higher education and professional careers for the second or third generation and direct encounters with different value systems, prepared more Chinese to choose between preserving their Chinese ways and accepting features of an alien culture. In most cases, however, unless there had been intermarriages and intensive social exchanges, it was possible to live as Chinese among non-Chinese for two or more generations. Since the 1950s, however, with increasing numbers of *huayi* adapting to local cultures and polities or remigrating elsewhere when they were no longer willing to adapt to discriminatory policies in the countries where they had originally settled, living with non-Chinese has now become multifaceted in ways never before experienced.

It is difficult to generalize about the *huayi* experience in Southeast Asia. In terms of social and cultural differences, Buddhist societies in mainland Southeast Asia provided one set of values and Islamic and Christian societies on the archipelago another; there were also local variations in Vietnam, Malaysia, Java, and Kalimantan (Borneo) that offered the local Chinese still other problems of acceptance and adaptation. On the mainland, for example, the Chinese were familiar with

Buddhist ideas of charity and compassion and found little difficulty fitting them into their own ideas of philanthropy and family welfare, especially in Thailand. Even praying and playing together were not unfamiliar, and eating together posed no problem. Islamic values in Indonesia and Malaysia, however, with different prayer habits and prohibitions on food and drink made social interaction inconvenient if not prohibitive. These foreign values also challenged Chinese attitudes about child rearing, the role of the family, rules of inheritance, and even birth, death, and marriage customs. This was also true of Christianity to a large extent, but insofar as Christian values in the former colonial territories were identified with the powerful, wealthy, modern, and progressive West, they seemed to have been more acceptable. Particularly attractive to Chinese women were the strictures and guarantees of monogamy.

Another major social difference was the size of the population that could be identified as Chinese in any way. Singapore and Malaysia are therefore exceptional countries: about 75 percent of the population is Chinese in the former and about 35 percent in the latter. In both countries, class differences within the Chinese communities are noticeable, but ethnic differences have been so politicized in Malaysia that neither government has allowed the class differences to endanger the necessary framework of racial harmony and cooperation.[26] Elsewhere, however, the picture is different; smaller numbers of Chinese (less than 5 percent of the population) have meant that most Chinese have become educated middle-class traders, technicians, professionals, and entrepreneurs. They associate and live in the same neighborhoods as their indigenous counterparts, and the more successful among them have even became part of the modern national elite. In this way, they live modern lives similar to those of the national elites and, consciously or not, play down their Chineseness, except perhaps when they live in Chinese enclaves in newly developed residential areas. Their occupations and education have edged these Chinese toward modern bourgeois identities. Such identities project their economic strength but, in areas where class and ethnic envy coincide, they also could expose their vulnerability. Living among non-Chinese elites can be comfortable and secure, but the pressure to assimilate is likely to be greater; if this is resisted, the cost of remaining Chinese may become higher.[27]

Much of this cost is political. It ranges from supporting the ruling political party and, to a lesser extent, the opposition parties, to trying to appease the local media and improve the image of the Chinese community. At the same time, living with non-Chinese politics and institutions in evolving nation-states has educated the Chinese in processes quite different from those of China, whether Nationalist or Communist. Insofar as each of the nation-states claims to be democratic and modern in its own way, the Chinese who learn to live with these claims are likely to acquire skills and experiences that increase the gap between themselves and things Chinese. If they face discrimination, however, and do not care to live with what is unfair and unjust, some have the option to remigrate. Because of their education and exportable skills, those who do remigrate have preferred to move as *huayi* to the West, notably to the English-speaking migrant countries in North America and Australasia, rather than return as *guiqiao* (returned overseas Chinese) to China or Taiwan.[28]

The modern bourgeois identity, legal protection of rights and property, educational opportunities, and upward social mobility in free and secular societies are some of the ideals and values that *huayi* remigrants from Southeast Asia to the West have acquired during the past few decades. These seem to have been the same qualities that the *huaqiao* from Hong Kong, Taiwan, and China also sought in the West. They migrate not so that they may become better-off, but because they hope to find these qualities in the non-Chinese peoples among whom they will have to live. They might expect these qualities to enable them and possibly their descendants to be Chinese in their own ways as long as possible.

There are, for the moment, great differences between Western societies and those of Southeast Asia. The greatest difference can be found in North America, where more Chinese have migrated since the end of the Second World War than any other region. The great number of emigrants has not only served to rejuvenate old Chinatowns and create new ones. The quality of these migrants, educated men and women often with ambitious children well prepared for studying abroad, and the self-conscious literati-type concern for the Chinese heritage that some brought with them have aroused expectations about what they could do for all Chinese abroad, as well as for the future of Chinese civilization. They are a new breed, who—when they are not despairing about how their descendants might still be Chinese—have closely observed the non-Chinese with whom they have lived, studied, and worked. They continue to have links, often quite close, with Taiwan, Hong Kong, and China. Unlike the *huaqiao* of the past, they move freely among the *huayi*, as well as among many varieties of non-Chinese. Unlike *huayi*, they have lived and have been educated as Chinese, and some have taken on the mission to preserve high standards of Chineseness among Chinese everywhere. They are well equipped to do so precisely because they have lived among both non-Chinese and *huayi* and appreciate the urge among young Chinese within China itself to bring modernization quickly to their country.

*   *   *

The Chinese abroad on whom I have concentrated have been limited to those in Southeast Asia (where most *huayi* now are) and North America (where most new *huaqiao* have gone). The perspectives on how to be Chinese, how to remain Chinese, how to become Chinese, or how to lose one's Chineseness vary greatly between regions, and even within each region. There are also other perspectives, from Sydney, London, Paris, Tokyo, Calcutta, Lima, Mauritius, Fiji, Tahiti, or the West Indies, where an even greater variety can be found. Despite these varying historical experiences, some common strands continue to run through the story of the Chinese outside China.

Some are not peculiar to the Chinese at all. Like others who have left their respective countries to settle elsewhere, there have been grim struggles for survival and many failures. Perhaps the Chinese are marginally better organized to care for the failures and the weak, but, for most new migrants, the main objective has been to use education as the ladder for success toward a modest professional, middle-class status. Like others who have adopted new nationalities, most members of the second or third generations would like to be proud of their new-found loyalty. Again, the Chinese may be slower and less willing than others to reassess their original identity, but during the past three decades, many have turned away from what the government of China represents. This does not mean they have denied their Chineseness (most live in countries where denial would be useless), but they are able to distinguish between Chinese culture and the Chinese state, and many now identify with the culture and not the Chinese regime. This is not a totally new phenomenon. In the nineteenth century many of the southern Chinese who sojourned overseas identified with Chinese civilization at one level and with their home towns and villages at another, rather than with the governing Qing empire.

Although they share many similarities with other groups of migrants, there are differences that distinguish the Chinese today. Two beliefs are important, if not essential, for the growth and quality of Chinese community life on foreign soil. The first is the primacy given by the Chinese to education, which can be seen not only in the spectacular successes of Chinese children in meeting the challenges of science and technology, but also in their ability to master the economic, financial, and managerial bases of the mature capitalist system. As long as the overseas Chinese live in societies that guarantee education, reward merit, and have legal structures to protect minority rights, there is little reason for them to fear living indefinitely among non-Chinese and to hope to return to China. Instead, new kinds of loosely structured Chinese communities, increasingly professional and bourgeois, may emerge in the towns and cities where they have chosen to settle.

The second belief rests on an interdependent world economy, which has been strengthened dramatically in recent decades by advances in communications and information technology. The ability of many Chinese abroad to turn multinational trading systems to their advantage has been remarkable. The massive growth of international trade has enabled these Chinese, especially in the Asian-Pacific region where they are so numerous, to combine cosmopolitan culture with an increased capacity to associate and trade with other Chinese—both in China and around the world—in ways never before seen.

Their faith in education and their position in the world economy invariably enhances the ability of the Chinese to live and prosper with equally committed non-Chinese. What this does to the quality of their Chineseness is open to question. One may even wonder how long being Chinese will continue to be relevant under such circumstances. A great deal will depend on where China, Taiwan, and Hong Kong will be in the future world economy. What the last century has shown, however, is that the Chinese outside China are adaptable and versatile. If it is possible to live among non-Chinese in the modern international economy and still achieve the social autonomy needed to sustain essential parts of their Chinese identities, there should be little doubt that the Chinese will find ways to do just that.

It is as if one-fourth of humanity carries much weight, and yet is totally silent, in the sense that there is very little articulation of recent Chinese history. For years I have been thinking of that incredible asymmetry, the importance of China, the numerical weight and size, and the lack of powerful articulation of Chinese experience in literature, in art, in philosophy, or even in history. There are so many reasons, political, economic, social, but one of the reasons is that the spiritual backbone, if I may use that awful term, of the Chinese intelligentsia has been broken, maybe not once, but a few times.

Tu Wei-ming
From the Conference on the
Meaning of Being Chinese
Honolulu, October 1990

Especially in the world to come, we will have a Chinese culture in the making, emerging, not necessarily as the descendent of traditional Chinese culture. . . . The Chinese culture will not be the culture we understand, the Chinese culture we identify with. We are overseas Chinese and there are many in China, equally marginal. We have a responsibility to interpret the objects we wish to identify with, to justify this identification as legitimate and comfortable.

Cho-yun Hsu
From the Conference on the
Meaning of Being Chinese
Honolulu, October 1990

7

The Construction of Chinese and Non-Chinese Identities

David Yen-ho Wu

Concepts of Chinese and non-Chinese as the Chinese perceive them are complicated. The single English word *Chinese* not only misses certain meanings but may cause confusion. In Chinese, in both the spoken and the written language, many terms are used to reflect racial, cultural, ethnic, and national attributes (*Zhongguoren, Zhonghua minzu, hua-ren, huaqiao, tangren, hanren,* and so on). These terms have evolved through time; some are recently invented; some originated before the Christian era but are still popular among Chinese. Such singular terms alone, however, cannot describe the complex situations of Chinese identity. The modern cultural concept of "Chinese," for example, must be understood in the context of China's recent political history. In order to create a modern identity to cope with conditions created by China's confrontation with the Western world, the Chinese were obliged to deal with foreign concepts, including that of nation, state, sovereignty, citizenship, and race; more recently, with cultural and ethnic identity. Chinese officials and intellectuals since the end of the nineteenth century have had difficulty in accepting these Western concepts, especially as they apply to Chinese living abroad, who are often regarded as foreign nationals under international law. The Chinese have also had to deal with the powerful national and racial groups who are not themselves Chinese, but who at one time or other conquered parts or the whole of China and continue to live today in China's vast frontier territories. Both of these peripheral situations not only raise interesting intellectual questions about the nature of being Chinese and the formation of Chinese identity, but also reveal cultural and political constructs of identity that have had local, national, and international interpretations, leading to negotiations about identity and manipulations of policy by the governments of China and other nations.

To ordinary Chinese, the traditional view of being at the center of existence has always been an important aspect of being Chinese. This anthropocentric view is based on a deep-rooted sense of belonging to a unified civilization that can boast several thousand years of uninterrupted history. Such a sense of unity and continuity was, until recently, common among all Chinese, even among those who had moved abroad permanently to settle among non-Chinese people. What is the reality of such sentiment today?

Let us first recall the movement of Chinese within the territory of present-day China. Throughout history, the Chinese have moved southward, from the center to what is today the southwest, traditionally perceived to be the location of the kingdoms of the southern "barbarians." Then, of course, there has been the migration and settlement of the Chinese abroad. In the last two centuries, hundreds of thousands of Chinese have left their homes in southeast coastal China to work and eventually settle in, primarily, Southeast Asia, Oceania, and North and South America. The physical separation of many Chinese from their homeland—the center of their culture—has not precluded the continuity of a Chinese identity. Although it seems natural for Chinese emigrants to maintain their cultural heritage, to emphasize their home-oriented identity, in the last sixty years this sentiment has been reinforced from the "center" through deliberate efforts by the Communist government in China to promote a state version of Chinese identity. As a result, many Chinese in the periphery share common sentiments, though they are physically far removed from China.

Two sentiments identify all who see themselves as Chinese. On the one hand, as *Zhongguoren*, which carries the connotation of modern patriotism or nationalism, they feel a connectedness with the fate of China as a nation. Associated with this is a sense of fulfillment, of being the bearers of a cultural heritage handed down from their ancestors, of being essentially separate from non-Chinese. Such primordial sentiments were very common among Chinese in the peripheral areas, especially among those living in the frontier lands, but also among the overseas Chinese, who were forced to intermingle with non-Chinese.

The Chinese also see themselves as being members of *Zhonghua minzu*; a close but inadequate English translation would be "the Chinese race" or "the Chinese people." Since ancient times, the Chinese have viewed themselves as being at the center, surrounded by culturally inferior barbarians on the peripheries—the Yi in the east, the Di in the west, the Rong in the north, and the Man in the south. *Zhonghua minzu* is a rather modern concept that emerged only at the turn of the twentieth century.[1] The term *minzu* (*min* for people and *zu* for tribe or clan) was adopted from the writings of the Japanese Meiji period, although the two characters used separately were borrowed by the Japanese from classical Chinese writings. By 1895 *minzu* began to reappear in Chinese revolutionary journals, but it was not until 1909 that it became popular among intellectuals.

The term *Zhonghua minzu* was first used by intellectuals during the time of the early Republic of China, where it was often associated with nationalistic writings warning the Chinese people of the danger of annihilation under Western invasion. In his article entitled "The Explanation of the Republic of China" (*Zhonghua minguo*), the leading intellectual of the time, Zhang Taiyan, proposed an authoritative definition of the Chinese people—*Zhongguoren* (people of the central country).[2] He writes that the ancestors of *Zhongguoren* (the ancestors of the Han) have, since ancient times, been centered (*zhong*) in North China (yet no mention of territorial boundaries), and have called themselves Hua Xia. His article, later cited by leading ethnohistorians, concluded that Hua, Xia, or Han could be used interchangeably to mean China the nation-state, Chinese the race (or tribe), and China the geographic location. According to his word and logic, and that of many Chinese intellectuals who supported him, Hua, Xia, or Han formed a unity— an undifferentiated race originating in North China, which emerged during the legendary Xia dynasty and was in the process of becoming a modern republic. Zhang Taiyan's vague and inclusive definition marks the beginning of a modern concept of Chinese national identity. Later efforts were made both in and out of China, through intellectual discourses and government promotions, to construct a Chinese identity based on his nationalistic view.

Both *Zhongguoren* and *zhonghua minzu* represent an identity based on concepts of cultural and historical fulfillment rather than the more conventional modern notions of nationality or citizenship. Since most

Chinese have believed that the Han people were *the* race of China, one that had absorbed people of all languages, customs, and racial and ethnic origins, the meanings of being Chinese in the sense of ethnicity, culture, citizenship, or residence were almost never addressed. According to the intellectual discourse in the early Republic, *Zhongguoren* was thought to be the same as *Zhonghua minzu*—meaning the five major stocks of the Hua people of the middle land—an idea that is still deeply rooted among many educated Chinese today. By the early twentieth century this concept of a "Chinese people" included four major non-Chinese races, descendants of what were formerly referred to as barbarians: the Man (Manchus), the Meng (Mongolians), the Hui (ethnic groups of Islamic faith in northwestern China), and the Zang (Tibetans). It was also believed that these minority groups, like hundreds of others in the past, had been assimilated into the Chinese culture because of the irresistibly superior Han civilization that had carried on unchanged for thousands of years. For several decades the perception that racial and cultural composition delineated Chineseness dominated the minds of Chinese under Nationalist education and party propaganda.

Recent studies, however, have shown that the existence of a superior Chinese culture is, at best, a myth. The Chinese people and Chinese culture have been constantly amalgamating, restructuring, reinventing, and reinterpreting themselves; the seemingly static Chinese culture has been in a continuous process of assigning important new meanings about being Chinese. However, the Chinese people have not been conscious of using such a cultural construction, and it has significantly affected Chinese individuals in peripheral areas because they are socially and politically situated on the border between the non-Chinese and the category of people considered Chinese. Chinese, be they *hanren, tangren*, or by the 1980s *huaren* (the Han people, the Tang people, or the Hua people), in the peripheral areas have embraced an unspoken but powerful mission: to keep themselves within the acceptable definition of Chineseness and to engage other members of the Chinese community in the preservation of Chinese civilization despite their non-Chinese environment. Although these processes of identity construction have occurred both in and out of China, they have been seldom documented by Chinese scholars within China.

CONSTRUCTION OF CHINESE IDENTITY OVERSEAS

In the Chinese mind the overseas Chinese or *huaqiao* (the Hua sojourners) are natural members of *Zhonghua minzu* as well as *Zhongguoren*.
Following the traditional thinking of the Chinese people and state,
overseas Chinese (regardless of racial mixture) remain Chinese in the
fullest sense as long as they are able to claim a Chinese male ancestor,
a homeplace in China from which this ancestor supposedly emigrated,
and observe some manner of cultural practices.

For ordinary people in China, the term *huaqiao* invokes the image
of a certain type of Chinese—one who is Chinese but partly alien,
wealthy, often associated with America and the Cantonese—but, in
some instances, with Nanyang, the South Seas, and the Hokkienese.
Overseas Chinese refer to themselves using a variety of terms in Chinese
as well as in other languages, with and without political connotations;
these include *huaren* (Hua or Chinese persons), *huayi* (descendants of
Chinese), and *huaqiao* (Chinese nationals living overseas).

Rising nationalism since the early Republic, the threat of Japanese
invasion, and discrimination against the overseas Chinese in most host
countries all created the necessary environment for a strong China-
oriented identity outside of China. After the Nationalist government
was established in Nanjing in 1928 following the northern expedition,
China entered a period of "political tutelage" under the authoritarian
rule of the Kuomintang (KMT) party. The entire school system of China
became a major arena for nationalist indoctrination—especially allegiance to the KMT party and its leaders.[3] Nationwide inculcation of
Kuomintang ideology in school classes included the teaching of Sun
Yat-sen's Three People's Principles and speeches of KMT leaders along
with lessons on citizenship and patriotism. Outside the schools, the
KMT introduced the daily flag salute and national anthem and sponsored weekly gatherings in the name of Dr. Sun Yat-sen for lectures on
KMT teachings and military training. This kind of nationalist indoctrination was also brought to overseas Chinese schools via branch organizations of the Kuomintang party and other overseas Chinese organizations, including the Overseas Chinese Commission of the Nationalist
government. Even today the commission regularly sponsors cultural
and educational activities in North America and Europe, under the

guise of promoting Chinese cultural tradition, in order to induce loyalty to the Nationalist government in Taiwan.

The case of the Chinese living on the remote islands of Papua New Guinea illustrates how Chinese in the center, primarily government officials and intellectuals, were able to forge a Chinese nationalist identity overseas. I conducted research there from 1970 to 1973 on people recognized by themselves and others as "Chinese."[4] During our first encounters they often complained that they had suffered for years from discrimination by the European colonists or, in Cantonese, the *lou-fan* (barbarians). They maintained that they were a people without a country to look after them (*guojia*), although the majority had become Australian citizens during the 1960s.

When I first arrived in Rabaul on the island of New Britain, I was astonished to find the New Guinea KMT headquarters, which was also the center of local politics as the majority of the local Chinese elites were KMT members. Only after a year of study did I realize that the New Guinea Chinese had been recruited and initiated by the KMT during the 1930s, when about one-fifth of the total Chinese population of New Guinea joined the party. In addition to the KMT headquarters in Rabaul, three branch offices were set up in Kokopo (on New Britain Island), Kavieng (on New Ireland Island), and Madang (on the New Guinea mainland). KMT leaders, primarily wealthy Chinese merchants, functioned as political representatives of the Chinese population vis-à-vis the Australian colonial administration, and represented the central power of China in presentations of Chinese culture and education. Until the late 1950s all Chinese in New Guinea were educated in Chinese schools under the wing of the KMT, who recruited teachers from China to infuse New Guinean Chinese youth with a proper understanding of Chinese language, culture, and national identity. These Chinese schools appear to have had a profound influence on the New Guinea Chinese in their formation of a nationalist Chinese identity. A photograph taken in Rabaul in 1953—which I obtained from a family album—depicts a community gathering on a playing field, with New Guinea Chinese Boy Scouts parading through a Double Tenth celebration arch. The inscription on the poles of the arch reads: "Donate generously to fill up the national treasury: To counterattack the [Chinese] mainland is the duty of overseas Chinese."

During my stay in New Guinea, I was introduced to KMT members or managers through KMT networks. The organization appeared to still be intact and KMT branches in Port Moresby, Lae, Madang, Kavieng, and Rabaul were in close contact with the KMT headquarters in Taiwan. New Guinea Chinese not only sent representatives to the annual Double Tenth celebration in Taipei, but, according to one regional KMT head, they were sometimes invited to sit in on the National Assembly of the Republic of China to show global support for the government of Taiwan. At the time neither I, then a student of anthropology, nor the Chinese in New Guinea had begun to understand the concept of *huaren* (used to mean ethnic Chinese without political connotations). The New Guinean Chinese considered themselves either *huaqiao* or *Zhongguoren*, using expressions like *ngo de wuakiu*; *ngode jonggokyan* (we overseas Chinese; we Chinese nationals). They accepted Chinese patriotism as a matter of duty to one's fellow man, though they were predominantly naturalized Australians. After the Second World War (and until the Republic of China's withdrawal from the United Nations in 1971), the Rabaul Chinese celebrated the Double Tenth holiday each year by performing a lion dance or, as they called it, a dragon dance. Each year they organized a party at the KMT hall that was sponsored by the KMT party of New Guinea and was attended by the Chinese community on the island of New Britain.[5]

During this period the Chinese in New Guinea publicly expressed their association with the KMT and the Nationalist government in Taiwan, but they also quietly gossiped about the rise of the People's Republic of China as a world power. By the late 1960s Chinese merchants gradually increased their imports from China—first through Hong Kong and later through direct trade. Because of the conservative, anticommunist sentiment of the Australian people—especially the colonial administration in New Guinea—the Chinese never openly expressed their pride about being Chinese and their continuing association with the mainland, although their "ancestral land" had successfully tested the atom bomb, had sent a satellite into orbit, and had reportedly cured the blind and the deaf with traditional Chinese medicine.

The influence of Chinese schools in teaching a China-oriented identity has been even more profound in the larger countries in Southeast Asia that have a substantial ethnic Chinese population. Indonesia is a good example. Before 1957 there were two thousand Chinese schools in Indonesia. These schools were divided between those that were pro-

Taipei and those that were pro-Beijing: "In 1958 there was an anti-Kuomintang campaign in Indonesia because of Taipei's involvement in the regional rebellion. The Chinese schools associated with the Kuomintang were closed down. In 1965 there was an abortive coup in which the Communists were involved. Beijing was implicated in this coup, which resulted in the closing of pro-Beijing schools, marking the end of Chinese education in Indonesia."[6] The five million ethnic Chinese in Indonesia considered themselves divided into two ethnic subgroups: the *peranakans*, predominantly locally born and residing on the outer islands; and *totok*, or in Chinese Fujian dialect *sinke* (new arrivals), which included a large proportion of non-Indonesian-born Chinese people concentrated in Java. However, in 1965 the government suppressed the use of Chinese languages, theatrical performances, and religious practices in public. By the 1970s, with the closing down of Chinese schools, the majority of the Chinese children in Indonesia, including the less acculturated *totok*, had lost their ability to speak Chinese.

CONSTRUCTION OF CHINESE AND NON-CHINESE
IDENTITIES IN FRONTIER CHINA

It was not until the 1960s, under a Marxist ideology and a Russian model of policy, that the People's Republic established a new concept of being Chinese, which clearly demarcated the Han (ethnically and racially Chinese) and the non-Han (a number of exclusive groups of people representing different cultures, languages, races, and territorial boundaries).

In the 1980s I did research on the minorities in China that raised serious questions about the meaning of being Chinese and non-Chinese inside China. The term Chinese—*Zhongguoren*—officially consists of fifty-six *minzu*, or nationalities. The majority of Chinese, who once called themselves *Zhongguoren*, now consciously refer to themselves as *hanren* (of the Han nationality), although the Han Chinese are only one of the fifty-six nationalities in China. The Han constitute almost 94 percent of the entire population of China, but the remaining fifty-five minority nationalities—including the Man, the Meng, and the Hui, well known since the early Republic—reside in over 60 percent of China's territory.

Does being Chinese (or non-Chinese) mean the same thing for the

Han, the minority nationalities, and the Chinese overseas? Stevan Harrell, in a recent discussion of ethnic group conflict in China, provides an
interesting observation.[7] He proposes that the distinctions between the
Han and the minorities in China and those between two groups of Han
from different regions of China are "ethnic" differences (in the contemporary social scientist's understanding of the term). But he makes the
important point that being Han (ethnic Chinese) does not include a self-
perception of being "different" from the mainstream of Chinese culture. The regionally defined groups of Han—Cantonese, Shanghaiese,
and Taiwanese, including those living overseas—have obvious ethnic
differences in speech, dress, customs, religious beliefs, and so on. Any
expert on ethnic studies today will notice that the difference between
two Han groups can, in some cases, be more pronounced than that between a Han and a so-called minority nationality group. From their
ethnocentric view, however, the Han do not believe that the culture and
territorial claims of minority groups are equal to those of the superior
Han civilization.

In view of these rather confusing senses of ethnic and cultural identity among the "Chinese" and "non-Chinese" in China, what is the
meaning of the resurgence of minority cultures? Government authorities in China, as in other modern nations, have played an active role
in changing and promoting ethnic or national identities. To classify a
group as non-Chinese in China today is to reinterpret the meaning of
minority culture rather than to preserve parts of a past tradition. The
present cultural system has been undergoing constant change, and is
the reinterpretation or creation of an already changed system, similar to the case of the modern Hawaiian or other "native" American
cultures. The new classification of nationalities in China officially emphasizes that each of the minorities has its own language, culture, and
history. China's State Nationalities Affairs Commission has even published an official ethnography, linguistic study, and ethnohistory for
each nationality. Furthermore, one can observe officially sponsored
festivals, officially sanctioned religious celebrations, and officially approved songs, dances, and costumes in minority regions to represent
the distinctiveness of the newly named non-Han groups.

Such concerted efforts by the government have been necessary given
the fact that under the new ethnic classification many previously anoma-
lous groups, whether by tribal name or by cultural characteristics, have

now been subsumed under single ethnic labels. As a result, the revival of minority culture in China has required the creation of new unified, centralized, and pannational sets of cultural symbols and activities. Thus, official efforts to promote Chinese minority groups have also included giving assistance to minorities to create a written language, compile a minority history (glorifying legendary heroes), and restore minority medical practices, and for the composition of minority music, opera, and literature. Field data gathered in the summer of 1985 on one minority group, the Bai in Yunnan Province, illustrate the above processes of cultural construction and interaction between the Han Chinese and the non-Han minorities.

The Bai are the second largest minority of Yunnan, with a population of 1.2 million (the largest minority group, the Yi people, numbers 3 million). The core of the Bai population resides in northwestern Yunnan, surrounding Erhai Lake, in the Bai Autonomous Prefecture. The capital city includes the ancient town of Dali, which has long been a trade center in the region and has recently become a popular tourist attraction for foreign visitors. The rest of the Bai people are scattered in east Yunnan, including Kunming—the capital city of the province.

Bai as an ethnic label was unknown to both the Bai themselves and others until 1958, when an official list of nationalities was compiled. Before 1958 the Bai had been known by a number of names, depending on where they resided and whether they were referring to themselves or being referred to by neighboring groups. The most commonly used name was Minjia, literally meaning "the civilians," a term developed during the Ming dynasty when the Han military settlers were distinguished from the local residents. In the 1940s one Chinese sociologist observed that the Bai were "not quite a minority, but not quite Chinese either."[8] According to ethnographic reports, the Bai who lived in towns and cities were so assimilated to Chinese culture that they were indistinguishable from any other so-called Chinese (or Han, in today's terminology). They maintained their own language only in the countryside (yet more than half of their vocabulary was Chinese) and practiced only a few customs that could be considered non-Chinese by anthropologists.[9]

The Bai assimilation to Chinese culture had been going on for centuries, perhaps millennia, even before their ancestors in the eighth century A.D. established a powerful kingdom—Nanzhao (Nan Chao)—

which dominated the Indochinese peninsula and influenced what is today Burma, Thailand, Laos, Cambodia, and Vietnam.[10] During the 1940s, when sociologists and ethnologists entered the Bai territory to do field research, the Bai people denied their non-Chinese origin and would feel offended if so regarded. Therefore, the Bai, until very recently, considered themselves to be ethnic Chinese and enjoyed treatment as such. One of the best-known works on Chinese culture, written by anthropologist Francis L. K. Hsu,[11] was based on fieldwork among the Bai people during the 1930s. Hsu's field site, in the heart of today's Bai Nationality Autonomous Prefecture, consisted of a township and several surrounding villages. It appeared to be a typical local Chinese center of commerce and agriculture. Local trading firms during World War II expanded their business to international ports as far as Calcutta. The "Chinese" in the Minjia territory (as it was known then) were so typically Chinese that their family and kinship systems as well as their rituals for ancestors, as described in Hsu's book, were thought to be the ideal representation of Chinese society and culture from the late 1940s through the early 1970s.

In 1985 I did field research in a Bai autonomous district, a cluster of five villages situated in a hilly valley, with a total population of two thousand. The majority of the villagers were farmers who grew rice, vegetables, and some fruit, but a small percentage were employed at local factories in the neighboring districts. Local legend had it that the original Bai families migrated here from Dali—the heart of the Bai territory—about 250 years ago. Most villages had once been dominated by one or two surnames, but since the Communist Revolution the local patrilineal clans had officially been dissolved, although local politics continued to revolve around prominent figures of those surnames.

My initial concern was to collect general ethnographic data. As is the convention in my discipline, I expected to find and document a minority culture which was quite distinct from that of the "Chinese"; I did not expect to make a connection between this "minority nationality" and Hsu's Chinese (the Minjia). I soon noticed that the Bai villagers did not appear to be different in physical features, appearance, behavior, or custom from other ethnic Chinese villagers in the region. I therefore inquired how a Bai, or the Bai people as a whole, could be distinguished from the Han—the ethnic Chinese. No one was able to answer the question save for mentioning language differences. The Bai claim to be bilingual—speaking the Bai language and Chinese Mandarin (Yunnan dialect) with a distinct Bai accent. Linguists have long argued about the likeness of the Bai language to other minority languages in the region, but all have agreed that it is basically a Tibeto-Burman language with a high percentage (60 percent) of its vocabulary adopted from the Chinese. The Bai language has always been easily accepted by other people living in and around the area as a local, rural dialect, since it is common in other parts of China for people to speak mutually unintelligible dialects or languages in places of close geographical proximity.[12] In terms of both language and culture, the Bai themselves believe they are different from others, especially the ethnic Chinese, yet they could not give a convincing explanation for these differences.

Further observations also failed to reveal cultural characteristics that could differentiate the Bai from the ethnic Chinese. Bai family and kinship structure, and their social and political organization at the village level, are all similar to those of the ethnic Chinese villages in the region. Although they used to be Buddhists and practiced rituals for Chinese deities on special occasions, these religious activities had stopped in the 1950s. Since the early 1980s, however, some villagers, usually women, have resumed the worship of gods at home and in restored temples. Rituals in memory of ancestors and marriage and funeral ceremonies—all traditional Chinese practices—have become popular for every family. Furthermore, since ancient times the Bai have celebrated folk holidays and festivals celebrated by Chinese elsewhere. Even the Bai architecture shows an adoption of traditional Chinese construction styles. A few wealthier families have even torn down their old houses (of mud bricks) and built modern cement houses, thus making their village houses less distinctly Bai.

All these observations leave an outside observer with the impression that the Bai people have little cultural uniqueness. What is clear, however, are the many cultural elements, though distinctly "Chinese," which have been associated with the claim of Bai ethnicity in the writings of Chinese ethnologists.

There are great similarities between Hsu's interpretations of the 1930s and my own findings in 1985. Most of the change in the Bai's self-perception has occurred because of their officially named identity; where they previously claimed to be ethnic Chinese, they now claim to be a minority—"non-Chinese." The case of the Bai reveals how the official policy of advancing a minority group's social status and the minority's acknowledgment of their new status have had a profound effect on ethnic identity in China.

Our research in China demonstrates how policy can influence the passing on of ethnic identity from Han (Chinese) to non-Han (non-Chinese) for an entire ethnic group. Such a move by a group, or rather the changing of official labels under an authoritative policy, does not require members of the group to change their culture; but it does require a change in their perception and interpretation of their culture so they can justify a new identity. This is the essence of being Chinese or non-Chinese in China today. Such a scenario has applied to many other minority nationalities in China, such as the Miao-Yao groups in southwest China, the Zhuang in Guizhou and Guangxi provinces (the largest minority, with over 13 million), the Tujia (2.8 million in Hunan and Sichuan), some of the urban Mongols, the She (in Zhejiang and Fujian), almost all the Man (Manchu) in the northeast and elsewhere in China, and the Hui (the assimilated Muslims residing in urban centers).[13]

BECOMING CHINESE OR NON-CHINESE: PERANAKANIZATION

Throughout the long history of Chinese civilization, Chinese cultural chauvinism notwithstanding, many non-Chinese have been absorbed both culturally and racially into the Han Chinese group, since traditional values have held that being Chinese is culturally and socially superior to being non-Chinese (barbarian). Therefore, we rarely find statements in Chinese literature of Chinese becoming acculturated with non-Chinese. Many in the overseas Chinese communities, however, have long observed that some of their members have "gone native," and have developed special terms to distinguish them. Many examples can be cited from Southeast Asia, where the migrant Chinese are numerous and have had a long history of settlement.

Peranakan is a Malay word popular among ethnic Chinese in Indonesia to refer to the native-born Chinese who have gradually lost their mother tongue and cultural characteristics. *Peranakan*s may speak the indigenous language of the host country (or a creolized version of it), observe some very old Chinese customs and ceremonies as well as acquiring indigenous ones, and are regarded by both the unassimilated Chinese migrants (the *totok*) and the indigenous people as belonging to neither group. While the "pure" Chinese may question the legitimacy of the *peranakans*' claim to being authentic Chinese, the *peranakans* themselves are quite confident about the authenticity of their Chineseness. They are often heard referring to themselves as "we Chinese." Conspicuous examples of *peranakan* communities are also found in Malaysia and Singapore, where they are known as the "Straits-born," or *baba*.[14]

Until recently, it was inconceivable for the Chinese in China to admit that it would be possible for a Chinese within China gradually to give up superior Han Chinese cultural practices, adopt the native way of life, and eventually become a *peranakan* or "native." However, owing to the change in minority policy to favor minority groups in China and the apparent advantage of having a new minority status, as promoted by the authorities, the acculturated Chinese settlers in some minority regions have even sought official recognition as a distinct ethnic minority. "Peranakanization" (migration out of China, acculturation to an indigenous culture, and subsequent loss of one's Chinese identity) has occurred repeatedly throughout history. The following is one example of how a Han family became acculturated to the indigenous culture in Yunnan, as described in a prewar ethnographic report.[15]

A Chinese man arrives in a minority region and becomes an itinerant trader. After toiling on the road among local villages and market towns, he saves enough money to settle down. He either purchases a piece of land or opens a shop in a market town and marries a native woman. As he prospers and the family grows, he decides to send one of his mixed-blood sons or grandsons to a school in the regional capital, or even the capital city of Yunnan, to acquire a proper Chinese education and eventually to become an official. The idea is that this son, if successful, will carry on the honorable Chineseness of his family, although the other sons who stay at home may eventually become natives.

To be established in a native-dominated region, a Chinese merchant or landlord must become acculturated to the indigenous culture and use his sociocultural abilities to build friendships with the natives—such a settler is usually a bilingual and bicultural man. The Chinese ethnologist Tao, who did fieldwork in Yunnan in the 1940s, was not ashamed to admit that a Han settler as such, as opposed to a truly native person, was usually the best informant for visiting ethnologists.[16] It is not unreasonable to assume that some of the Han Chinese settlers Tao observed might have, in a generation or two, changed their ethnic identity to become members of the minority group they lived with, as many Chinese colonists in Yunnan did during the fifteenth and sixteenth centuries (the Ming and Qing dynasties).

It is highly possible that some of the Bai people described earlier were descendants of early Han migrants who acculturated with the indigenous people when the Chinese were not as numerous or as powerful as they later became. These "indigenized Chinese," or Bai, may have later become reacculturated to the Han when further waves of Chinese migration and domination reached the old Bai territory. Turning to the Chinese communities in Southeast Asia, we begin to understand that a comparable process of peranakanization has repeatedly occurred among Chinese migrants overseas.

There was a Hokkien (south Fujian dialect) saying among the early Chinese settlers in Malaya: *sa dai sheng ba*—in three generations a Chinese will become a *baba*.[17] If a Chinese man married a Malay woman and their son also married a Malay, it is unlikely that the grandson would maintain his Chinese language skills and practice of Chinese customs. What Chinese ethnologists observed in Yunnan appears to be typical of early Chinese migration and settlement in Malaya. Ethnographic reports in recent years still document the process of Chinese (considered pure) incorporation of Malay customs, language, and other cultural practices. One interesting example is the way the Malayan Chinese have included Malayan gods, spirits, and non-Chinese figures in the traditional Chinese cosmology and religion. In other words, although the Malayan Chinese continued to live as Chinese on foreign soil, many foreign elements became part of their existence. Anthropologist William Newell reports that the Chinese "hierarchy of gods was parallel to the government hierarchy in the world. The gods were sometimes regarded as subordinate to officials in this world."[18] In the 1950s, for example, a tree spirit was making trouble for workers during road construction work in a Chinese village in Malaya:

In desperation, the Chinese community and the workmen petitioned the [British] District Officer to come and order the tree to be cut down. The District Officer took the axe and gave the tree one stroke. After this, the tree was easily destroyed. In another village the [British] District Officer had to perform a similar task. Underneath the present new village, there used to be a cemetery. Each time the cemetery was cleared, mysterious rumblings and groans were heard so that the workmen became frightened. Finally the District Officer had to sign a notice ordering the spirits or ghosts to remain quiet. From then on no trouble was experienced. [Incidentally, this notice was written in English.]

Chinese flexibility in cultural and religious identity can be seen in the inclusion of native gods in their worship. In north Malaya, Chinese peasants worshiped local tutelary gods. Newell writes: "One family has built four shrines to [the local gods] in each corner of their property. In other cases, the earlier Malay inhabitants of the land have worshipped a tree or other object believed to have mystical power, and the Chinese inhabitants have continued to worship the same object."[19]

I observed similar patterns of Chinese becoming non-Chinese in Papua New Guinea, which parallel the case of the Yunnan Xian described by Tao as well as that of the Malayan Hokkien mentioned above. The Chinese settled in New Guinea at the turn of the century. By the 1970s, at the eve of the country's independence from colonial rule, the Chinese community of some three thousand included a minority group of mixed-blood descendants (numbering about seven hundred) whose identity depended on the other's labeling and interpretation.

The example of a particular family further illustrates the peranakanization process. At the turn of the century, a Chinese migrant worker from Taishan, in Guangdong Province, arrived on New Ireland. He became a coconut plantation manager for a wealthy uncle, married a native woman, and had three sons. His eldest son (who was least noticeably of mixed blood) was sent back to China for education at the age of eight and was raised there. By the time he reached his forties, life in China had become less acceptable to him. He returned to New Guinea with a Chinese wife and their children, where they were received as "Hong Kong Chinese" by the locally born Chinese and the native people of New Guinea. His two younger brothers stayed on the island and both married mixed-blood women. One of the brothers became a local politician and was successful enough to serve a term as prime minister of this newly independent nation. His dark skin and physical features made it difficult for people to distinguish him from the rest of the Melanesians on the islands. Yet, during his recent visit to China with a government delegation representing Papua New Guinea, he spoke Cantonese—a common language of the island Chinese community, which he had learned as a child. He was treated, in one sense, as an overseas Chinese returning home. The youngest brother of the three, whose physical appearance was obvious enough to be recognized as a *bun tong* (a Chinese translation of the colonial English term "half-caste"), became the proprietor of the family business established by his father. In three generations, a Chinese migrant's offspring had become Chinese, New Guinean, and mixed-blood New Guinean-Chinese; each could claim any one of these multiple identities.

In the early 1970s almost one-third of the locally born Chinese in Papua New Guinea (second and third generation) were of mixed blood. Wu observed that, "Judged by its ethnic as well as its cultural characteristics, the Chinese population in Papua New Guinea is not a homogeneous group. Among the Chinese included in my survey only 77 percent are *chin tong* (the Cantonese word for pure Tang people), the rest are *bun tong*." [20] The Chinese on these remote islands were able to construct a Chinese identity using very flexible criteria. Irrespective of the extent of ethnic mixture in a person's progenitors, if he was descended from a Chinese man, maintained a Chinese surname, and spoke a little Chinese, he was accepted by the Chinese community as a Chinese—*tongjan* (in Cantonese, Tang person). In Kavieng all the Chinese, regardless of ethnic makeup, lived in the Chinese quarter of town. We often heard the Sino-Niuginians, who closely resembled indigenous people in appearance (in one instance a man's complexion could be described as charcoal black), refer to themselves as "we Chinese." For many communities being Chinese depended on one's wealth and social status, not one's skin color or degree of knowledge about Chinese culture. A mixed-blood Chinese, if poor, was regarded as a member of the *bun tong* community; however, if he owned a prosperous commercial business, he was accepted as Chinese. [21] No matter how well the New Guinea Chinese could demonstrate their Chinese language skills or their knowledge of Chinese culture (as by reciting stories from the *Romance of the Three Kingdoms* as some did to show off to me, a person of the center), they all ate with a plate, a spoon, and a fork, as opposed to the "universal" bowls and chopsticks.

The Indonesian Chinese are another example of Chinese who may have lost all possible ethnic and cultural traits, including language, but are still able to improvise a Chinese identity. Media reports, for example, have revealed that recent government relaxation has allowed the revival of public displays of Chinese identity in the form of temple renovations and celebrations of Chinese folk festivities. A recent article in the *Far Eastern Economic Review* reports that although there has been a revival of Chinese culture by the *totok* in the performance of *po-te-hi* (hand puppet theater, which originated in Fujian, the homeland of the Indonesian Chinese), these Chinese puppet theaters now perform in the Javanese language. "In the early 1960s one could still watch *po-te-hi* performed entirely in Hokkien, but now only the chanted parts are in the dialect, and even then only if the puppeteer masters it. Otherwise, he merely chants nonsense syllables."[22]

CONCLUSION

For centuries the meaning of being Chinese seemed simple and definite: a sense of belonging to a great civilization and performing properly according to the intellectual elite's norm of conduct. This is what Wang Gungwu referred to as the Chinese "historical identity." The Chinese as a group traditionally believed that when a larger Chinese population arrived in a frontier land, Sinicization was the only possible course. It was inconceivable that any Chinese could be acculturated by the inferior non-Chinese "barbarians"; however, such acculturation has been a common course of development for Chinese in the frontier lands and overseas, although people still insist that an unadulterated Chinese culture is maintained by the Chinese migrants.

Wang, in an article in which he reviews social scientists' concepts of identity and ethnicity and applies them to the Chinese experience in Southeast Asia, points out how complex the Chinese identities are from multiple perspectives of ethnic, national, local, cultural, and class considerations.[23] My discussion has focused on how Chinese conceptualize their own Chineseness in the peripheral situation, demonstrating the complex process whereby they are able to incorporate indigenous language and culture without losing their sense of having a Chinese identity—not even their sense of having an authentic Chinese identity. A comparison of the situation of overseas Chinese with those living on the frontier of China allows us to understand how similar processes of acculturation can have very different political interpretations. Within China, official policies alone can label acculturated Chinese as non-Chinese. In the situation overseas, owing to the politics and conventional thinking about race and culture, many Chinese who have acculturated to the indigenous population are still labeled Chinese and subject to suspicion, discrimination, or exclusion from sociopolitical participation. In part, this suspicion is not unreasonable given that identity for the overseas Chinese has been inseparable from a China-oriented nationalist sentiment for most of the twentieth century.

Since the formation of the early Republic of China, nationalism has preoccupied Chinese intellectual thought both in and out of China. The organizational efforts of the KMT and the Nationalist government, through the activities of the Overseas Chinese Commission, continue to exert their influence in many parts of the world where large numbers of ethnic Chinese reside. This nationalism has been defined in Western terms and is manifested in modern organizational activities such as the KMT party and its affiliated associations, such as the Boy Scouts and summer camps for Chinese cultural learning, national anthems, and other rituals and ceremonies for public demonstration of the ties between the Chinese overseas and their ancestral land of China.

The China-oriented identity of the overseas Chinese will continue as long as the Chinese government—whether Nationalist or Communist—as well as Chinese intellectuals and community elites overseas, continue to recognize its significance. Despite continual cultural change among the peripheral Chinese, the official interpretation of their Chineseness will sustain their meaning of being Chinese.

ACKNOWLEDGMENTS

The author gratefully acknowledges the useful comments at the October 1990 conference from Tu Wei-ming, Wang Gungwu, Cho-yun Hsu, Mark Elvin, Wang Ling-chi, and other participants at the October 1990 author's conference at the East-West Center in Hawaii.

I was absolutely serious when I said that for the last forty years, things written about China in English and Japanese may have exerted more shaping influence on our conception of China—not outside China, but inside China—than things written in Chinese. This is changing, I am sure, but it tells us something about the overall intellectual situation that we are in.

Tu Wei-ming
From the Conference on the
Meaning of Being Chinese
Honolulu, October 1990

I am searching for reconfigurations. I am not interested in whether the twenty-first century is to be a Pacific one, or a European one, but I am certain that the world is going to be very different. We are remapping the world, and here I see provincialism in Chinese studies as they are pursued in the world today that I find unacceptable, needlessly parochial. As a modernist, I feel this acutely.

Leo Ou-fan Lee
From the Conference on the
Meaning of Being Chinese
Honolulu, October 1990

8

The "Evil Wife" in Contemporary Chinese Fiction

Zhu Hong

> There are enough women in the world, Mr. Tulkinghorn thinks—
> too many; they are at the bottom of all that goes wrong in it.
> —Charles Dickens, *Bleak House*

What do the images of women in recent Chinese writing reveal of the culture and politics and status of women in the People's Republic?

From 1949 to the end of the Cultural Revolution, the image of woman in Chinese literature and the arts served largely as a vehicle to demonstrate the blessings of Liberation. Under socialism, it would seem, woman was no longer chattel. The former slave was delivered by the Party. During the last forty years, innumerable variations on the theme of the emancipated woman have been advanced by the ruling ideology. We were familiar, for example, with the stereotype of the vacillating young person, the "weaker vessel," guided by the strong male on the path of Revolution. The widely publicized novel *Song of Youth* (1958), which was almost required reading in the late 1950s, is a good example. The self-immolating woman on the altar of revolution is another familiar model often held up for emulation. Thus are female images—victims, objects, tools—manipulated to serve the ends of the Party-state.

The end of the Cultural Revolution signaled a new era for Chinese writing. In the 1980s, writers explored ways of dealing more truthfully with the realities of social, political, and emotional life. One positive result was to demystify the ideal revolutionary female and present her in ways that contrasted sharply with her submissive self-immolating predecessors.

Even so—and this is the burden of my paper—the old stereotypes persist, or, to put it another way, a new one no less misleading and no less denigrating to women has taken over. To be sure, the new female image is active rather than passive; the woman is no longer a tool but an agent. Yet her new presentation is by no means an indication that the status of women in Chinese literature has markedly improved.

A look at a popular performance would be revealing.

The lunar New Year's Eve television festival is always a big national event, prepared for months in advance. The heroic effort to meet all tastes and still satisfy the censors usually results in a medley of song, dance, acrobatics, snatches of Chinese opera, and the like. But the comic skit inevitably carries off the crown. One such memorable skit of the liberal 1980s was "A Gift-Offering to the Bureau Chief." As the scene opens, a toadlike fellow presents his humble offering to the well-dressed woman who opens the door, presumably the wife of the bureau chief. As he bows and scrapes, it is evident to the audience that they are about to see another of many satires on the prevalent practice of bribing officials for personal favor. This is a popular theme. The joke is always on the seeker of favors, so there is no slur on the system. The audience gets a good laugh from the bodily and linguistic contortions of the bringer of gifts. No one notices anything out of step in the behavior of the woman, played by a veteran actress. Then, the action takes an unexpected turn. The woman turns around, spurns the gift, and gives the man a verbal thrashing. One can imagine his discomfiture. More contortions, to the audience's delight. Of course this is the treat saved for the ending, one assumed. But then comes the climactic turn of the plot—the woman announces that she herself is the bureau chief. The man staggers and reels in disbelief. This is adding insult to injury. The audience, too, is riveted by this revelation. But now the mood shifts. The bringer of gifts is no longer the butt. The audience identifies with him in marveling at this rare bird, a female bureau chief, and one who refuses bribes to boot!

It would be interesting to find out how many people stopped to think, "Now why am I laughing?" "What am I laughing at?" "A Gift-Offering to the Bureau Chief," shown to an audience of tens—hundreds—of millions on a national holiday, is a good example of the "familiarization," or "naturalization," of the unnatural that goes on in everyday culture. Susan Suleiman said in a recent interview: "What feminists really have accomplished with their work is to make people aware that many things that we consider as natural are really not natural, that they are part of the whole cultural baggage, which needs to be looked at."[1]

As in "Gift-Offering," it is taken for granted that an official would have a wife and that his wife would accept bribes on her husband's behalf; it is "natural" and as familiar as the mole on one's own face. On the other hand, a woman who is a bureau chief in her own right, and moreover does not take bribes, is a singular anomaly. The New Year's Eve performance, instead of making people question their assumptions, was actually banking on their pervasiveness and propping up this "cultural baggage."

Suppose we put popular entertainment aside and enter the realm of more serious writing. Take, for instance, the literature that sprang up in the late 1970s and early 1980s after the end of the Cultural Revolution—prompted by a social conscience, concerned with social issues, loosely termed the literature of reform.

Millions of readers of the book and viewers of the film got a good cry out of Shen Rong's "At Middle Age" (1980), one of the outstanding novellas of the early 1980s. "At Middle Age" is the story of a woman doctor, Lu Wenting, who suffers a heart attack under the combined pressure of overwork, household responsibilities, and harassment by a representative of the Party. The story, told through Dr. Lu's flashbacks as she drifts in and out of consciousness, is a string of episodes that lead to her collapse. One might call it the modern Chinese intellectual's "stations of the cross." In the story, Dr. Lu is not a symbol of oppressed women; she stands for all of China's beleaguered professionals, men and women alike. The writer underscores this point by making the husband in the story uncharacteristically helpful and understanding. The straw that breaks the doctor's back is the fuss over the operation on a government vice-minister. This focus on social factors, rather than marital relationships, is all the more evident if we compare "At Middle Age" with a Soviet short story on the same theme. In "A Week Like Any Other," a Soviet woman scientist is also on the verge of collapse for more or less the same reasons, but the curse of a selfish husband is very much in the foreground. In contrast, "At Middle Age" carefully eliminates any hint of marital discord in order to highlight the social issue. To put the situation crudely, it is the professional on the one hand and the Party on the other, poised in tension. One would assume, of course, that the vice-minister seeking special treatment is emblematic of the Party.

What is of real significance in the story is that the person who pushes Dr. Lu over the edge is not the vice-minister himself but his wife, Qin Bo. She it is who insists on interrogating the doctor who is to perform the operation, much as Mr. Dombey inspects the "deserving object" when hiring a nurse for his son and heir Paul;[2] she it is who inquires after the doctor's "political background" as she weighs the latter's credentials for the job; she it is who proposes to outline a joint "plan of action," as if removing a cataract were a major military maneuver.

In the two examples, the television skit and the novella, a woman is presumed evil, or presented as downright evil. In the case of the comic skit, she appears to be the bribe-taking wife of an official before the audience is let in on the secret. In the novella, she is more subtly presented as the decisive factor in precipitating a catastrophe.

To be sure, "At Middle Age" is a heartrending plea and an angry protest on behalf of China's professionals. On the one hand, we see the appalling living and working conditions of the doctor's family. On the other, we see the privileges enjoyed by the vice-minister and his wife. To complete the picture, we also have the old peasant, who has to pay for medication out of his own pocket. The image of the old peasant not only serves as one of many bits of straw heaped on the doctor's back, but also as a backdrop against which the vice-minister's lifestyle is judged. But all these depictions pale beside the image of the vice-minister's wife, the straw that finally breaks the doctor's back.

The author has clearly given much thought to polishing the image of Qin Bo, the wife of vice-minister Qiao. Qin Bo is a compound of smugness, snobbery, downright selfishness, and manipulation—with a smattering of Party hack thrown in. It is clear from the outset that she manages her husband's affairs and is out for all she can get. She oversees everything and directs everything, usurping her husband's (the Party's) role. Qin Bo is individualized primarily by the way she uses language. In the original text, she begins all her harangues with "O Comrade mine." She undertakes to put everybody in their place: she reminds Dr. Lu that eye examinations must be conducted in a darkened room; she instructs the director of the hospital on the "appropriate" handling of the vice-minister's operation; later she blames him and herself for "bureaucracy" in the same breath, casually putting herself on a par with him, a noted surgeon and head of a major hospital; she takes it upon herself to speak for the Party as she encourages Dr. Lu to strive for membership; she even does some metaphorical hand-wringing over deteriorating morale and exhorts the Party to intensify ideological work among professionals—when she finds out that a highly qualified doctor she might have used has gone abroad. Every one of Qin Bo's four appearances leaves an impact. It is her fussing and meddling and bossing and scolding that sustains the story, and it is *her* image that drives home the point of the story—the victimization of professionals and intellectuals under the Party-state, the waste of talent.

"At Middle Age" has been attacked as "anti-Party," though it is hard to see why. As a protest on behalf of China's professional class, it points the accusing finger not at the Party, but at the *wife* of the Party. The Party, so far as it is embodied in the person of vice-minister Qiao, is untouched. This is effected by a tactic I would define as blocking the line of vision. Whenever the vice-minister, wielder of power and privilege, appears on the scene, we are distracted by the speechifying of his wife. The poor man can hardly get a word in. In contrast to his wife, the vice-minister himself is represented less through speech than through gesture. Thanks to this strategy of silence, he is mercifully spared the risk of self-exposure. In the couple's first joint appearance, the vice-minister angrily drums his cane on the floor as Qin Bo prattles on. The drumming of the cane, directed at Qin Bo's impertinent remarks, is the voice of the Party, and it is a righteous voice. Finally, in his last appearance, vice-minister Qiao seizes Lu Wenting's hand in gratitude when he realizes that she is the very doctor who had helped him ten years ago, under vastly different circumstances. This last handshake redeems the vice-minister in the eyes of the reader and seals a cordial relationship between the Party and the professionals. Significantly, this handshake occurs during the vice-minister's only solo appearance, while he is in the operating theater, where his wife cannot intrude.

Thus through various strategies of presentation, the symbol of power and the representative of the oppressed are reconciled and the reader is appeased. The wife alone is isolated.

Like a prism catching the rays of the sun, Qin Bo draws to herself all the darts of the reader's hostility. The quintessence of everything the person-in-the-street resents about the Party—the stark inequality, the privileges extending to family members and dependents, the discriminatory "class line," the spouting of political jargon—Qin Bo takes upon herself the persona of the Party. Socialist butterfly turned Marxist shrew, she is aptly dubbed the "Marxist old lady," a brilliant stroke on the author's part.

As the epithet captured the popular imagination and made its way into everyday language, it began to acquire the dimensions of a myth. Just as in the story the "lady" acts the part of the villain, so in the myth the archetypal "evil wife" is "at the bottom of all that goes wrong" in the world. The "evil wife" image functions as a kind of safety valve. All evil can be traced to its source through this image, from the "Marxist old lady" in everyday life to the "white-boned demon" on the higher plane of national politics. Popular anger and ridicule and contempt at the performance of the "Marxist" could be deflected from the real source of power—the Party—and directed toward the power holder's "old lady." It is in essence the "Marxist" making his "old lady" bear the burden of his guilt.

As an incarnation of the myth, Qin Bo is not a solitary figure. In fact she and her sisters took up permanent residence in the house of fiction of the liberal 1980s. Whenever an incurable problem related to Party misrule is raised, you may be sure this Socialist mermaid is behind it, flapping her ugly tail. She appears in a variety of shapes and colors, but all bearing the hallmark of the type.

In Yu Shan's "The Girls' Dorm" (1981), for instance, we catch a glimpse of the mayor's wife as she takes her daughter to school in the mayor's car. In just a few words, the writer conveys a striking image of a privileged woman, another Qin Bo, used to getting her way. What is remarkable here is the way her evil influence is taken for granted even though the story does not have the remotest bearing on her role as the mayor's wife. "A piece of advice for her ladyship your mother!" growls one student who has caught a glimpse of her, "Keep within bounds. Observe the proprieties. Try not to embarrass your father the mayor. And don't let yourself be influenced by her!" In the story, repudiating her mother becomes the key step by which the mayor's spoiled daughter reforms herself, and harmony in the girls' dorm is restored.

We might take another example, from Wang Meng's novella "Butterfly" (1980). Here the writer, among other things, sketches the outlines of another type of "evil wife," the siren—the young second wife of a high-placed cadre. Indolent, enervating, outwardly placid, Meilan is in fact shrewd and grasping. "Meilan is a slimy fish. Meilan is a snow white swan. Meilan is a shifting cloud. And—Meilan is a pair of pincers," the author comments in a successful merging of his own voice with the protagonist's. "He took up this soft and glittering new wife," the voice continues, "just as he took up his soft and glittering new sofa." On her part, "She took up the post of wife of the municipal party secretary as naturally as he took up his post of municipal party secretary. . . . Only occasionally did he vaguely feel that Meilan was ordering his life, leading him by the nose." With her husband's downfall during the Cultural Revolution, Meilan predictably "draws the line" and divorces him, taking all the family valuables. Later, when he is reinstated, she tries, just as predictably, to force her way back into his bed. The description becomes so pat one would suspect Wang Meng of parody were it not for the serious tone of his story.

Dai Qing's "No!" (1981) casts the image of the seductive young wife in another light. Compared with Meilan in "Butterfly," the description of Li Ying in "No!" is profuse with hints of sexuality—the soft embrace of the sofa, the sinking mattress, the clinging down quilt, the discreetly shaded lamp, the pots of health-giving potions, the plump white hands, the cloying scent of cologne. Like Meilan, Li Ying also shows her claws: it is she, not her husband, who insists that documents be sent to him, to preserve the myth that he is still active at his post, in order to retain all the privileges that go with it.

Meanwhile, the siren turns into a vampire in Jiang Zilong's story "The Visiting Hour." It is surprising how much the writer packs into a short story. Everything is seen through the eyes of a young nurse new to the hospital. As she threads her way through the three pages of the story, she finds her way around the hospital and learns about human relationships in Socialist society—all in less time than it takes her to wipe a pane of glass—the glass door of the VIP ward, with its television sets and sofas. "Just like fairyland," thinks the girl. The inhabitant of this fairyland is a "shrunken, diminutive, dried-up" mummy, a breathing corpse with all sorts of tubes and appliances stuck into parts of its anatomy. He is the Deputy Provincial Governor, who has been enjoying this special treatment for over a year and might continue to do so for another year. At the "visiting hour," his wife stands outside the door and takes one hard look through the glass pane to make sure he is still breathing—to make sure, that is, that she is entitled to stay on in the governor's mansion and draw the governor's salary. That is why wiping the glass pane until "it feels like looking straight through" is crucial to the success of the visit, which has a ritualistic quality. As for the husband, he seems to be strapped down solely for his wife's benefit. The point of the story, of course, is the transparency of the wife. As she looks through the glass door, she herself is seen through. As an added thrust to bring home the point, this wife is pointedly described as a solid, impenetrable mountain of flesh, a not very subtle allusion to her as a bloodsucking vampire.

In many other works of the mid-1980's, such as Zhang Xuan's "The Woman Up Bamiao Mountain," Shen Rong's "Everlasting Spring," Lu Xiner's "Tombstone," Han Ying's "The Funeral," Bai Hua's *Herland*, Chen Ruiqing's *The Call of the Great Northern Wilds* and Bai Fengxi's dramatic *Trilogy on Women*, the figure of the senior Party man is invariably shadowed by the figure of his wife, seeking gains, working schemes, kneading him under her clever fingers. The ultimate power she strives to hold over her husband is the power of life and death. "To die or not to die, if not up to the individual, is at most between the individual and almighty heaven, but Li Ying [his wife] has made it her business to meddle," the political commissioner in "No!" thinks angrily. The wife is nothing in herself: whatever power and privileges she has she enjoys through her husband. She makes him cling to life in her own struggle for survival.

Thus from the slave waiting to be delivered, the female character has evolved into an active agent, but an agent of evil. These images of women come from writers of both sexes, of different styles and affiliations, but all avowedly committed to reform. Yet when they approach the sensitive area of Party misrule, they invariably take refuge in the image of the "evil wife." With the best of intentions, they are overtaken by the myth and contribute to it by erecting more variations on the "evil wife" image.

One might argue that stories of Communist old guards being captured and manipulated by insidious young women are reflections of historical reality, as the noted writer Dai Qing claimed when the subject was first brought up at a conference to commemorate Women's Day at the Institute of Foreign Literature in March 1989. Indeed, on the eve of Liberation, the Party issued regulations by which all cadres who had served a certain number of years and reached a certain rank could automatically invalidate their marriages with their old country wives—who happened, incidentally, to have waited eight years or more through the horrors of the anti-Japanese war and the civil war that followed. And then right after Liberation, the Party passed the much-vaunted New Marriage Law, by strength of which those who could not take advantage of the Party regulation just mentioned could liberate themselves from their old wives by claiming that theirs was a "feudal" marriage. The implementation of the Marriage Law met with stiff resistance at local levels and had to slow down, owing to the "tens of thousands of murders and suicides that had resulted from the lack of support for women who wished to annul betrothals or free themselves from unhappy marriages."[3] But by then the Party elders had consolidated their own "liberation" and were enjoying its fruits with their brand-new young city wives. The "feudal" wife got a brief notice from the local authorities, or none at all. In the 1980s, stories like "No!," "The Ex-Wife," "The Funeral," "The Woman Up Bamiao Mountain," and others dragged this skeleton out of the Party closet. What better subject than the privileged VIP wife, especially the pampered young wife, when the writer holds up the mirror to a corrupt ruling hierarchy?

In the sensitive sphere of social exposé, it is interesting to observe the shifts in location when tracing the root of evil. It used to be the class enemy (or the wife of the class enemy, as in Zhou Erfu's *Morning in Shanghai*). It moved on to mistakes in ideology, under the umbrella of the impersonal tag "ultra-leftism." Finally it nestled in the "bosom" of the Party—the "wife of his bosom." As a historical process, the target is certainly getting closer. But it is still clouded in myth.

As in the case of "At Middle Age," putting the spotlight on the "evil wife" can be self-defeating as social exposé if the wife is shown not as the end product but the source of Party misrule. But then, in order to reverse this point of view, to transcend the limitations of the myth, the writer must start from a wider framework, one in which the "evil wife" is seen in a different perspective and her role is largely reduced, thereby undercutting the concept of the "evil wife" altogether. The image of the "evil wife" is a stereotype, surviving under artificial narrative conditions. The array of "evil wives" in recent fiction profusely illustrates the tension between the pull toward the innate logic of truthful description on the one hand and the demands of myth on the other. As writers bend to meet the demands of the myth, they lose their grip on reality and slide into narrative conventions that prop up the stereotype.

The "evil wife" stereotype follows a highly controlled pattern. To drive home the moral, she must be positioned only from a certain angle, highlighted only at a particular moment. She is usually presented when her husband is at the end of his career, when the moral authority of the Party is significantly on the wane and he himself as a Party elder is totally disillusioned. Against a setting of illness and decline (sickbeds, hospital wards, emergency situations) she intrudes, bringing discordant associations of creature comforts and worldliness with her. Her figure hovers in the background as the Communist old guard reviews his life and wonders whether it was worthwhile. In many of the stories, he looks at her fading beauty with distaste and recalls with nostalgia the wholesome life of the country. He feels that the betrayal of his faithful old country wife and acquisition of this "bit of fluff," so to speak, is inextricably linked to his own moral decline ("Butterfly," "No!," "The Woman Up Bamiao Mountain").

In the progress of such stories, the husband—the Party elder, the wielder of power—is invariably presented at a moment of repentance, while the wife is caught in the act of petty scheming. In "The Tombstone" the bureau chief "cannot forgive himself." In "Butterfly" he reviews the life he led with his first wife and thinks "I ask to be judged for my crime," "My agony is that there is no one to punish me." In "The Woman Up Bamiao Mountain" the revolutionary old guard finally faces up to the fact that he is "a coward." In "No!" the political commissioner sees his career as a series of betrayals—of his former bodyguard, his old wife, the folks in his home village, the homeless petitioners huddled in the streets. As he does his mea culpa act ("I am ashamed to face . . ."), the reader is drawn into a sentimental complicity. Now that his sexual urge has waned, he sees his young wife for what she is, and the reader sees her through *his* eyes. Silently, he blames her for his "loss of innocence": his revolutionary goal was deflected by her petty demands, his Party integrity was compromised by her seductiveness. The reader, meanwhile, is seduced by his surge of repentance and suspends judgment.

The penitent wielder of power may even be given a moment of "transcendence." In "The Woman Up Bamiao Mountain," as Liu Gang, the deputy commander of the military zone, lay dying, his spirit flies back to his youth, when he was pure. He was a hero, preserver of his people, a legendary figure, his name on every lip. And the woman he had betrayed long ago, she who had saved his life and given herself to him and had borne him a child, comes back to him in his dreams. "Because of this experience, Liu Gang now goes through a spiritual crisis, a purging of the soul, whence he sheds his old self and looking at himself, seems to see a stranger"—an epiphany. But crude reality intervenes as he is recalled from his trance by his wife. "It is she, she again, who has dragged him back from the world he yearns after," he thinks as he looked at her as on a stranger. "You have become another person!" she exclaims in alarm. He smiles aloofly: "Yes, I have changed, changed back to my old self, my true self!" His years of marriage to her were an aberration. Now that his spirit has rejected her, he is restored to his true self. The narration acquires overtones of the sublime as the veteran Communist is "transported." As to the forty years of bloody striving that got him where he was, they have receded into insignificance with his change of heart.

Similarly, Wang Meng's theme in "Butterfly" is also transcendence, or rather, metamorphosis. Through suffering, the vice-minister in the story has acquired two identities and alternates between them; Vice-Minister Zhang Siyuan and Old Man Zhang the peasant. Wang Meng uses the ancient philosopher Zhuangzi's famous dream of the butterfly as a metaphor to bring the moral home. Zhuangzi asks himself after his dream: Am I awake and the butterfly a dream? Or is the butterfly awake and I myself a dream? Have I changed into a butterfly in my dream? Or am I a butterfly dreaming that I am the man Zhuangzi? Wang Meng's vice-minister leaves his vice-minister self in Beijing and takes up his identity as Old Man Zhang the peasant as he travels incognito back to the countryside. There, he draws strength from the people. When he returns to his minister's desk, he rises phoenixlike from the ashes of his bureaucratic persona to become a true son of the people. Meanwhile, he has of course also shaken off his guilt. "Tomorrow will be a busy day." Apparently he has the author's blessing to keep the wheels of power rolling. But one must concede that in its ambiguity "Butterfly" breaks out of the convention of repentance and transcendence. Is Zhang Siyuan the vice-minister resurrected as the peasant Old Man Zhang? Or did he wriggle out of the cocoon of Zhang the old peasant to relapse into Zhang the bureaucrat? Is he transformed into a true "servant of the people," or is he only dreaming that he has turned a new page? Wang Meng's endorsement of his protagonist's metamorphosis leaves room for ambiguity.

To bolster the stereotype of the "evil wife," the husband is always given the last word and the last victory. Witness how on his deathbed the political commissioner in "No!" is irritated by the small talk of his wife and "the wife of his son." Note how the wording itself conveys his hostility to the idea of "wife": "These women can always find common language when it comes to clothes and hairstyle." He has finally shed himself of his wife's coils. "So to keep going thus was all for her sake, this woman who was so clever, and yet so stupid." He already thinks of her in the past tense. She thinks she is in control, but he sees through her as he lay dying. Thus in the power struggle, he is the ultimate winner. He still has the last say—by force of moral superiority, which he has managed to recapture at the last moment, thanks to the narrative conventions that help him on his moral journey.

Basic to all the strategies and conventions that sustain the image of the "evil wife" is what one might define as the strategy of "alienation" and "rejection." She is the alien element, to be rejected before he can be redeemed. Her hold on him is pried loose. Just as he had been "liberated" from his old wife to enjoy the new in the first flush of power (sexual and political), now in his decline (again sexual and political), he is "liberated" from his degrading association with her and restored to purity. The concepts of "alienation" and "rejection" are embedded in the very epithets used to denote the "evil wife." The "Marxist old lady" implies a travesty of Marxism. It reinforces the idea of a true Marxism while holding the travesty up for contempt.

"No!" is a good example of this rejection, brought out in the title itself. To whom is the political commissioner saying "No!" at the end of his life and career? Not to the misrule of the Party. He reviews in his mind all the disastrous policies of the last forty years and acknowledges that he had followed docilely along: "Who am I to say nay when everybody else follows?" "What he was unwilling to commit, he had lacked courage to refuse." He has never said "No!" to the Party. It is to his wife that he says "No!" in a ritual of rejection, making her the emblem of his guilt. He rejects her as a possessed man rejects the devil, and having rejected her, he is cleansed and redeemed.

The "evil wife" is after all but a foil for the final redemption of her husband. When this is effected, she is cast out. She is punished for the worst of feminine offenses, appropriating a man's power. We always see him at the end of his career, on the verge of a change of heart, never in action. There is a strange reversal of roles. It is she who is seen in action, as in "At Middle Age." She even enacts his betrayals ("The Girls' Dorm," "Butterfly," *Herland*), while in most cases, *his* betrayals of the interests of the people on an incomparably larger scale are forgiven and forgotten as the reader is swept along by the high-tragic tone of the narrative. In keeping with the requirements of the stereotype, the wife is cut out to be what her powerful husband was supposed to be; she does his job as he is supposed to do it, and ultimately she is punished for it.

Of course there is the untold story, the suppressed voice. What, for instance, was she like when he first married her? "No!" mentions that the young woman burst on the rising political commissioner like a "budding bean sprout" when he was first tempted. Thus even in retrospect she is seen only *as he remembers her*. But people are products of history and environment; even "bitches" are not just born but are mostly made by a system that breeds parasites among the powerful and the privileged. Owing to a failure of the imagination, however, the wife's story is encoded in a narrative that usually merges the voice of the narrator with that of the husband. Her image is securely imprisoned in the stereotype and neatly pared to evade larger issues.

Rather than a reflection of reality that she is claimed to be, the "evil wife" is a highly artificial contrivance, and at best offers only a glimmer of the problems that the writer means to grapple with. In these various images of mermaids, shrews, and vampires, the pattern embedded in "At Middle Age" is repeated again and again, wherein the stereotype contributes to the myth and the myth confirms the stereotype in a vicious circle. Thus is anger at the privileged deflected from the male patriarch to the subordinate female figure, from Mr. Murdstone to Miss Murdstone.

But if the "evil wife" stereotype is hardly a truthful mirror of social reality, it is a faithful reflection of a mentality that tends to see a woman behind every disaster. We are familiar with the "evil concubine" of history and legend who ruins empires and cuts short dynasties, notably the Royal Concubine Yang Guifei—the Chinese Helen who allegedly set the Tang dynasty rocking on its foundations by sheer sexual power. So deep-seated is the notion of the sinister powers of female sexuality that in Chinese writings "the female factor" has been formally listed among the strategies of power politics of ancient times,[4] conspicuously absent in Machiavelli. And in a twentieth-century version of the myth, we have Mao's wife, the "white-boned demon" Jiang Qing, largely a symbol of the destructiveness of the Cultural Revolution and a convenient scapegoat for the excesses of Mao's last years. Such women are traditionally regarded as the "*huoshui*" (disaster factor) or "vipers disguised as beautiful maidens" in modern vernacular usage. It is a fixation of the national consciousness, this perception of the root of evil encapsulated in the image of a woman. If the fiction of the 1980s, with its wide-ranging themes of social exposé, could be compared to opening up the magic bottle and letting out the genie, then the eventual ascendance of the "evil wife" myth could be compared to the genie recaptured and returned to the bottle.

Of course one could say that this is not a specifically Chinese phenomenon. After all, the West has its myriad sirens, mermaids, witches, shrews, and femmes fatales, its Helen of the thousand ships and its Eve of the fatal bite. And then we were further exposed to its modern "dominating bitches" when first looking into Norman Mailer. But the difference is there. Granted the similar perception of the destructive power of female sexuality, in the Western tradition it is more individualized, less tied to political power, less compulsively linked to the deterioration of the state and loss of empires. After all, the sirenlike Beatrix Esmond lured the young Stuart Pretender *away* from the throne, not toward it; evidently nothing was further from her thoughts than to manipulate the future king and influence affairs of state. Actually it was her seductiveness that effectively destroyed the hopes of the Jacobites, at least according to William Makepeace Thackeray. Of course there are images of strong and evil women swaying affairs of state—Lady Macbeth, notably. But instead of being cut down to the size of scheming concubines, they are glorious villainesses and reach queenly stature: after Ellen Terry, it is hard to imagine Lady Macbeth without the crown hovering over her brow. There *is* a man in English fiction who said that women "are at the bottom of all that goes wrong,"[5] but the price he paid for that remark was death.

Only in the Chinese imagination—with its perception of women as on a par with "base persons" (Confucius) and with its extreme fear of female power—is the image of the "evil concubine" such a fixation of the popular mentality that we have no second thoughts about laying the roots of our national disasters at her feet. The irony, of course, is that the perpetuation of this myth is in itself an exaggeration of female power. Be that as it may, the image of the "evil wife," assimilated in popular imagination and embodied in catchwords, is still an effective weapon of thought control.

Under the best possible circumstances, that is, leaving aside the constraints of official censorship, the Chinese writer is hampered by the constraints of a ruling ideology, from which he (or she) must consciously disengage. The danger is that the writer might unconsciously be caught up in myths the ruling ideology has quietly adapted for its own purposes, the "evil wife" being one among many.

"One thinks one's own thoughts but speaks the thought of others," one of the interviewees in *Legacies: A Chinese Mosaic* said regretfully.[6] The greater problem, however, is that one might think the thoughts of others even as one thinks that one is thinking one's own thoughts. To return to *Legacies*, a man persecuted by Madam Mao says "At first, I wanted to commit suicide, and imagined how I would do it. There would be thousands watching. I would sing: 'Cuff in irons, I bid farewell/Living is not dear to me.' But my faith in the Party cannot be quelled. . . . Later I changed my mind and decided to live for the day the Party would vindicate me. And it did. Madam Mao is the one in jail now." The double irony lies in the fact first that the victim can find no other language except quotations from his hated enemy's concoctions in her infamous "model operas," and second that he feels vindicated after Jiang Qing is locked up, as if that were the ultimate guarantee: "Madam Mao's in jail and all's right with the world."

This is an example of what is so unsettling in the image of the "evil wife," the underlying assumptions behind it, the air of finality that it carries. In the new fiction of the reform period, should the image of the "evil wife" provide a closure, or an unlocking of the imagination? Is there a danger that her image, be she the "Marxist old lady" or the "white-boned demon," will be familiarized and adapted as part of our "modern" cultural baggage and offered as the all-purpose answer to our questions? In the light of recent events, such naïveté seems unlikely, yet the persistence of the image of the "evil wife" in the works of some of our most influential writers is undisputable evidence of sexist attitudes prevailing in the culture. It points to other similar assumptions in the cultural baggage that defines being female and Chinese in a state-controlled society with an ancient tradition behind it and Western influences flooding in.

The Socialist Party-state claims to have eliminated inequality between the sexes by nature of its basic principles, going back to Marx and Engels and August Bebel, the emancipation of women being a measure of the degree of general emancipation. One of the best-known songs of the immediate post-Liberation days was the "Funü Fanshen Ge" (Song of the Liberated Woman), a female rhapsody of gratitude to the Party. Blessed by Liberation, men and women share the sky, in accord with the official slogan "Women Hold Up Half the Sky."

But in hindsight it seems that the problem of inequality for women has not been eliminated. The reform policy of Deng Xiaoping's New Era three decades later opened up the space for a new discourse on the Woman Question. The issues raised have to do mostly with practical problems facing women, now thrown onto the market with shrinking social supports. That the reform policies should hit women harder than men is proof that equality between the sexes has not been realized. More pernicious, and more to the point of my argument here, is the fact that this continued state of inequality continues to be taken for granted, to be a familiar, seemingly natural, aspect of Socialist culture under the Party-state.

With the growing articulation of calls for women's empowerment and the new discourse on women's problems in this New Era, China has witnessed an epidemic of "bronchitis" among its male population. This refers to the pun on the term "bronchitis" in Chinese (*qi guan yan*), homonymous with a newly concocted popular term *qi guan yan* (wife in control). This squeak of protest as men feel threatened by women's voices is as good as a public declaration of male chauvinism.

The most damning evidence of the society's pervasive sexism are spontaneous manifestations of it among proponents of the new modernity. In their anxiety to be Westernized and modern, they rush in to market Freud and many other modern and not so modern theories, with no second thoughts about their latent sexism. In the translation of Western writings, D. H. Lawrence was at one time the archetype of the modern writer, furiously competed for by many publishers. The 1988 exhibition of nude paintings, touted as a challenge to orthodoxy, was basically an all-female show, visited predominantly by men for reasons one must assume were not primarily aesthetic. In creative writing, one still remembers the flurry of excitement over Zhang Xianliang's *Half of Man Is Woman*, acclaimed as a dual breakthrough for descriptions of both sexuality and life in a labor camp. This novel closely resembles the Song Jiang episode in the classical novel *Outlaws of the Marsh*. In that episode, Song Jiang's paramour Yan Poxi blackmailed him over his correspondence with outlaws, driving him to kill her and throw in his lot with the outlaws. In Zhang Xianliang's version of the story, the woman threatens to turn in her husband for writing seditious thoughts in his diary. At the end, having overcome his sexual and political impotence, Zhang Xianliang's hero renounces his wife and escapes from the camp to become a political fugitive in pursuit of social justice, presumably a male pursuit that women can only hinder. The two stories, written hundreds of years apart, share a view of women as sex objects and threats to men's higher aspirations.

In the liberal New Era, as far as social and economic problems are concerned, women have become a social group with special needs to be dealt with and thus a burden on the state. This "enlightened" view of women has led to such measures as the notorious experiment of Da Qiu Zhuang village, in which women were ordered to quit their jobs, stay home, and be happy.[7] In the cultural realm, by contrast, woman can still be perceived as a sex object despite the trappings of avant-gardism. The examples are omnipresent, part of the air we breathe. We have a wide field for decoding, or deconstructing, the sexism weighing down our cultural baggage. The "evil wife" fixation is, alas, just one of many.

But criticism is not an exact science. The "evil wife" image may be seen as an essentially conservative literary device in a particular historic and political context. But in another context, for a study of the evolution of the literary image of women in state-controlled writing, it may be seen as a step forward in breaking down the contrived idealization of women. In a still wider context, superseding the confines of a particular history or society, the pervasive image of the evil wife could provide fertile ground for a study of female power, the power of the weak, the power of insidious influence, in contrast to male rule by force.

9

Roots and the Changing Identity of the Chinese in the United States

L. Ling-chi Wang

In the United States as well as in China, a single perspective has guided the study of the Chinese in America. The notion of assimilation has dominated American discourse on "the Chinese Question," while the question of their loyalty has preoccupied the study of the Chinese overseas in China.

The political and scholarly concern over the ability of the Chinese to assimilate surfaced in many forms in different periods in American history. During the second half of the nineteenth century and the early decades of the twentieth, the overwhelming public sentiment was to exclude and expel the Chinese from American soil on the grounds of their "nonassimilability." Politicians, labor leaders, and Christian ministers all thought that Chinese racial, cultural, and personality traits, seen from the prevailing religious and biological perspectives on race, were incompatible with the "American character."[1] Exclusion of the Chinese became the dominant public policy for about one hundred years. In the post–World War II period, however, the preoccupation of social scientists and journalists alike has been the "success" of Chinese Americans in achieving "total assimilation," measured by such indicators as educational achievement, occupational status, and income. Chinese American success has been considered so phenomenal that since the 1960s, politicians and the press have been calling Chinese Americans the "model minority."[2]

In China, by contrast, the primary concern has been the loyalty of the *huaqiao* or the Chinese in diaspora. During the nineteenth century, loyalty was understood generally as an unbreakable bond between the Chinese abroad and their cultural roots in China. But culture was infused with political content in the twentieth century as China confronted the growing encroachment of Western powers and Japan. From the point of view of the Nationalist Chinese government (the Guomindang) and China's leading intellectuals, the *huaqiao* were first and foremost an economic asset as sources of remittances and promoters of international trade.[3] They were also considered a leading force for China's modernization and a significant political element in the legitimization of the regime in power. Cultivating and ensuring the loyalty of overseas Chinese to the homeland—both cultural and political— has thus been a primary task of successive governments since the late nineteenth century.

Both the American and Chinese views on overseas Chinese briefly sketched above are important because each has greatly influenced public policy—both within the two countries and in their interactions with each other. These, in turn, have had enormous impact on the collective experience of the Chinese in the United States and the formation of their identity. However, both views ignore history and erroneously assume the homogeneity of the Chinese Americans. As we shall see, Chinese identity in the United States has been shaped by the dominant ideas of assimilation and loyalty, but other ideas—which evolved out of actual encounters between Chinese and Euro-Americans—have molded and transformed that identity; and that identity has, in turn, influenced public policy.

CHINESE "ROOTS" AND IDENTITY

The word *gen* (roots) carries several meanings. Aside from its basic biological meaning, it symbolizes the genesis and maintenance of life. At another level, it is used to designate one's birthplace, ancestral village, or native place, and the source from which one derives one's personal identity. Identity here is inextricably tied to and equated with one's ancestral village. The bond to one's roots is unique, sacred, and eternal. At still another level, especially among overseas Chinese, *gen* takes on additional meanings as Chinese culture and a geographic entity called China, one's *zuguo* (motherland). It is this bond between overseas Chinese and China that undergirds the unique racial and cultural identity of the overseas Chinese. With the rise of Chinese nationalism, especially since the beginning of the twentieth century, roots came to denote also a political entity, the Chinese nation-state, headed by a government, from which overseas Chinese derived their legal status as Chinese citizens and to which they owed allegiance.[4] In short, the notion of roots has changed and expanded over time. Its historical transformation is intimately tied to the experiences of the Chinese in diaspora and China's emergence as a nation among other nations.

In the postwar world, both at home and abroad, there are two competing paradigms for interpreting the history and life of the overseas Chinese in general and the Chinese in the United States in particular. Since the establishment of the People's Republic of China in 1949, these two paradigms—represented by two widely used Chinese phrases, *luoye guigen* and *luodi shenggen*—have dominated political, legal, and intellectual debates. Roughly, the former characterizes the Chinese abroad as fallen leaves that must eventually, even inevitably, return to their roots in Chinese soil, while the latter depicts them as seeds sown in foreign soil, taking root wherever they have emigrated. One definition describes the overseas Chinese as sojourners imbued with an irresistible urge to return to China one day and to live out their retirement there; the other describes them as permanent settlers in a foreign country, becoming an integral part of that country.

The word *gen*, central in both phrases, thus simultaneously carries opposite meanings: one refers to a geographic location or cultural entity called China, while the other signifies the planting of one's roots in foreign soil. The two paradigms thus epitomize two different mindsets, two different views of China, two different survival strategies, two different chosen destinies for the Chinese residing overseas, and indeed, two different interpretations of overseas Chinese history and identity. The idea of permanent settlement on foreign soil, however, is not the same as the notion of assimilation propounded by social scientists in the United States. Prior to the 1960s, Chinese in the United States rarely perceived themselves to be a racial minority. Planting one's roots in the United States, except for American-born Chinese and such assimilation-oriented social scientists as Rose Hum Lee, Robert E. Park, and William C. Smith, hardly meant abandoning one's racial and cultural identity in favor of total assimilation into the dominant society.[5]

Behind these two competing paradigms are conflicting and changing views of China—as a geographic entity, a nation, a government,
a people or race, a culture—and the way Chinese in diaspora view,
relate to, and identify with these conflicting views of China. Like en-
tangled roots and twisted branches, *pangen-cuojie*, to use a Chinese
expression with the word *gen*, the status and self-perception of Chinese abroad, regardless of their survival strategy and chosen destiny, is
further complicated by China's highly institutionalized policies toward
the overseas Chinese and also by immigration policies and racial politics in the host countries.[6] Moreover, the fate of *huaqiao* of all classes—
from the Cantonese and Fukienese peasants shipped to the Americas
and Southeast Asia as cheap labor in the second half of the nineteenth
century to the *zhishifenzi* (the intelligentsia) and *liuxuesheng* (Chinese
foreign students) in the elite institutions of higher education in Japan,
Western Europe, and the United States in the post-Tiananmen era—has
frequently been a source of diplomatic dispute, international intrigue,
and governmental deal-making.[7] In short, the identity, status, and destiny of an estimated 36 million people of Chinese ancestry abroad are
neither homogenous nor static. Their status and destiny abroad depend
as much on the ever-changing domestic racial sentiment and public
policy of their host country as on the diplomatic relations between
China and that country. We should also not assume that only the intellectual class and political leaders can legitimately participate in the
discourse on Chinese identity and culture.

While these paradigms are useful for understanding the development and identity of overseas Chinese communities in various countries, they are oversimplified and ahistorical. The actual experiences of
the overseas Chinese since the emergence of China as a modern nation
have also shaped their self-perceptions and their attitudes toward their
homeland. Political and intellectual debates over the future of China
as a nation and over the nature and viability of Chinese culture itself
have also been important in the quest for self-understanding and identity. However, unlike those of the pre–World War II period, when the
debates were confined largely to the intelligentsia and gentry serving
the interests of the state, the post-1949 debates have been taken up
increasingly by Chinese around the world.[8]

In this essay, I suggest that five types of identity have appeared
among the Chinese in diaspora: (1) the sojourner mentality; (2) assimi-

lation; (3) accommodation; (4) ethnic pride; and (5) alienation. Each is represented by a Chinese phrase with the word *gen* in it, and each is defined by its perception of, and relation to, its Chinese roots or *gen*. Here, I shall confine my discussion to the Chinese in the United States. While parts of this analysis are also applicable to the experience of Chinese in Southeast Asia, Latin America, Africa, and Europe, the particularities of Chinese American history, and the global power of the United States vis-à-vis China in the post–World War II era, make the Chinese American experience unique.

To set the stage, I shall begin with a sketch of Chinese immigration to the United States. This will be followed by an analysis of the five types of Chinese identity in both their historical and contemporary manifestations. I shall conclude the essay with a discussion of the future direction of overseas Chinese identity, especially in relation to China as a nation and to traditional Chinese culture in our shrinking world.

PATTERNS OF CHINESE MIGRATION TO THE UNITED STATES

According to the 1990 census, there are 1.8 million Chinese in the United States, a mere 0.5 percent of the total U.S. population.[9] This number is negligible when compared with the size of other racial groups in the United States, but in terms of its growth rate and sociological importance, this small population—which has increased dramatically from the 237,292 counted in 1960—has had a good deal of influence on American science and diplomacy in recent decades. Far from being homogeneous in terms of geographic, linguistic, and class background, this population now comprises both American-born and foreign-born, southern and northern Chinese, and most notably, Chinese from around the world—the most prominent among them being Chinese from Taiwan and Indochina. Virtually all the major dialects and regional cuisines of China can now be found in the United States, and many Chinese are conversant in several other languages as well. The diversity is further reflected by their class background; there are peasants, workers, small businessmen, world-class capitalists, artists, writers, students, scholars, and professionals. The Chinese-language press and a network of national organizations link this diverse population, which is dispersed throughout the United States. Newspapers, periodicals, books, and audio-visual materials from China, Taiwan,

TABLE 1

Chinese in the United States, 1850–1990

Year	Number	Year	Number
1850	789	1930	74,954
1860	34,933	1940	77,504
1870	64,199	1950	117,629
1880	105,465	1960	237,292
1890	107,488	1970	431,583
1900	89,963	1980	812,200
1910	71,531	1990	1,800,000
1920	61,639		

and Hong Kong are brought daily to the Chinese in the United States and vice versa. Because of the disproportionate influence of the United States in global politics and economy, the affairs and accomplishments of Chinese Americans are habitually and closely watched by the governments in China, Taiwan, and Hong Kong, and are widely reported in mass media as well.

The growth, decline, and resurgence of the Chinese population in the United States can be seen in the census figures reported in Table 1. Behind this fluctuation lies a history of periodic opportunities for and restrictions against the Chinese, China's turbulent history and its changing policies toward overseas Chinese, and unequal diplomatic relations between China and the United States.

Chinese immigration can be divided roughly into three periods. The first, 1852 to 1882, began shortly after gold was discovered in California and ended abruptly thirty years later with the passage of the 1882 Chinese Exclusion Act.[10] During this period, the immigrants were almost exclusively young male peasants dispossessed from their land in rural counties around Guangzhou in the Zhujiang delta in Guangdong province. An estimated 200,000 came as laborers to seek new opportunities, to meet the demand for cheap labor in the American West during a period of rapid ascendancy of industrial capital along the Eastern seaboard and Westward expansion. In the American West, Chinese laborers were employed to extract metals and minerals, to construct a vast railroad network, to reclaim swamplands, to build irrigation systems, to work as migrant agricultural laborers, to develop the fishing industry, to build a university (Stanford), and to operate highly competitive, labor-intensive manufacturing industries.[11]

The manner and terms of their employment, along with strong anti-Chinese sentiment, precluded most of them from becoming permanent settlers. Detached from their roots—meaning, at this juncture, their families and villages—the laborers had only limited objectives: to advance their economic well-being on behalf of their families during their sojourn and to return to their ancestral villages to enjoy the fruit of their labor in retirement. From their employers' point of view, detached Chinese laborers, without resident families or domestic responsibilities, meant substantially lower labor costs and higher productivity.[12] It seemed to be a mutually beneficial arrangement for the development of the American West.

During this initial period of Chinese migration, two major problems inhibited the smooth functioning of this arrangement. First, the Qing government, preoccupied with domestic revolts and imperialist incursions, prohibited Chinese emigration.[13] It possessed neither the political strength nor diplomatic will to protect the overseas Chinese, whom it branded as outlaws. Second, the Chinese presence in the western United States, though eagerly sought by expansionists in Washington, D.C., and employers and developers in the West, was vigorously opposed by the white working class and by local and state politicians.[14] Frequent outbreaks of anti-Chinese violence and the passage of anti-Chinese state laws and local ordinances threatened the steady supply of cheap Chinese labor.

These two problems were temporarily resolved with the signing of the Burlingame Treaty in 1868, which committed the Chinese government to legalizing the free flow of Chinese to the United States and required the American government to extend federal protection to Chinese laborers persecuted by local ordinances and state laws. However, the treaty failed to protect the Chinese from mob violence and economic and social repression; it also included no provision for Chinese in the United States to become naturalized citizens. Under intense political pressure, the United States eventually forced China to renegotiate the Burlingame Treaty, paving the way for Congress in 1882, over China's protest, effectively to ban further Chinese labor immigration and explicitly to deny the right of naturalization to Chinese.[15]

Anti-Chinese prejudice and political agitation continued into the second period, that of exclusion, from 1882 to 1965. This long span can be divided into two subperiods: one of near-total exclusion between 1882 and 1943, and one of partial exclusion from 1943 to 1965. From 1882 to the 1920s, in the face of unrelenting anti-Chinese sentiment, many immigrants were forced to return to China or chose to do so, thus contributing to a steady decline in the Chinese population over these four decades and to a rising Chinese nationalist sentiment. China's boycott of U.S. imports in 1905 was a concrete expression of this emergent sense of nationalism. Those who stayed in the United States were confined, through both legal and social segregation, to congested, dilapidated ghettos in large cities and were relegated to menial jobs and small businesses that were noncompetitive with or rejected by white Americans. During this period, Congress as well as local governments continued to enact harsh discriminatory laws, including anti-miscegenation laws, that systematically evicted Chinese from jobs, businesses, and land. These laws thus subjugated the Chinese economically, segregated them socially, and disenfranchised them politically. Even though these laws were challenged by the Chinese in the courts, the only recourse available to them, the constitutionality of many of these laws was upheld by judicial interpretations that permanently suspended Chinese rights, privileges, and sanctuaries in white society. Within the ghetto, a predominantly male, transplanted Chinese society, dominated by clan, village, and district associations, was gradually transformed in its self-perception, political consciousness, and social organization. Daily encounters with American racism and a growing concern over the fate of China in the face of Western and Japanese imperialism haunted their lives, transforming them into sojourners and later nationalists.

The declining population trend was slowly reversed and its demographic characteristics were gradually transformed beginning in the 1920s. Two factors contributed to this reversal. The first was the arrival of members of the "exempt classes" under the exclusion laws, which included merchants, students, tourists, and diplomats, as well as their spouses and children. Members of the exempt classes were allowed to enter the United States as visitors and to bring their families with them, but they were still regarded as aliens ineligible for citizenship. In terms of class background and emigration objectives, the new arrivals differed significantly from the peasants of the first period. Torn between loyalty to China and the stark reality of China's backwardness and vulnerability, they became China's vanguard for modernization. Second, the birth of an American-born generation gradually reversed the declining population trend after 1920. Brought up in the ghettos, despised and oppressed by the dominant society but exposed to American values through the public schools, the American-born Chinese were forced to choose between being Chinese and being American. Most opted for assimilation, or Americanization, rejecting their cultural heritage in the hope of gaining acceptance by white society.

It was against this setting that modern nationalism among overseas Chinese gradually emerged, notably among the students and merchants in the United States. They attributed the mistreatment of the Chinese in the United States to China's backwardness and powerlessness. In order to gain respect and equal treatment, they believed China had to be modernized and Westernized. It is not surprising that the leaders of the reform and revolutionary movements—led respectively by Kang Youwei and Sun Yat-sen—found enthusiastic support in American Chinatowns at the turn of the century.[16] After Japan invaded China in 1931 Chinese nationalism intensified, as did dissatisfaction with the corruption and impotence of Chiang Kai-shek's regime.[17] Nationalist sentiments were expressed in concrete terms by the contribution of professional skills toward China's modernization.[18]

But the advent of overseas Chinese nationalism also led to repressive policies, first of the Qing and later of the Chiang Kai-shek regime, designed to ensure the loyalty of overseas Chinese to the regime in China and their compliance with its policies. Overseas nationalism, while politically and diplomatically useful at times, was more frequently greeted by the Chinese government with suspicion because anti-government tendencies and rhetoric were inherent in the movement. As a result, the government in China formulated policies and established institutional channels to keep overseas communities under constant surveillance and to suppress—by a variety of means, including violence—all social and political movements not directly sponsored or controlled by the government. For example, the 1905 boycott to protest the mistreatment of the Chinese in the United States was halted by government coercion.[19] Similarly, political exiles working among the overseas Chinese—such as Kang Youwei, Liang Qichao, and Sun Yat-sen—were constant targets of government repression, including kidnapping attempts and threats of assassination.[20] The combination of racial oppression in America and the extraterritorial and repressive rule of the homeland government effectively placed the Chinese community in the United States under a structure of dual domination.

American attitudes and policies toward the Chinese in the United States during the second part of the exclusion period did not change until China became an indispensable ally of the United States in the fight against Japan during World War II. Only then, in 1943, did Congress repeal the Chinese exclusion laws, allowing a token 105 Chinese per year to enter the United States as immigrants and permitting very small numbers of Chinese residents who met stringent eligibility requirements to become naturalized citizens.[21] Unfortunately, these positive but limited wartime gestures yielded few measurable gains for Chinese in the United States: they had virtually no impact on removing the discriminatory laws and practices that still existed at the state and local level.

Thus, from 1943 to 1965 the exclusion of Chinese remained basically in effect. Several remarkable demographic and political changes did occur, however. First, in addition to the other Chinese granted the right of naturalization, some 15,000 Chinese who had served in the U.S. armed forces during World War II also became eligible for citizenship. Second, under a 1947 amendment to the 1945 War Brides Act, some 10,000 wives of Chinese American G.I.s came to the United States, contributing to a significant increase in the number of women and children in the Chinese American population. Third, the Cold War and the consequent hostile relations between the People's Republic of China and the United States abruptly terminated all ties and communications between Chinese Americans and their families in China from 1949 to 1972, and, in effect, forced Chinese in the United States to permanently plant their roots in American soil. Fourth, under the various Refugee Acts, several thousand Chinese with strong educational, professional, and commercial backgrounds were admitted into the United States. Among these were five thousand of the best and the brightest graduate students sent over by Chiang Kai-shek's government to be trained for China's postwar reconstruction and modernization. Finally, liberal American policies toward foreign students attracted a large number of highly qualified Chinese students (*liuxuesheng*) from Hong Kong, Taiwan, and Southeast Asia. Many found legal loopholes that enabled them to stay after completion of their graduate studies, while others became undocumented aliens employed in research, business, industry, and higher education. Thus, in spite of continuing immigration restrictions, the Chinese population increased steadily. In the process, its relatively homogeneous composition was gradually transformed as Chinese immigrants of both sexes and of diverse geographic origins and class backgrounds joined those already in the United States. Together, they planted myriad roots in American soil.

The historic, sweeping changes in American immigration law that occurred in 1965 ushered in the third and final period, a period of diversity with a notable influx of intellectuals. Rooted in two principles— the promotion of family reunification and the recruitment of skilled and professional personnel—the immigration law of 1965 replaced the discriminatory, race-based quota system with a new system of preferences that allowed thousands of Chinese Americans to be reunited with relatives long separated by the exclusion laws.[22] Furthermore, the admission of thousands of Chinese students (*liuxuesheng*), many of them top students from Taiwan, Hong Kong, and various Southeast Asian countries, brought the most important immigration of intellectuals to the United States since the influx of Jewish intellectuals in the 1930s. According to the 1987–88 report of the International Institute of Education, in 1987 Taiwan and the People's Republic of China ranked first and second in the number of students they sent to study in American colleges and universities, with 26,000 from Taiwan and 25,000 from China. Hong Kong ranked seventh with 10,600, and Malaysia was fourth with 19,000, about one-third of whom were ethnic Chinese. Among the students from China and Taiwan, three-quarters were graduate students, more than 50 percent of whom were in the sciences and engineering. In other words, there were approximately 68,000 Chinese students enrolled in American colleges and universities in 1987 from these four countries alone, about one-fifth of all foreign college students in the United States. (In 1955, only 10,000 foreign students from all Asian countries combined were studying in the United States.) Since 1950, Taiwan alone has sent more than 100,000 of its most able students to the United States.

It is extremely difficult to determine the exact number and types of Chinese immigrants to the United States since 1965 because they have come not just from China, Taiwan, and Hong Kong, but also from countries in Southeast Asia and Latin America. We do know that some 460,000 Chinese quota immigrants and 150,000 non-quota immigrants from China and Taiwan (including spouses, parents, and children of U.S. citizens) have come to the United States since 1965.[23] This sharp increase of Chinese immigrants has been aided in part by a 1979 amendment to the 1965 immigration law, creating separate annual quotas of 20,000 each for Taiwan and the People's Republic of China, following the normalization of U.S.-China relations. Congress also raised the annual quota for immigrants from Hong Kong from 600 to 5,000 in 1988. In preparation for the return of this British colony to China in 1997, Congress is considering raising this quota again, to 20,000 per year. To these numbers must be added several hundred thousand ethnic Chinese among the one million refugees from Vietnam, Laos, and Cambodia who have been admitted to the United States since 1975. In addition, anti-Chinese discrimination and political unrest in Southeast Asian and Latin American countries in the last three decades have led many affluent, longtime Chinese residents there to seek a more secure investment environment and better educational opportunities for their children in the United States. The decision by President George Bush to offer protection from mandatory return to China of some 30,000 Chinese students pursuing graduate degrees in the United States after the Tiananmen massacre of June 4, 1989, will also have a profound impact on the future composition of the Chinese American population. Thus international relations, geopolitics, and race relations in host countries have shaped the patterns of Chinese immigration during the third period and will continue to do so.

When President Richard Nixon decided to reverse the policy of containment of China in 1972 with his historic visit to Beijing, he sent shock waves through the countries of East and Southeast Asia whose security and stability had been guaranteed by the United States. His diplomatic initiative instantly caused a geopolitical realignment throughout the region vis-à-vis China and established a framework for the eventual withdrawal of the United States from the costly Indochinese conflict. In addition, the dictatorial regimes of South Korea, Taiwan, the Philippines, and South Vietnam found they could no longer count on the military support of their sponsor, which had enabled them to resist possible external aggression and internal unrest. The human rights and national liberation movements within these countries—long ruthlessly suppressed by the likes of Park Chun Hee, Chiang Ching-kuo, Ferdinand Marcos, and others—found new alliances and constituencies and began to agitate for democratic reform and the ouster of these corrupt dictators. The ensuing changes occurred less dramatically but in a manner not unlike the collapse of the Soviet Union's client regimes in Eastern Europe in 1989.

The response to this internal strife in the 1970s and 1980s was more repression, political and economic instability, and still more intense struggles between the reformers or dissidents and those determined not to yield power. As a result, many of the well-educated, professional, and entrepreneurial Chinese in Taiwan and throughout Southeast Asia began to look for secure investment opportunities in the United States and also began to move their families out of the political turmoil.[24] Political instability greatly aggravated the already tense relations between the Chinese and the indigenous populations in Southeast Asia. Chinese immigrants and their capital poured into the United States all the way from Taiwan to Burma immediately following Nixon's trip to China. After the United States pulled out of Vietnam in 1975, the exodus of Chinese immigrants and their capital accelerated and continues to this day. The trend slowed down somewhat during the 1989–92 recession in Canada and the United States.

Adding to the influx of the middle- and upper-class Chinese from the region was the arrival of ethnic Chinese refugees from Indochina during the "boat people" crisis that began in 1978. Vietnam's anti-Chinese policy forced hundreds of thousands of Chinese to flee, about a quarter million of whom were repatriated to China in accordance with China's 1957 policy toward overseas Chinese.[25] The remainder tried to flee to nearby countries, but only about half of them survived the ordeals at sea. Several hundred thousand entered the United States as Indochinese refugees. By 1990, more and more of these refugees began to identify themselves as Chinese Americans (*huayi*), a phenomenon that contributed to the significantly higher count of the Chinese population in the 1990 census.

TYPES OF CHINESE IDENTITY

Thus far I have briefly surveyed the history of Chinese immigration to the United States and some of the major factors contributing to the different waves and types of Chinese immigrants. I shall now discuss how this history impacts the formation and transformation of Chinese identity in the United States. In my view, there are five basic types of Chinese American identity. Each is connected to a different notion of *gen*; none is static. Change has been brought about by changes in China, in the United States, in U.S.-China relations, and in Chinese perceptions of themselves in relation to all the above. Although each type emerged from a distinct historical setting, all five are found among the Chinese in the United States today, and all are still changing and interacting constantly with one another, sometimes in peaceful coexistence and at other times in conflict. Depending on the circumstances, a person may move from one identity to another. Each is dynamic yet never ceases to have its focus on *gen*, whose meaning also changes as time passes and spatial reference moves.

Luoye guigen: The Sojourner Mentality

Among the most enduring images of the Chinese abroad since the mid-nineteenth century, from the point of view of the host countries, has been that of "aliens" or "sojourners." [26] Words most frequently used to characterize Chinese living in countries outside China include foreigners, outsiders, strangers, pariahs, outcasts, visitors, temporary residents, and nonnatives—because natives or citizens of the host countries frequently do not consider the Chinese in their midst to be immigrants, permanent settlers, or naturalized citizens, integral to their populations. Instead, they see Chinese as parasites, arrogantly or chauvinistically holding onto their peculiar culture, reserved and clannish mannerisms, and austere lifestyle and strange habits, incessantly siphoning off the host country's assets and resources. To add insult to injury, most Chinese yearn eventually to return to their native village in China to retire. In the predominantly Christian countries of Europe, Australia, and the Americas, the sojourner image of the Chinese is reinforced by the perception that Chinese are "heathen" and nonassimilable.[27] Neither actual activity nor change in legal status can effectively distract the host country's single-minded focus on their racial or national origin in the host countries. Whether the perception is with or without basis, most countries have formulated domestic and foreign policies that severely limit Chinese efforts to earn a living and to achieve integration; not infrequently, these countries even deny Chinese basic legal and human rights.

In California, led by Governor John Bigler in 1852 and later by other political and labor leaders, the first wave of Chinese immigrants were labeled "nonassimilable," people unable to take part in the emerging free, democratic society of the Pacific coast. Politicians and labor leaders advocated total exclusion of the Chinese "race," and they won passage of many discriminatory local ordinances and state laws that stripped Chinese of any basic rights and privileges and discouraged their continuing presence in many localities.

For the Chinese peasants recruited to work abroad and merchants seeking economic opportunities overseas, the hostile reception was bewildering, if not shocking, in light of what they knew to be the privileged treatment white foreigners received in China. It is fortunate that, in most cases, their motivation in coming to the United States was to secure a financial state and to return to their villages once this mission was accomplished. Thus they came with the culture-bound notion of *luoye guigen*, and they perceived themselves as *huaqiao* or Chinese sojourning abroad. In short, the American perception of Chinese as aliens and sojourners resonated with the Chinese notion of *huaqiao* and with the Chinese government's *qiaowu zhengce*, or policies toward the Chinese in diaspora.

It should be pointed out, however, that *huaqiao* and *guigen* described only a certain mentality, belief, or desire. In practice, not all Chinese who emigrated beyond the borders of China returned. In fact, throughout Chinese history Chinese have migrated and settled in foreign lands as immigrants, notably in Southeast Asia.[28] Even in the United States, a small minority of Chinese immigrants managed to settle down quietly, mostly in rural areas such as the Monterey Bay region of California and in certain southern and southwestern states where their services and labor were needed.[29]

While the deeply held value of *luoye guigen* or the *huaqiao* mentality was reinforced by the hostile reception of Chinese immigrants in the first period, most of them accepted their alien and sojourner status. Most Chinese were willing to tolerate discrimination and abuse because they considered their suffering temporary. They also set up parallel social institutions, such as family (*gongsuo*) and district (*huiguan*) associations, to protect their well-being and maintain their lifestyle. Before 1878 China had no embassy or consular office in the United States to protect her nationals. In fact, the Chinese government was indifferent or unsympathetic toward those who were being persecuted abroad during the mid-nineteenth century.[30] The only protection the Chinese in America received was from the American judicial system, to which they frequently appealed and from which they occasionally received relief.[31]

With the emergence of China as something resembling a modern nation-state and the establishment of diplomatic missions toward the end of the nineteenth century, China began to develop policies (*qiaowu zhengce*) and establish government agencies—notably the Overseas Chinese Affairs Commission, called the Qiaowu Weiyuan Hui by the Nationalist government and Huaqiao Bangong She in the Communist government—at home and abroad to deal with the overseas Chinese, especially with problems arising from their maltreatment. The ruling Guomindang of the Nationalist period even set up a special section to enlist political and financial support from overseas members, especially those in the United States and Southeast Asia. Consistent with Chinese ethnocentrism and the notion of *luoye guigen*, the Qing, the Nationalist, and the early Chinese Communist governments each adopted policies based purely on race and claimed full jurisdiction over all overseas Chinese, regardless of where they happened to reside or whether they had become citizens of their adopted lands. In other words, the successive governments of China specified a system of dual citizenship for Chinese outside the nation's borders.[32] By Chinese laws and through various law enforcement apparatuses, Chinese communities overseas were treated essentially as colonies of the Chinese government, subject to its extraterritorial rule. It was not until 1957 that the Chinese Communist government officially renounced the policy of dual citizenship and replaced it with one that emphasized the free choice of citizenship, integration into the adopted country, and repatriation if necessary.[33] However, the Chinese government in Taiwan continues to hold to the old policy to this date.

Several factors can be identified in the continuing maintenance of the sojourner mentality. First and foremost is the high social and cultural value assigned by Chinese society to returning home (*jiaxiang*) to the Chinese cultural environment. This loyalty to one's home village and pride in one's culture, inculcated from childhood on, is vital to the structuring of one's existence and to the formation of one's identity. It has both a racial and a cultural basis, and at times may be ethnocentric, chauvinistic, and racist. Second, racism and discrimination against the Chinese have led many, including some American-born Chinese, to conclude that their presence is not welcome in their adopted land. This fact is most dramatically demonstrated by the declining population trend of Chinese in the United States immediately after the enactment of the Chinese Exclusion Act. Third, nationalism prompted overseas Chinese to return to China either to help defend her territorial integrity—as, for example, during the Sino-Japanese War (1937–1945)—or to assist China's effort to modernize, as occurred during the early Nationalist period and immediately after World War II. Last, the policies, propaganda, and activities of the Chinese government in the overseas Chinese communities and in their home districts in China have often provided incentives for emigrants to return. Instilling pride or guilt is one tactic, applying coercive pressure or dispensing attractive inducement is another. Establishing government-controlled institutions such as Chinese-language schools and newspapers is yet another way of indoctrinating and ensuring loyalty. In the past, the Chinese government succeeded in attracting overseas Chinese to return and invest in housing, industries, transportation, utilities, and in health and educational facilities. Since the U.S.-China détente in 1972, many Chinese American scientists and engineers have contributed their knowledge and skills to universities, research institutes, government agencies, and special projects in the People's Republic of China.

The sojourner mentality therefore is inextricably tied to cultural roots in China and is the basis upon which many overseas Chinese have structured their existence and identity. The mentality is also reinforced by the racial discrimination they encounter. In its original form it was purely cultural. But over time, it took on new meanings with legal and political consequences. Indeed, the meaning of *gen* changed from time to time, as did the specific response to the goal of returning to China.

Zhancao-chugen: Total Assimilation

Opposite the sojourner mentality stands the assimilationist mentality most commonly associated with the first American-born generation. As mentioned earlier, during the pre–World War II period of exclusion, American-born Chinese represented only a minority of the population of Chinese ancestry in the United States. Nevertheless, they had become visible as an identifiable group in major Chinatowns by the early decades of the twentieth century. Even though this group was born and brought up in segregated Chinatowns by China-oriented parents, its members were nevertheless exposed to a largely American environment and, most important, were given an American education either through domestic Christian missions or American public schools, which typically had as a primary objective Americanizing immigrant children.

Through education the American-born Chinese became aware of the sharp difference—racially, culturally, socially, and legally—between them and their Euro-American peers. These differences soon led to comparisons and the making of value judgments and choices. The overwhelming superiority of the dominant white society over their community, perceived as repressed and backward, dictated their choices. Very quickly, they became ashamed of their personal appearance, the values and behaviors they were taught by their parents, and the communities from which they had emerged; self-hatred and the need to be accepted by white society became their primary obsession. In practice, this meant the rejection of their parents' language and culture, and the pursuit of white values in an attempt to become thoroughly Americanized. They vigorously pursued their education, joined Christian churches, and participated in the social and recreational activities of their white peers. This choice also meant the need to acquire a new personal identity, one based on what they thought to be desirable and acceptable to whites. Their sole objective, therefore, was to be accepted by and assimilated into mainstream American society, which, ironically, was the very institution that had been instrumental in the creation of the inferior conditions under which they were brought up.

The assimilation mentality, or survival strategy, and the process through which American-born Chinese sought to gain acceptance by their superior white peers is well depicted in the autobiographies of Pardee Lowe and Jade Snow Wong—two Chinese Americans born and raised in the San Francisco Bay Area before World War II—and has been analyzed by social scientists like R. D. McKenzie, Robert Park, Eliot Mears, William C. Smith, and Edward Strong.[34] It is a mentality that is well captured in the Chinese phrase, *zhancao-chugen*: to eliminate the weeds, one must pull out their roots. In other words, to gain acceptance into white society, Chinese Americans must erase and uproot all traces of their Chinese cultural heritage and thoroughly conform to the values and behaviors of Euro-Americans. This is why some went so far as to anglicize their Chinese family names, suppress their Chinese language ability and accent, dissociate themselves from their relatives and Chinese friends, move out of Chinatowns if possible, and take advantage of modern cosmetology, some by dyeing their hair, others by undergoing plastic surgery to alter their eyelids, nose, and lips.

The strategy of denying one's racial and cultural identity tragically failed to gain American-born acceptance in the period before World War II, even for those who managed to wipe out their linguistic and cultural heritage and to complete a college education at reputable universities. Most found themselves still shut out of the mainstream and prevented from competing for jobs commensurate with their education and ability, solely on account of their race and culture. Disillusioned, they began to wonder whether their future lay in the United States, which rejected them, or in China, which could greatly benefit from their skills and knowledge. Unfortunately, staying in the United States meant accepting second-class citizenship, while going to China for these thoroughly assimilated Chinese Americans was as dauntingly foreign an experience as it would have been for their Euro-American peers.[35]

This catch-22 situation was partially resolved with the outbreak of World War II. The war changed the negative images of China to that of a friend and trusted ally; it opened new job opportunities, enabled thousands of Chinese to become citizens by joining the U.S. Army, and created a favorable political climate for the repeal of the Chinese exclusion laws in 1943, which, as mentioned earlier, allowed 105 Chinese per year to immigrate to the United States and granted the right of naturalization to eligible Chinese already in the United States.[36] All these milestones signaled the inauguration of a new era of acceptance, which the Chinese American sociologist Rose Hum Lee hailed in 1942 as the complete assimilation of the Chinese in the United States.[37] In retrospect, however, the wartime optimism proved exaggerated and the promise of equal opportunity failed to fully materialize. Even the repeal of the exclusion laws failed to assure equality and justice for the majority of Chinese Americans, who continued to be separated from their loved ones across the ocean and to endure both covert and overt discrimination in the next few decades.

In short, social progress was slow. For each new generation of American-born Chinese after the war, even in today's much more open and enlightened society, the racial and cultural difference and social distance between the dominant society and the small Chinese American community has continued to present difficult choices in values and perspectives. The inherent identity crisis facing Chinese Americans still persists today. Self-hatred and the blind pursuit of an ambivalent identity will continue as long as racial and cultural differences are not accepted and appreciated, and as long as public policy, media depiction, school curricula, and academic disciplines continue to provide preferential treatment for Euro-Americans. In the postwar era, the assimilationist perspective was most dramatically reinforced by the massive exodus from Chinatowns into white neighborhoods and suburbs—although social integration has never been achieved. While many Chinese Americans have been employed as technicians and professionals in high-tech industries, the most visible evidence of their educational and occupational success, they have also been effectively prevented from moving further up in the occupational ladder (the so-called glass ceiling phenomenon) and have frequently been willing to accept their second-class status without protest because they subscribe to the postwar ideology of assimilation and are still obsessed with winning acceptance.[38] It was not until the late 1960s and early 1970s that a segment of this middle-class population surfaced to fight racial discrimination, under the auspices of Chinese for Affirmative Action, a community-based civil rights organization in San Francisco, and the Organization of Chinese Americans, a national organization based in Washington, D.C.

Luodi shenggen: Accommodation

While there have been some Chinese immigrants who successfully planted their roots in American soil since the gold rush era, the vast majority of first-generation Chinese in the United States before 1949 identified themselves as Chinese, lived in Chinatowns, and planned to return to China before they died. However, their intention and hope were totally and abruptly shattered with the collapse of the U.S.-backed regime of Chiang Kai-shek in 1949, the advent of the Cold War, and the U.S. policy of containment of China by military means. The United States declared China "Public Enemy Number One," imposed a total economic embargo against it, and eventually fought two costly wars in Korea and Indochina to contain what was then seen as Chinese expansionism. The abrupt change in China's status, from that of friend and ally of the United States during World War II to abhorred enemy during the Cold War, had a devastating and traumatic effect on the Chinese in the United States. In 1951, the U.S. government immediately prohibited Chinese residing in the United States—who until then had maintained ties with family members in China who could not come to visit the United States because of exclusionary immigration laws—from maintaining contact with or sending remittances to their relatives in China.[39] Their relations with their *gen*, in all its meanings, had to be severed. Moreover, at least 5,000 government-sponsored Chinese students pursuing advanced degrees at American universities were stranded, much as the thirty thousand Chinese students here at the time of the Tiananmen incident in June 1989 have been stranded. Most of these earlier students were prevented from returning to China either in fear of political persecution upon their return (their education having been sponsored by Chiang Kai-shek's government) or because their knowledge of science and technology was deemed too valuable to China.[40]

In short, the older generation's option of returning to China to live out their old age and the students' plans to serve China with their newly acquired knowledge of science and technology were abruptly, and in many cases traumatically, taken away. Their sole option was to settle permanently in the United States, to begin to restructure their existence, and to reshape their identity and destiny, because China—the homeland, the fountainhead of Chinese culture, the political entity to which they had pledged their loyalty and with whom the United States had formed a political alliance during World War II—had overnight become an enemy of the United States. In fact, to avoid the fate suffered by 120,000 Japanese Americans during World War II, when they were put in concentration camps because their loyalty was deemed questionable, leaders of the Chinese American community went out of their way to prove their loyalty to the United States by forming anti-China organizations and, with the help of Chiang Kai-shek's agents in the United States, suppressing all dissident views within the Chinese American community during the McCarthy era.[41]

Settling down in a foreign land and accommodating to the host society (*luodi shenggen*), planting seeds in foreign soil and allowing them to take root, had not been an option for most Chinese in the United States before World War II or in the policies of the Chinese governments toward their overseas nationals before 1957. In this case, however, accommodation is quite different from the assimilationist mentality discussed above, in that it calls for a commitment to permanent settlement in the United States, which includes renouncing Chinese citizenship, accommodating to American life styles at least in public without fundamentally changing private Chinese lifestyle and cultural values, and contributing to the well-being of American society. Accommodation here also differs from Robert Park's use of the word in his cyclical theory of race relations in that both the initiative for and the terms of accommodation come not from the host society, but from the Chinese themselves. Accommodation, in this instance, is a survival strategy in an alien setting one is unable to leave, a pragmatic approach widely adopted by Chinese in Southeast Asia. More important, it can take place even if American society continues to show intolerance or hostility toward Chinese Americans.

It is quite conceivable that, over time, accommodation could lead to assimilation, if the Chinese in the United States lose contact with China over an extended period or if hostile relations prevail between China and the United States; this has been the situation of Chinese in Southeast Asia in the past few decades. Accommodation could, on the other hand, revert to the sojourner mentality if Chinese nationalism were to resurface. It is also possible that American society may someday choose to accept Chinese Americans as they are, both racially and culturally, if we can achieve a form of cultural pluralism or multicultural democracy.

In short, the Cold War created a climate under which Chinese in the United States and in countries outside the Soviet bloc were compelled to drastically change their sojourner mentality and life style, to plant their roots permanently in foreign soil, and to become an integral part of their adopted country. Their success in making the transition has depended largely on the receptivity of the host societies and on the changing relations between the host countries and China.

Xungen wenzu: Ethnic Pride and Consciousness

An indigenous movement to develop a distinct Chinese American identity began only in the late 1960s and early 1970s, as part of a broader movement of Americans of Asian descent.[42] As a political movement, it owed its genesis to and derived its inspiration, agenda, and tactics from the Black civil rights and Black power movements. However, its content was rooted exclusively in Chinese American and Asian American experiences. Its objective was not only to reconceptualize Chinese American identity, but also to demand a rightful place in the United States for all Chinese Americans. Toward these ends, the movement set as its goal the liberation of Chinese Americans from the structure of dual domination—i.e., freedom from racial oppression by white society and freedom from the extraterritorial rule of the Chinese government in Taiwan and its representatives in the United States.

College students who participated in this movement have been inspired to study and understand Chinese American history and cultural heritage and to reidentify with the Chinatowns that had been rejected and forgotten by their assimilationist parents following World War II. Students pressured a number of universities to establish Asian American studies programs that would provide opportunities for research and teaching about the past as well as the present conditions of Chinese America.[43] They also established civil rights and social service organizations in Chinatowns across the nation to fight for justice and to provide needed services for the poor and the elderly. Over the last twenty years, this new ethnic pride has inspired many young Chinese American scholars and students to reinterpret Chinese American history and to reexamine the problems and needs of Chinese American communities. From San Francisco's Chinese for Affirmative Action (CAA) to New York's Chinatown Planning Council, from the National Association of Chinese Americans (NACA) to the Organization of Chinese Americans (OCA), local and national organizations were created to redefine and rebuild Chinese America.[44]

Many Chinese began to reconstruct their family histories in the United States and to trace them to the villages in China from which their ancestors had come; others began to express their feelings and perspectives through literary and artistic creation. A new breed of Chinese writers—Maxine Hong Kingston, Amy Tan, David Wong Louie, Gish Jen, and Fae Myenne Ng, playwrights Frank Chin, David Hwang, and Genny Lim, musicians/composers Fred Ho and Jon Jang, and filmmakers Wayne Wang and Peter Wang—have achieved national prominence.

This new development was a historic break with earlier perspectives. The reconceptualization of Chinese American identity based on a Chinese American past with roots in the United States is best described by the Chinese phrases *xungen wenzu* (searching for one's roots

and ancestors), and *zhuigen qiyuan* (pursuing one's roots and looking for one's origins). A graphic example of the fruits of this tireless
search is Frank Ching's *Ancestors: 900 Years in the Life of a Chinese
Family.*[45] *Gen* in this case is not just China, but Chinese America, past
and present, in addition to the ancestral villages from which the fore-
bears of today's Chinese Americans came and from which the culture
of Chinese Americans was derived. The approach makes it clear that
the new identity is not based on an uncritical, wholesale transplant of
Chinese culture, as was maintained by the *luoye guigen* approach. Nor
is it rooted in the wholesale denial of the Chinese American past, as
in the *zhancao-chugen* approach. Instead, it is grounded in the concrete collective experiences of Chinese in the United States, in a newly
conceived community with shared interests and a common destiny in
America. The movement's participants are intensely proud of being
Chinese Americans. They are committed to building a Chinese American community based not on a transplanted Chinese society, but on
past experiences in the United States and on the principles of justice
and equality. From these roots in both China and the United States,
new life, new culture, and new identity have emerged and flourished on
American soil (*gensheng yemao*).

Shigen qunzu: The Uprooted

As mentioned in the section on immigration, the most noteworthy
feature of Chinese immigration to the United States in the third period
(since 1949) is the large concentration of highly educated Chinese who
have chosen to abandon their roots in China, Taiwan, and, increasingly, Hong Kong and Singapore. Some came to the United States ini-
tially as *liuxuesheng* (foreign students), others as immigrant *zhishifenzi*
(intelligentsia). Together they constitute much of the educated elite of
their native lands. The Tiananmen massacre has turned the steady flow
of Chinese intellectuals into a massive hemorrhage, forcing China to
impose severe restrictions in its *liuxuesheng* policy. In Taiwan, Hong
Kong, and Singapore, the governments have been devising incentives to
lure back their lost talent, including lucrative salaries, generous research
support, and the promise of at least limited intellectual freedom.

Sending the best students to study in the United States, Japan, and
Europe is not a recent phenomenon. In the mid-nineteenth century,
Yung Wing and others were sent by the Chinese government to study at

Yale University and other leading institutions in the United States. Since then, there has been a steady stream of select students sent abroad each year—notably in the last decade of the Qing dynasty, the early years of the Nationalist period, the first few years following the conclusion of World War II, and the last twenty years.

By far the most significant difference between the earlier waves of *liuxuesheng* and the recent one is the fact that most of the former eventually returned to serve China. The purpose of studying abroad was, historically, to help modernize China, hence the notion of *liuxue jiuguo* or *chixin baoguo* (to study abroad to save China). Patriotism motivated progressive intellectuals to seek knowledge overseas. Indeed, the desire to deliver China from Western domination inspired the educated elite to seek knowledge in the West. In this respect, the earlier students were sojourners as well. But the vast majority of the latest wave of students have failed to return to China, Hong Kong, Taiwan, or their home countries in Southeast Asia, contributing to a phenomenon that has been deplored by the governments in Beijing, Taipei, Hong Kong, and Singapore as *rencai wailiu* or *chucai jinyong* (brain drain). The 1980s marked the largest exodus to date of the educated elite seeking greener pastures in the United States. The Chinese press characterizes the exodus as *chuguochao*, *chuguore*, and *chuguobing*—a stampede or sickness. Clearly, many Chinese intellectuals have lost their faith not just in governments in Taiwan and the People's Republic of China, historically their patrons, but also in the viability of Chinese elite culture, which had flourished through countless upheavals from one dynasty to another up to the present day.

Three major factors may be identified as the causes behind this significant departure from tradition. First, many Chinese intellectuals have lost faith in China's ability to achieve modernization under either of the political and social orders on both sides of the Taiwan Straits. As a group or class with rare privilege and power—the scholar-officials (*shidafu*), the forerunners of modern intellectuals—were the standard bearers and custodians of Chinese cultural values and political institutions; they were the only group with access to new knowledge and exposure to new ideas from abroad. Since the second half of the nineteenth century, the progressive wing of this group has made numerous valiant attempts to introduce new ideas and a new political order to China, beginning with Lin Zexu and Wei Yuan's opposition to foreign incursions and the Westernization movement (*yangwu yundong*) to make China strong and prosperous (1860–1885), through the reform and revolutionary movements at the turn of the century, to the May Fourth Movement and the Communist liberation of the twentieth century. Each movement made some progress, but each also met strong resistance from traditionalist rivals. Each time, the defeated segment of the intelligentsia was sacrificed at the repressive hand of the victors. The ideological and military conflicts of the Cold War period, represented by competing models of development in China and Taiwan, aggravated the growing disenchantment and loss of faith in China. It was inevitable that as many forward-looking young people became increasingly aware of the backward and repressive conditions in China and Taiwan in relation to other countries, many lost faith in their government and in China's ability to modernize and to become a full-fledged member of the family of nations. Exhausted and disillusioned, many ceased to see themselves as able to play any role in China's modernization and cultural regeneration.

Second, the opportunity to pursue advanced degrees and develop careers in research and teaching abroad stimulated many frustrated intellectuals to migrate to the United States. The liberal admissions policy for foreign students and the preferential treatment of scholars under the 1965 immigration law provided the legal framework for these motivated intellectuals to enter the United States. Third, the freedom of expression in America—a privilege seldom accorded Chinese intellectuals and artists, whether in China, Taiwan, Hong Kong, or Singapore—was especially attractive for those who had never experienced it. Although some have been unable to change their medium of expression from Chinese to English, many have come to the United States and established themselves as leading writers and intellectuals in the Chinese-speaking world. With the aid of new printing technology, modern telecommunications, and efficient worldwide distribution networks, they have found a sympathetic following among diaspora Chinese. Many have become leading Chinese intellectuals, whose works frequently penetrate even the stringent censorship imposed by the governments in China, Taiwan, and Singapore.

The influx of Chinese intellectuals is likely to continue for some time, and China will continue to lose its leading scholars as long as this crisis of confidence persists. The crucial question is whether these intellectual exiles will be able to function with the same creativity and vitality outside the Chinese cultural milieu of China, Taiwan, and Hong Kong, as Jews in Europe and the United States and the Spanish in Latin America have been able to do for centuries outside their respective cultural fountainheads. For now, in the wake of the Tiananmen massacre, thousands have become "wandering intellectuals" cut off from their roots in historic China, *shigen qunzu*. Some have been able to take advantage of their training and background in China to function well— like trees transplanted with intact roots, *yishu daigen*—while others, discovering and exploiting a market for their dissident opinions, have been peddling their works or views for financial and personal gains, *genwai zhuifei* (bashing China for personal gain). Still others find it impossible to pursue their intellectual or artistic work outside China. In spite of obvious restraints and political repression, some choose to return to China or Taiwan. Most, however, opt for accommodation in the new environment, trying to survive; they make the best of a very difficult situation and hope someday to anchor their roots in receptive and compatible soil, whether in China or in the United States.

CONCLUSION

It is clear that there is no single Chinese identity in the United States or in the world of the Chinese diaspora. China's preoccupation with the loyalty of the overseas Chinese and the United States's pursuit of total assimilation for the Chinese are, at best, simplifications that disregard history and the rights of Chinese in the United States. The tendency on the part of Chinese intellectuals to disregard the concerns and aspirations of nonintellectuals has severely limited the scope and context of the discussion of Chinese identity in diaspora. Of the five major identities I have suggested, each emerged from a concrete historical situation and in some form has persisted to this day among the Chinese overseas.

Each identity is dynamic in character, constantly undergoing transformation. Motivating this transformation are factors such as race relations in the host country, public policy toward the Chinese, the state of the host country's diplomatic relations with China, and China's policies toward overseas Chinese. At the personal level, racial identity is decisive, but even more important is one's perception of one's own *gen*, whether it is seen as a geographic entity, a nation, a government, or a culture, and whether it is planted on Chinese or American soil. The Chinese notion of *gen* is what gives rise to the varied, often conflicting understandings of Chinese identities; it contributes to the shaping of the destinies of Chinese in foreign countries. China itself is an important base for structuring overseas Chinese identity, especially for intellectuals now residing outside China, but it is not the sole basis. Different classes of overseas Chinese, including the American-born generations, have been struggling over the issue of identity since the nineteenth century. Their perspectives must also be included in the global debate now under way.

By virtue of her size, history, power, and culture, China will continue to play an enormous and dynamic role in the formation and structuring of Chinese identity abroad. Its influence on the Chinese in diaspora can be either positive or negative, depending on China's own ability to modernize and make herself a credible member of the family of nations. The Tiananmen massacre has made China look barbaric to the global community and alienated large segments of the Chinese population worldwide. Overseas Chinese nationalism, long cultivated by successive Chinese governments, is not likely to surface anew without a massive reversal of current policies in both Taiwan and China.

The continuing influx of Chinese intellectuals into the United States is bound to have a lasting impact on both the United States and China. Intellectuals from China, Taiwan, Hong Kong, and Singapore have established their base in the United States, in a new climate of freedom, and have begun to produce works depicting the contemporary conditions of Chinese at home and abroad and debating the future of China and Chinese culture. Their work has gained acceptance among the Chinese worldwide and, by virtue of their stature and the political importance of the United States, their voices are gaining influence around the world. Without question the United States has rapidly become an intellectual center for the people of Chinese ancestry. Just how this center will shape the future identities of Chinese is impossible to predict. In the meantime, the debate over the roots of Chinese culture and identity will continue as conflicting views surface in dialogues both outside and within China—anywhere with a sizable Chinese population.

10

From Qiao (僑) To Qiao (橋)

Victor Hao Li

I AM SOJOURNER (僑)

Leaving

Virtually all started as sojourners. We left a place we wished to leave, whether for economic or political reasons. We went to a place we thought we wished to go, whether for a better livelihood or education or safety. That was true for laborers, students, traders, spouses, or refugees. Leaving the Central Kingdom was a difficult physical act, of course. Moving was never easy. In addition, at times during China's history, emigration was illegal; and immigration to some places was illegal as well.

Even under the best of circumstances, newly arrived immigrants found that the barriers of language, race, status, and economic condition were formidable. Often the circumstances were not the best, and hosts were not hospitable. Laborers and others arrived with little education and meager financial resources. Refugees, the most reluctant of emigrants, usually came with empty hands and heavy hearts. For people who have crossed national and cultural boundaries, there is often a sense of severed roots or rootlessness that can be very painful. Many were lonesome, even forlorn, contemporary strangers in a strange land. I still remember a very sad book written by a Chinese tutor I had as a young boy, *Nowhere Is My Home*. He left his home in China, with both himself and his country scarred by the Japanese war; and spiritually he really never did arrive in the United States.

Leaving the Central Country was also an important symbolic act. In mainstream Chinese culture, a person was not defined by individual attributes as in the West, where "I" carried my persona and my soul with me and could establish a New World wherever I went. Instead, the individual was at the nexus of a broad network of relationships that connected the person to ancestors and descendants, family, the community, and the state. All persons regardless of social or economic status knew that there was one specific spot on the earth that was, and would be for all time, their "place," linked by generations of life, existence, and death. Weakening or severing these links diminished or even destroyed a person.

Sojourners could handle these problems more readily than emigrants. Sojourners were, in theory, physically away for a time and spiritually away only in part. At the symbolic plane, they yielded almost nothing and never really left. Host countries also found it easier to deal with sojourners. So long as a person was only a temporary resident, at least in theory, society did not have to face up to issues of language and cultural policy, intermarriage, education for the young, and other such questions of integration.

From the perspective of China itself, sojourners did not reject a culturally and spiritually superior land; these persons were only temporarily absent to carry out some practical activity. Their social and economic obligations to family and community remained. Also remaining were the political obligations that sojourners had toward the state. For centuries, China regarded overseas Chinese, *huaqiao*, as Chinese nationals who were temporarily abroad. With the advent of regular contact with the West, China adopted the convenient practice of some European countries (often those that had a significant number of emigrants) of dual citizenship. In this system, a person had political obligations to both China and the host country. Needless to say, this greatly disturbed many host countries, such as Malaysia or Indonesia—which feared subversive activities on the part of their large Chinese communities on behalf of the People's Republic—or Burma, which had concerns about the influence of the Taiwan government.

It was not until the 1970s that Chinese government terminology changed from "overseas Chinese" to "American" (or some other nationality) "nationals of Chinese descent." This defined much more clearly a person's political (as contrasted with cultural or social) loyalties and obligations. The Nationality Law passed in the PRC in 1980 formally renounced the dual nationality concept. Taiwan still follows the practice.

Returning

Many sojourners did return: some after their education was completed or their fortune made, even if this required many years; others to marry or to die. Even if they did not move back permanently, important ties were maintained. Money and persons passed back and forth, births were duly entered in the family register, and important rituals were performed.

But many more did not return. With the passage of time and the improvement of circumstances, the sojourner was increasingly becoming a settler. Businesses and careers were gaining success. Usually local families were established. Language and educational barriers declined. Intermarriage or adoption of indigenous local names eased integration into majority society. The sojourner was developing a new set of relationships in the host country. These relationships may not have displaced the ones in China, but they were real nonetheless. They added to the definition of "I" for the people concerned, or even began to establish a new or additional "I."

Some host countries accepted this shift from sojourner to settler grudgingly and slowly; others were more welcoming. But the direction of movement was clear. As the sojourners expanded and deepened their local ties, de facto settlement was taking place. De jure settlement, however incomplete and hesitant, would follow.

Some of the greatest changes were occurring in the sojourners themselves. Many ties with China remained but were stretched progressively thinner. Developments in the home country, such as the Revolution of 1911 or 1949, altered both the practical and the symbolic rules. Very importantly, successive generations of children found that they were increasingly losing their ability to function as Chinese in China. Their commonality with people in China was shrinking, as they became more involved in local affairs elsewhere, and as they began to establish an "indigenous Chinese" culture there or were increasingly merging with the local majority culture. They still admired things Chinese and might search for their roots, but they were also losing their ability to go and interest in returning home. Indeed, the meaning of "home" began to change. The cultural home was China, while the physical home was in the host country. The spiritual home was in both, with the mix and the degree shifting with the times and the individual.

The traditional Chinese sense of "returning" is illustrated by a Tang dynasty poem. The world had changed, but the lack of understanding was the children's, not the old man's. He knew his "place" on the earth:

> I left home young and returned old.
> My dialect had not changed but my hair had thinned.
> Young children greet me yet do not know me.
> And smiling ask from where the stranger came.

The second poem, drawn from the Arabic, conveys a very different perspective. The changes are fundamental and probably forever:

> Returning to the land of my birth
> I joyfully cried,
> "Where are the friends of my youth?"

> "Where *are* the friends of my youth?"
> The shadows replied.
> And again I cried.

In American culture, Thomas Wolfe was much more explicit. Individuals can change and old ties break. For many, you can't go home again.

I AM BRIDGE (橋)

The United States

For myself and many, many others, the United States has been a most hospitable and admirable host. In spite of all the difficulties—exclusion laws, Japanese internment, the murder of Vincent Chin, racial conflicts in Koreatown, and many other painful episodes—this country has opened its arms to immigrants, or at least has aspired to do so. It has set a standard of humanity toward which the rest of the world must move. There is, nonetheless, a basic problem. The melting pot is European and white. Blacks, who have been here for centuries, and more recent Hispanic and Asian immigrants, do not melt well into this pot.

For European immigrants, cultural similarities greatly exceed differences. Religious beliefs and rituals are familiar. Everyone also looks more or less the same. A loss of accent by the second generation or even a change in name can erase most distinctions. But that is not so for Asians, and of course also not so for blacks and most Hispanics. I remember my first teaching job—at a very fine university. Just after I arrived, a member of the faculty came up to me and said with great care and warmth, "Do you . . . speak . . . English?" I replied, "I do the best I can; it's my Chinese that needs help." But what I thought was, "He cannot look past my skin to see who I am." My face and color are Asian; I am happy with that. But the point is that I will always look different from the majority. The same is true for my children. Depending on whom they marry, the same will probably remain true for several more generations. Of course, physical appearance is just one aspect. There also are vitally important differences in religion, language, institutions, and even values.

Given the problems of dealing with race, this society is at a near total loss on issues that involve both race and economics. The "model minority" concept focuses on successful Asian Americans, and in the process chokes the help that should be extended to the very deprived and needy members of the Asian American communities. This concept also has a more pernicious effect on society as a whole, by trying to represent a half truth as the whole truth. Its underlying message is that all minorities can be successful in the majority culture if they study and work hard. But that is only partly true; we cannot gloss over issues of racism, psychological and economic deprivation, and institutional inequality. This society also frames race issues in terms of majority/minority relations. We have great difficulty thinking about, much less dealing with, minority/minority conflicts, such as street gangs or the Los Angeles riot.

But we should not allow the above comments to make us lose sight of the larger picture. Of course there is discrimination, stupidity, and injustice. (Asians, by the way, are among the worst in discriminating against other groups.) Certainly there is need for improvement. Nevertheless, the guiding principles of this country recognize equality and diversity and, on the whole, these principles are observed, or at the least aspired to. Our focus, rather, should be on how to change and improve American society. The people of this country already come in many shades and colors. In a growing number of cities, the majority is no longer the majority, at least in numbers. One of this nation's great social tasks in the coming decade will be to work out both the theory and the practice of increased racial and cultural diversity. Does the melting pot concept still hold as the racial and ethnic make-up of this country substantially changes? If not, what is the theoretical foundation for the alternative concept of a mosaic? What needs to be done in very practical areas such as language policy, education, housing, and employment?

In carrying out this great task, minorities have an especially important role, and with this, an added burden. We have to be willing to take on the task and the burden. Those of us of Chinese cultural heritage have to expand our concepts of self and obligation to include relationships that go well beyond family and ethnic group. We also have to get more directly involved in the public sectors of society.

China

Changing the Nationality Law to remove dual nationality was an important step: the Center relinquished one of the most powerful bonds. We now have to see how the severing of this bond will work in practice. Even more, we need to define the scope and content of the remaining cultural and spiritual bond. In doing so, we can draw wisdom from the experience of others, from Jews to Poles and Irish to Native Americans.

Let me focus on one aspect. China now is actively reaching into the rest of the world, just as the rest of the world is actively reaching into China. Its international trade is growing at an extraordinary rate, and foreign investments are not far behind. Millions of people are traveling to and fro, and tens or even hundreds of thousands are studying in one another's countries. Not just people but news and information flow extensively across borders, as do ideas. While the volume and variety of transnational activities are very impressive, their actual conduct has not been easy. Problems are caused by language and cultural barriers, differences in institutions and methods, political tensions and economic competition. Adding to the difficulty is the shortage of persons on both sides who have the experience and skill to deal with transnational and cross-cultural matters. There is a great and growing need for people, ideas, and institutions that can bridge national and cultural gaps.

I Am Bridge (橋)

Like many others, I have often wondered who I am. Part of the answer is fairly easy. Having come to this country very young, I had little ambivalence about where my home was: here. I should add that although I was a member of a minority, I felt no special disadvantage. I never had the slightest doubt that the culture I came from and carried within me was much superior to the majority culture I saw around me.

I looked to the United States. While this was home, I could not fully melt into this pot, nor would I want to. There was still a yearning, if you will, for a historically, culturally, and racially more complete home.

So I also looked to China. That did not satisfy either. For example, in 1964 I went to Hong Kong to work on my dissertation. I had looked forward to that trip, my first time back to Asia since leaving as a child. I thought that in Hong Kong I would find *my* people, who would speak my language and understand my ways. But once I arrived there, I felt very much out of place. The people were like me in one sense, but they were utterly different in many other important ways. I was really much more at home in Times Square. One day standing on Nathan Road, I saw a person walking down the street and knew that he was a Chinese American—because he walked, held his head, and looked about him in an American and not a Hong Kong way.

I had a different kind of experience in 1972, my first trip to China. There I felt even more out of place. I knew China could not be home. Something else also happened. In Guangzhou I went to find my family's old house, where we lived when I was four or five. Looking at it, I recalled playing on that porch and those stairs with the neighbor's children. It was a very satisfying moment, emotionally and intellectually.

When I returned to New York and told my father, he replied that not only did I find the wrong house, I had even been in the wrong part of town. The next year, I went to the correct house. And again, I recalled that garden and those rooms. But I wondered, What do I really know and remember, and what am I constructing? Where *are* the friends of my youth? The initial reaction was a kind of shock. Uncertainty added to the possibility of rootlessness and homelessness. But shock also makes one think. Perhaps I am getting the wrong answers because I am asking the wrong questions.

The sojourner question: Am I Chinese? In some ways, but not in many others. The settler question: Am I American? In many ways, but certainly not completely. Is this discomforting? Of course. But it also is very comforting and exciting. The incompleteness of the answers leads one to reformulate the question.

In times past, countries and cultures were much more self-contained, especially those in Asia separated from others by long distances and hard terrain. Despite periodic massive infusions of outside influences, the emphasis was on introspection. What was the core meaning of the Center? How should those on the periphery relate to the Center? These are the questions of both sojourner and settler.

There are points in human history when cultures and peoples cross old boundaries and build new ties at especially rapid rates and in important ways, and in the process civilizations are transformed. We are at one of those points. It can be described as the shrinking of the world or the globalization of human activities. The result is that the economic well-being and physical security of both individuals and societies are intimately linked with people and events in other countries. Even more, the opportunity for ideas from different cultures to interact holds the promise of enriching each one of us and all of humanity. At such a juncture, those who to one degree or another straddle two cultures have a special role, and with it a special responsibility. We are not simply sojourners dreaming of home, or people of the periphery trying to define our ties with our native "place." Nor are we minorities or outsiders in the host country, trying to establish our rightful position.

We are those things, of course. But even more, we are the bridges who will help bring about the Pacific era and build a global community and a New World Order. We are conveyers, not simply of goods and services, but of knowledge and understanding and trust. We have the skills and the interest to deal with cultural differences, linguistic barriers, and differences in values and institutions—all those problems that so often lead to misunderstanding and strife. We are, or can be, the bridge linking two societies, and linking the past with the future.

11

On the Margins of the Chinese Discourse: Some Personal Thoughts on the Cultural Meaning of the Periphery

Leo Ou-fan Lee

I

About five years ago an interesting movement raged in the literary circles of urban China. Known as *xungen*, or "searching for roots," the movement was launched mostly by young writers who for one reason or another felt the need to look for the source of their own cultural origins—and hence their creativity—in areas other than the political center as represented for over forty years by the Maoist ideology of the Chinese Communist Party. What makes this "anticenter" movement politically provocative is the argument that the strands of Chinese culture have been so severely ruptured by the ideological campaigns of recent decades, and by the Cultural Revolution in particular, that the younger generation has been cut off from its cultural roots and must go in search of them. In an intriguing act of symbolic reversal, their quest has led most of the movement's writers away from Beijing or other urban centers of political power into the remote countryside. Some of these regions they identify as their birthplaces, hence evoking an emotional feeling of nostalgia for their native land typical of most writers of this genre. For others, it came from their personal experience during the Cultural Revolution when as urban youth they had been sent "up to the hills and down to the countryside." But the spiritual process of discovering their roots is nothing less than an epiphany, which they seek to capture artistically in their reinvented fictional landscape. The ancient myths and rituals they have uncovered invariably impart a sense of grandeur and vitality against which the official Communist ideology pales into insignificance. From the angle of this new vision, the political peripheries are culturally richer than the center, which is further divested of its previous aura by de-Maoification.

The intellectual impetus of this literary movement has also given rise to a broader movement of "cultural self-reflection" (*wenhua fansi*), a critical reexamination of all aspects of Chinese culture and history.[1] In both cases, the dissatisfaction stems directly from a profound sense of disillusionment with the Cultural Revolution, which ironically reduced Chinese culture to rubble. It is out of this sense of void that these writers, artists, and intellectuals feel compelled to redefine their own culture as they seek to redefine themselves: How to find a meaning of being Chinese other than what the Party has defined for them?

The literary value of these new works has been affirmed by most scholars as far superior to the spate of works produced under the official Maoist brand of socialist realism, for these young writers, influenced notably by Gabriel García Márquez, the South American Nobel prize winner, have woven layers of myth into the tapestry of reality through a more inventive use of language.[2] Interestingly, none of them considers himself or herself to be "traditionalist"; rather they prefer the notions and techniques, however vague, of Western modernism. This new form of modernist art in the service of uncovering an ancient past again bespeaks an anticenter impulse. One detects even an artistic animosity against the Han culture, which, as they see it, has been suffused with both feudal and current authoritarianisms of Confucian and Communist ideology; its hegemonic status fails to conceal its cultural atrophy.

Some of these writers are from minority origins, such as the Muslim Zhang Chengzhi and the Tibetan Zhaxi Dawa. But they nevertheless write in the majority language of *baihua*, like their fellow Han writers. So the phenomenon is not one of minority rights or linguistic pluralism, but rather a new discourse on the meaning of modern Chinese culture— a new dialogue initiated by a group of self-disenfranchised young intellectuals who wish, so to speak, to "decenter" the oppressive political culture of the Party. I have called it a dialogue both as it is defined by the Russian theorist Mikhail Bakhtin (in which a new language or a new genre interacts "dialogically" with the established literary conventions, especially in the polyphonic structures of the novel),[3] and as a way to delineate the contours of their own psychological makeup. The process of searching for roots, as enacted in fictional terms, also becomes a quest for identities. In a typical work, such as Han Shaogong's story "The Homecoming" (Han comes from the "central" province of Hunan in the south—Chairman Mao's birthplace—which he turns into a "peripheral" landscape in his fiction), the "I" narrator, visiting a village for the first time, finds it vaguely familiar. He has, in reality, never been there before, but the villagers seem to recognize him and call him by another name. "All this seems familiar, yet strange too," the narrator muses, "like a word you've been staring at for too long— now it looks right, now it doesn't."[4] This identity confusion leads not merely to the narrator's mental search for a fictional double (a familiar ploy in modern Western fiction); of greater importance, it points to the presence of an "Other," not only another persona but an alternative realm that seems to convey a deeper meaning. One could also easily see traces of a "Peach Blossom Spring," an ancient Shangri-la immortalized by the poet Tao Yuanming. But Han Shaogong is definitely not invoking an ancient ideal. In this and in his other stories both realms clearly exist in the present and the ravages of the Cultural Revolution loom heavily in the foreground.

What does this all mean to a novelist like Han, a leader in the *xungen* movement? In Han's novella, "Ba-Ba-Ba," the protagonist is a mentally retarded boy whose entire vocabulary consists of two phrases— "Ba-Ba-Ba" (a child's sound for father) and the expletive "f - - - your mother!"[5] Like the hero in Günter Grass's *The Tin Drum*, the boy seems to utter a curse, an inarticulate *j'accuse* against the brutality of his surroundings—without, however, gaining any full consciousness of the situation. One prominent critic, Liu Zaifu, sees him as a latter-day descendant of Ah Q, the protagonist in the famous story by the most celebrated modern writer, Lu Xun, who constructed this nameless figure during the May Fourth period in order to probe the more perplexing question of the modern Chinese "national character." If Lu Xun reached a despairing conclusion some seventy years ago, that Ah Q as a psychological prototype has no "soul" and hence no sense of individuality or selfhood, Han Shaogong's more contemporary verdict is even more depressing: the boy not only becomes, like Ah Q, a victim of his historical environment but is in fact never given a chance to articulate his desires.

If the boy were able finally to have a voice, he would be like another boy figure in the film *Yellow Earth* (produced during the heyday of the searching for roots movement), who, after a long silence, finally bursts out singing a ditty about the Dragon King urinating and creating a flood—to the surprise of the revolutionary cadre who visits this patch of yellow earth to collect folk songs. The film's director, Chen Kaige, spent several months searching for a proper location for his film and discovered in northern Shaanxi what he thought to be the exact birthplace of the ancient Chinese civilization. The film's ironic reference to the present situation is even more pointed: the present-day dwellers of this ancient site, the peasants that the Communist cadre encounters, are both unbearably impoverished and mysteriously silent. To try to help the boy and his sister find a voice, the cadre begins by teaching them revolutionary songs from Yan'an, with tragic consequences: the sister, awakened and "liberated," wishes to join the departed cadre in the revolutionary headquarters on the other side of the river and is drowned in her journey.

The film, like Han Shaogong's stories, raises the question of the Other voice—a true voice of the people that seems muffled and suppressed by the sound and the fury of the Communist Revolution. Beneath the veneer of a revolutionary mode, Chen Kaige seeks through an original technique of evoking a "visual silence" to carry on a dialogue with this more "mysterious" realm that lies dormant under its impoverished socioeconomic reality. In Chen's film that dialogue is carried through songs. In Han's "Homecoming," the medium is words, words used in an archaic fashion by the villagers who seem to recognize the I narrator who, in turn, finds their words odd compared with the familiar modern vernacular. What then do these folk songs and archaic words signify? On one level, they represent the *xungen* artists' affirmation of a vox populi that, in a sense, springs from the Chinese earth. On another level, the use of the modern Western ploy of a narrator in order to gain some deeper insight—a technique, incidentally, first used by Lu Xun—itself bespeaks an uncertainty, an indeterminateness about the true message of the people. If we bear in mind the somewhat ironic fact that most *xungen* writers come from urban centers, it is not surprising that they too are strangers to these peripheral regions which they wish to uncover as authentic "centers" of Chinese civilization; the Other as the primordial source of their culture thus seems unfamiliar and even exotically "foreign." Herein lies their paradox: like exiles returning home after a long absence, they find the homeland of their own culture foreign, and the journey to their roots becomes one of increasing "defamiliarization."

However, what matters in this new cultural discourse is not so much its intellectual content as the mode of its inquiry. Whether this younger generation has attained any new insight about its own culture (in scholarly terms) remains to be seen, but one of the movement's by-products is the emergence of an imaginary boundary between the familiar real world in which they live, which continues to be dominated by the ideologies emanating from the Party center—be it Maoist Revolutionary canon or the Four Modernizations, or Four Insistences, championed by the post-Mao leadership—and the unfamiliar Other world they imagine to have existed, whether it be a relatively remote region such as Tibet or Heilongjiang or the ancient sites of Han or Chu cultures (northern Shaanxi in *Yellow Earth* or western Hunan in Han Shaogong's fiction). This imaginary boundary does not necessarily correspond to the official geographical boundary between center and periphery or the nationalistic boundary between Han and minority races. Yet by implication they raise new and profound questions about what it means to be a Chinese even *inside* China.

In intellectual terms, one consequence of the searching for roots movement is that it opens up the chasm between politics and culture. The impetus for cultural self-reflection has managed to stand on its head Mao's famous dictum to put "politics in command." This chasm is further widened by a generational gap between young and old, with the former expressing their cultural dissidence against the conservative orthodoxy of the older generations. These two broadening gaps have served further to separate society from the Party-controlled state. It is in the domains of society (if not "civil society") that the young leaders of cultural dissidence have launched their purposefully "apolitical" assaults against Party authoritarianism while attempting to carve out new spaces for their artistic creativity. In this connection, their works describing exotic peripheries become in turn a symbolic "presence," to reinforce as well as to demarcate new boundaries. What we are witnessing is a phenomenon unlike any other since the establishment of the People's Republic. The student demonstrations in Tiananmen Square in 1989 dramatized this split, and although the Party-state has reasserted its power by military suppression, the gap between state and society can no longer be bridged. This post-Tiananmen state of affairs has led to new configurations of intellectual power and a rethinking of the issues of cultural identity, especially among those Chinese intellectuals compelled to leave China as voluntary or involuntary exiles.

II

This new state of affairs inside China has brought me, as something of a voluntary exile situated forever on the fringes of China, some-what closer to the homeland I left some forty years ago. I find myself strangely in tune with the young writers of the searching for roots move-ment on the mainland, though I would define my own search for roots differently.

The word *exile* in Chinese is often associated with negative or pas-sive meanings—banishment as a form of punishment by government (*fangzhu, liufang*); seldom, if ever, does it connote the meaning of self-exile, or exile by voluntary choice as an act of protest by an individual. The closest equivalent in traditional China for voluntary self-exile is eremitism, or voluntary withdrawal from political service in order to maintain one's own integrity or for the more practical reason of sur-vival in times of great upheaval such as the change of dynasties. Often, however, an elegant way of seeking eremitism from the political center of power was, in fact, a return to one's home region, to indulge in such cultural pursuits as art, literature, and scholarship. This stance, partly inspired by Daoism, formed a counterpoint to the Confucian ethos of sociopolitical engagement. But it did not, in my opinion, constitute exile in all its implications of alienation and dislocation. In modern Chinese the phrase *liuwang*, literally "wandering in escape," comes perhaps closer to the dictionary definition of exile, prolonged separa-tion from one's country or home, as by force of circumstances. The phrase often refers to circumstances of war or famine, connoting almost the state of a refugee. In premodern China, in fact, given the Central Kingdom syndrome, it was all but unimaginable, even as punishment, to be exiled out of the country; rather, the faraway lands to which a criminal (and sometimes a guilty official) was banished were always on the peripheries of the nation's power center—for instance, Xinjiang in the northwest or Hainan Island in the far south. In post-1949 China, the well-known region of banishment was Beidahuang (literally, "the great northern wilderness") in Manchuria, where leading Party intellectuals who had been castigated as rightists, men and women like the writer Ding Ling, spent years doing hard labor under miserable physical conditions. With hindsight, one may even consider the movement to send youths "down to the countryside" during the Cultural Revolution as a collective form of banishment or internal exile.

In modern Chinese history, education abroad is a largely twentieth-century phenomenon. Waves of Chinese intellectuals first went to Japan at the turn of the century. They were followed by students seeking education in Europe and the United States in the early 1920s. By the end of the Second World War, the Chinese student population in the United States was sizable, their ranks soon being swelled by massive numbers of college graduates from Taiwan coming to pursue graduate education. This has been a well-documented, familiar story. Equally familiar, but not adequately analyzed, is the concomitant phenomenon of voluntary exile resulting from the majority of Chinese students choosing not to return to their home country. For an older generation of students abroad, this was certainly related to the watershed moment of 1949, when the triumph of the Communist Revolution and the establishment of the People's Republic presented them with a compelling choice. A great number, fired by patriotism, chose to return to serve the New China; even larger numbers chose, for one reason or another, to stay in their adopted country, in most cases, the United States. For younger generations of students from Taiwan, going abroad does not carry the same momentous trauma of choice. Still, it may entail other psychological consequences.

In an article written in English and published in 1976, the famed novelist from Taiwan Pai Hsien-yung (himself a self-exile now resident in America), characterizes such voluntary self-exiles as the "Wandering Chinese":

Deprived of his cultural heritage, the Wandering Chinese has become a spiritual exile: Taiwan and the motherland are incommensurable. He has to move on. Like Ulysses, he sets out on a journey across the ocean, but it is an endless journey, dark and without hope. The Rootless Man, therefore, is destined to become a perpetual wanderer. . . . The Chinese Wanderer yearns for the "lost kingdom," for the cultural inheritance that has been denied him. . . . He is a sad man. He is sad because he has been driven out of Eden, dispossessed, disinherited, a spiritual orphan, burdened with a memory that carries the weight of 5,000 years.[6]

These depressing remarks are partially triggered by Pai's reading of a novel by another writer, Yü Lihua, who first applied the then fashionable term, "rootless generation," to Chinese students, intellectuals, and professionals who had chosen to stay abroad. Yü's popular work, *Youjian zonglu (Again the Palm Trees)*, depicts such a person, a young professor who teaches elementary Chinese at an obscure American college (a Chinese version of *Pnin*, without the ironic touches of its master, Nabokov). The novel is a heavily sentimental account of his journey back to Taiwan, his "hunger for cultural identification," his incessant nostalgia for the lost mainland, and his final mental debacle, being unable to find spiritual anchorage in Taiwan. The journey exemplifies the familiar truism: You can't go home again.

Is the Wandering Chinese so spiritually dispossessed that he or she is utterly incapable of either rediscovering or (as the *xungen* writers have done) reinventing his roots? I may perhaps offer my own experience as a case study. When I first came to the United States as a graduate student some thirty years ago, the term exile never occurred to me, nor did the term émigré. The phrase which obsessed me during my first twenty years in the United States was *identity crisis*, defined, not only in Erikson's terms as a psychological stage of youth in the human life cycle, but also as a matter of culture. Instead of feeling culturally deprived, I was more concerned about a self-perceived "threat" from the other side: was I becoming too Americanized, thereby losing my Chinese identity? My psychological confusion stemmed from a deep-seated ambivalence (perhaps even more acute than that of most of my contemporaries) toward the established forms of Chinese cultural practice at that time—a structure of conventional ethics and wisdom in the name of Confucianism with which I became profoundly disenchanted. This antitraditional frame of mind, curiously reminiscent of the familiar ideological stance of the May Fourth Movement (which eventually became the subject of my first scholarly pursuit), made the other May Fourth position, total Westernization, a distinctly viable alternative to forge a new identity as my American sojourn became lengthened into permanent residence.

However, as the years went by and I came to middle age, I out-grew this identity confusion. I realized that my sense of being Chinese, though it has undergone several subtle ideological transformations, is so deeply rooted that it practically rules out the possibility of total Westernization. This has not led me to return to Chinese cultural con-servatism; I continue to find certain of the intellectual "temptations" from the West—particularly from Central and Eastern Europe—irre-sistible. Such a psychological state is by no means uncommon among exiled Chinese in the United States, but it has not been fully articu-lated as an issue *beyond* the parameters of what is known as Chinese-American ethnic or minority discourse. Simply put, I would call this stance Chinese cosmopolitanism—a loose epithet, but one that em-braces both a fundamental intellectual commitment to Chinese culture and a multicultural receptivity, which effectively cuts across all con-ventional national boundaries. It is, in other words, a purposefully marginal discourse, intended to recontextualize the margins.

My emotional affinity with the Wandering Chinese and the *xungen* writers lies, of course, in a shared self-perception of marginality, ex-cept that my marginality has a double edge vis-à-vis the centers of both China and America. On the peripheries of both countries, I feel com-pelled to engage actively in a dialogue with both cultures. Perhaps it was this perceived need for intellectual engagement that saved me from feeling totally "lost" between two continents, like the protagonist of *Again the Palm Trees.*

The one novel that most vividly dramatizes this double dialogue is Hualing Nieh's *Mulberry Green and Peach Red* (*Sangqing yu tao-hong,* translated into English as *Two Women of China*),[7] discussed by Pai Hsien-yung as providing an example of the Wandering Chi-nese syndrome. In this novel, written in high-modernist style, the two personas—divided selves—of the same protagonist address her dual marginal fate. As Peach Red narrates her recent journey as an exile in America in a series of letters to the American immigration officer, her former self, Mulberry Green, confronts a much larger historical ex-perience of modern China—her move from central China to Taiwan (and, as Peach Red, to America). This tortured double journey infuses the novel with tremendous psychological power. Its prevailing pathos comes from an author equally committed to—and troubled by—both cultures "from the margins." Through a purposeful schizophrenic split of the two contrasting personalities, the author has not only described a heightened case of identity confusion but has located a special angle from which to decipher—and in a way to deconstruct—the master narrative of modern Chinese history. In doing so, the novel gives new meaning to being a self-exiled Chinese on the peripheries.

In the double frame of the novel, it is precisely Peach Red's tormented and anxiety-ridden outcry about her exiled existence on the edge of American society that compels her alter ego, Mulberry Green, to encompass the entire historical span of her personal past. In other words, it is her newly acquired American side—and the need to explain why she is in America—that forces her Chinese side to be engaged in a search for meaning through her personal journey in Chinese history. That journey, in both geographical and symbolic terms, is also a journey of chaos and fragmentation in which the protagonist invariably finds herself escaping from an endangered center. The beginning of the novel—set in wartime China (1945)—finds Mulberry Green as a young girl of sixteen who has just escaped from home only to join up with a boat full of refugees fleeing from the Japanese. The second part has her trapped in and then escaping from the besieged city of Peking in 1949, before the impending entrance of the Communists. In the third part of the novel, the setting shifts to Taipei, a peripheral city in the eyes of mainland refugees that became the new political center of the evacuated Kuomintang in Taiwan. Here Mulberry Green, her husband, and her daughter are locked in an attic which, according to one critic, "is highly symbolic of the island itself."[8] In addition to suffering from claustrophobia and temporal disjunction, they are being hunted by the police on charges of embezzlement of government money.

Only after Mulberry Green reaches the end of her journey to the periphery as she arrives in America is she able to recall her past experience in China. At the same time she rejects this old "historical" self by assuming a new name and identity, Peach Red. The most harrowing part of the novel concerns the escapades of Peach Red as she is hunted down by the U.S. immigration officers. Her identity confusion takes the form of both schizophrenia and nymphomania as she sleeps her way from man to man across the continental United States. Her rejection of Mulberry Green, the Chinese side of herself, plunges her into a state of "moral and sexual anarchy" which, according to Pai Hsien-yung, may be also "representative of the macrocosmic disorder of an entire nation"—China.[9] Peach Red's fragmented psyche is a reflection of her own confusion as an exile and of the historical fragmentation of her past experiences in China. Pai considers the novel an allegorical tale because it evokes the fate of the prototypical Chinese exile who, as a Wandering Chinese, becomes "eternally terrified, eternally uncertain, eternally on the run," because "this physical uprooting means also the spiritual dislocation."[10]

Unlike Nieh's emotionally disturbed Peach Red, I now realize, after more than twenty years of identity confusion, that the journey of exile need not be utterly traumatic, dark, and without hope. On the contrary, it is only on this marginal ground that I feel psychologically *secure* and even culturally privileged. By virtue of my self-chosen marginality I can never fully identify myself with any center. Thus, I do not feel any compelling need to search for my roots. I believe that the aimless anguish of Peach Red stems from the anxiety of loss and an inability to anchor her new identity on the margins of American society and culture. The feeling of self-torment, perhaps representing the negative side of a bicultural marginal person, can be turned into a positive character strength. Hualing Nieh's most recent work—a large-scale historical romance entitled *Qianshan wai shui changliu* (*Beyond the Myriad Mountains Flows the River*), in which a young girl of an interracial marriage arrives in America in search of her American roots—presents a more affirmative tone that embraces the values of both cultures and replaces the nihilistic mood of *Two Women of China*. I would also argue that even the *xungen* writers' search for roots stems from a psychological need for an alternative center. To that extent, their discourse is still within reach of the center no matter how much they wish to embrace the culture of the peripheries. Total freedom from such a centrist orientation should be both the privilege and the prerogative of a truly "peripheral" writer, a literary exile who chooses to be "unbounded" by his or her homeland.

The fact of the matter is often to the contrary: exiled writers, within their own communities or ghettos in their adopted country, tend to reproduce narrow facsimiles of the same habits and ways of thinking that they brought from their homeland. According to Joseph Brodsky, the Soviet poet in exile, this signifies the exile writer's peculiar vanity to retain his past—a desperate wish not to be forgotten by the homeland. My attitude toward exile writers is perhaps more charitable because I

can easily understand the reasons for this misplaced obsession, especially among Chinese writers whose "obsession with China" has been
something of a moral burden.[11] It is an obsession that privileges China's
problems as uniquely Chinese, which lays absolute claim to the loyalty
of Chinese in all parts of the world. This omniscient nationalism, easily
capitalized upon by every Chinese government to legitimize itself at the
center, has so dominated the literary imaginations of modern Chinese
everywhere that it is virtually impossible to imagine a Joseph Brodsky
who writes in both his native language and the language of his adopted
country in order to create an art that transcends national boundaries.
When one thinks of some notable examples produced by Chinese exiles
in the United States in addition to Hualing Nieh and Yü Lihua—Pai
Hsien-yung's own collection of fiction, *Niuyue ke* (New Yorkers), and
the post–Cultural Revolution writings of Ch'en Jo-hsi, for instance—
emotional attachment to the homeland seems like an "unbroken chain."
In the last two or three years a new subgenre has crept into mainland
Chinese writing, following in the footsteps of exile writers from Taiwan: *liuxuesheng wenxue* (literature of Chinese students abroad), in
which both author and subject are in America but the language remains Chinese and the work is published in mainland Chinese journals.
Again the stories take place, as in real life, in the Chinese communities;
American culture and characters make only an occasional, peripheral
appearance.[12] Needless to say, the Chinese characters' obsessions continue to be with China.

This excessive obsession with their homeland has deprived Chinese
writers abroad of their rare privilege of being truly on the periphery.
In my view, only by being on the true periphery of China—that is,
overseas—can they hope to rise above it, because a true peripheral perspective affords them a distance sufficiently removed from the center
of the obsession so that they can subject the obsession itself to artistic treatment. This can be done by turning this perspective into a new
form of fantasy or mythology, as is the case in the work of the Jewish-
Polish writer Isaac Singer (who lived mostly in New York), or it can be
turned into a kind of philosophical, metafictional discourse, as Thomas
Mann did when he created his version of *Doktor Faustus* while an exile
in southern California. The most recent example would be the Indian-
English writer Salman Rushdie (now in hiding in England), whose controversial novel *The Satanic Verses* subjects an entire religious tradition

to an elaborate, postmodernist satire. The boundaries are again not so much geographical as intellectual and psychological.

III

These (somewhat idle and diverse) meditations on the meaning of being an exile have been triggered, ironically, by my association with a number of Chinese intellectuals and writers who left China partly as a result of the Tiananmen incident. In reflecting critically upon the cultural activities and discourses that they had initiated or helped to promote in China—including the search for roots movement—they were struck by a notable lack of peripheral thinking, because for several years they had been at the center of a cultural movement that exerted great impact on urban intellectual society. For all its implications of breaking up the Party's monolithic hold on creative culture, the movement has not entirely changed their "centrist" frame of mind—the elitist belief that they can ultimately influence the reformist leaders in the Party to their way of thinking.

No longer at the center of action (and in a sense the failure of the student demonstrations signaled the failure of hasty action), these writers are turning inward to matters of thought and psyche. They are beginning to reflect actively on the internal ravages caused by the Cultural Revolution—the impact of the Maoist revolution on their individual souls. They have invented a number of metaphors in order to describe a situation for which their old language seems inadequate. The hegemony of the "official talk" has created "a prison-house of a language" that has "subjugated the soul." After repeated political campaigns in which they were ordered to "surrender their hearts" (*jiaoxin*) to Chairman Mao and the Party, they have no heart left—they have almost no inner resources with which to fortify their sense of self and to justify their individual existences, much less their dignity as human beings. The first step toward a reconstruction of the self has led them to the writings of Václav Havel in order to reaffirm what Havel has called "human identity" and the individual will to "live in truth." In a way, the elitist agenda of the Chinese intellectuals offers a sharp contrast to Havel's nonelitist philosophy of "small-scale work" starting from the "everyday, thankless and never ending struggle of human beings to live more freely, truthfully and in quiet dignity."[13] Beginning from this mundane baseline, Havel's movement built up great momentum, which shook the entire Czech society and finally led his "Charter 77" group to power— a journey, so to speak, from the periphery to the center.

Havel's emphasis on everyday life derives from the post-Enlightenment tradition in the West that began to place a high premium on the quality of life defined within the axis of bourgeois marriage and family. Concomitant with it is the well-known valorization of individual privacy, which forms the precondition for what the Czech intellectuals would call internal exile—the voluntary act of individuals to keep a private mental space that is immune from the power influence of the state. But the mentality of internal exile embraces a more activist ethos than the negative freedom of the right to privacy: it is a state of mind created willfully by an individual to resist pressures from the outside. To that extent it becomes a value like freedom. Coming from a tradition in which voluntary self-exile hardly existed (except as eremitic withdrawal), my newly arrived colleagues from China were at first understandably baffled by the concept of internal exile. At the same time they found it appealing because, I suspect, it fills a certain psychological gap by suggesting an alternative form of individual resistance to a far stronger central power than that which Havel confronted. Internal exile does not mean physical banishment to the peripheries of the country but rather to turn inward—the construction of a sanctuary of the soul that stands in a peripheral position vis-à-vis the omnipotent center.

Is it possible, then, to internalize the *xungen* movement by conducting a search for the roots of Chinese culture in the abode of an exile's soul? In trying to answer this question, I am reminded of Josef Škvorecký, a self-exiled Czech writer now living in Canada who wrote about Bohemia in an article for a recent issue of *Dædalus*: "I love her soul, which is in her culture. And that is in exile with me. That is my loyalty. . . . That has always been the loyalty of exiles. Only tyrants stress geographical patriotism." [14] Škvorecký also quotes these lines from the nineteenth-century Slovak poet Jan Kollar:

> Do not give the holy name of homeland
> To the country where we live.
> The true homeland we carry in our hearts,
> And that cannot be oppressed or stolen from us. [15]

These words carry a timely resonance, not only to perennial self-exiles like myself but also to those Chinese intellectuals who left their homeland because of the Tiananmen massacre. For the first time, nation and state become separate entities in their minds: it is the Chinese nation, instead of the state, that remains the central object of their loyalty—their motherland. In this regard, their thinking corresponds closely with that of their fellow intellectuals inside China, and offers an amazing parallel to the situation of Central and Eastern European nations before 1989. In the memorable words of Leszek Kolakowski (an eminent self-exile from Poland), "the split between the State, which people feel is not theirs, though it claims to be their owner, and the motherland, of which they are guardians, has reduced them to an ambitious status of half-exiles." [16]

It is this new self-awareness of being "half-exiles" that has led Chinese intellectuals from the People's Republic to reexamine their current situation in an international context of cultural exile and cultural migration. Here they are confronted for the first time with the familiar twentieth-century phenomenon of the "intellectual in exile" which, according to Kolakowski, can indeed "boast an impressive spiritual pedigree" in the Western traditions. In fact, Kolakowski considers exile to be "the normal and inescapable lot of mankind on earth" and finds the myth of exile not only in the Judeo-Christian religious tradition but in all religions: "The fundamental message embedded in religious worship is: our home is elsewhere." [17] Echoing essentially the same view, the young Chinese scholar Liu Xiaofeng, now studying theology in Switzerland, published recently a learned article entitled "Exile Discourse and Ideology" (*Liuwang huayü yü yishixingtai*) in which he juxtaposes the "homeless discourse" of exile and the "homed discourse" of authoritarian regimes and finds that somehow in this century the former has been invariably associated with "the knowledge-value discourse called socialism." [18] Liu singles out, in particular, the year 1922, when the new Soviet regime suddenly arrested and then exiled some 120 leading Russian scholars, writers, and scientists, thus marking the first massive intellectual migration (followed by the exodus of Jewish and other European intellectuals to America during the Nazi era and that of the East Europeans in the 1950s and 1960s). The post-Tiananmen exodus of Chinese intellectuals seems to complete this twentieth-century picture.

It is widely known that the European intellectual migrations exerted a powerful cultural impact on the countries of their resettlement. At the same time, a reverse impact—that of the diasporas on the homeland—has also taken place, especially when mutual communication is possible (such as between Jewish communities abroad and in Israel). Even in the case of East European countries before 1989, outside émigrés had always maintained contact with semiexiles inside through underground or unofficial channels to help create a powerful counterculture opposed to official ideology. Since 1989 many exiles have returned to assume key government positions or otherwise participate in the political transformation from the post-totalitarian systems to democracy. But the phenomenon of Chinese intellectuals' migration and its possible contribution to both the homeland and their adopted country is somewhat more complicated by the existence since 1949 of two rival regimes in two separate territories. Contending loyalties have tended to splinter overseas Chinese populations. It is only during the most recent decade, as mainland China and Taiwan resumed unofficial contact and Hong Kong emerged as an intermediary zone with a pressing future (its formal "return to the motherland" in 1997), that a different configuration of relations—and a different perspective on the problem of center and periphery—has become possible.

IV

In his classic essay titled "Center and Periphery," Edward Shils defined the center not as a spatial location but as a central zone of symbols, values, and beliefs that govern a society.[19]

The existence of a central value system rests, in a fundamental way, on the need which human beings have for incorporating into something which transcends and transfigures their concrete individual existence. They have a need to be in contact with symbols of an order which is larger in its dimensions than their own bodies and more central in the ultimate structure of reality than is their routine everyday life.[20]

It would seem that this consensus model has the opposite implication when compared with Havel's ideas, and the symbols of a larger order could easily be construed as ideology, which Havel calls "a specious way of relating to the world. . . . As the repository of something 'supra-personal' and objective, it enables people to deceive their conscience and conceal their true position and their inglorious modus vivendi, both from the world and from themselves."[21] However, Shils's set of values corresponds to ideology only in Mannheim's sense; he is careful to differentiate his concept from the specious and "super-transcendent" ideologies (utopias in Mannheim's formulation) "which are explicit, articulated, and hostile to the existing order" such as Bolshevism, National Socialism, and Fascism.[22] Thus, it would seem that they are in basic agreement about the utopian excesses of ideology—in Havel's case, of an ideology in the service of a post-totalitarian system. Both men stress the need of human individuals to be "in personal communion" with one another once they have "reached a certain level of individuation."[23]

Still, in a fundamental way, the consensus model—which emphasizes the necessity of an established center and (despite tensions) its beneficial incorporation of either rebellious individuals or the mass population on the peripheries of a society through the process of modernization—remains suspect. Havel has vividly described the frightening, anonymous power of the inhuman automatized systems found in both post-totalitarian and capitalist countries. In the case of post-Tiananmen China, the political scene clearly manifests the symptoms of an emergent post-totalitarian system in which control no longer comes from charisma (Maoism, for example) but from a central authority wielding anonymous power. What is to be done—even for those who, as Shils perceptively puts it, "have a very intense and active connection with the center, with the symbols of the central value system, but whose connection is passionately negative"?[24] The *xungen* writers have offered one alternative solution, by reinventing new centers on the peripheries. But even this reinvention has already split open the Maoist model of a popular consensus: it has "relativized" the significance of one center and paved the way for cultural pluralism.

In fact, the statement by Han Shaogong, one of the leading *xungen* writers, already intimated such a pluralism. He has argued that the orthodox Han-Chinese culture is merely a dead "crust" resting on the "hot and turbulent" seedbed of a mixture of several unorthodox ethnic cultures, and it can only be revitalized if it is able to absorb the magma of these unorthodox cultures.[25] In Han's view the search for roots is not a search for lost purity but rather an attempt to uncover the vital pluralism of this cultural hybrid. To rephrase Han's point further, it is clear that in Chinese history orthodoxy is to be found in the center, whereas heterodoxy is to be found in the peripheries.

To render Han's argument in a different way, it celebrates the un-orthodox cosmopolitanism that he has found in China's cultural past and contrasts it with the monolithic orthodoxy of present-day Chinese culture. The argument is not novel—the culture of the Tang dynasty comes readily to mind as a shining example of ancient cosmopolitan-ism. But its relevance to the contemporary world increases when the boundaries of the periphery extend to areas beyond the China coast. The prosperity of the Four Dragons may be used as an argument for the continuing influence of Confucianism. But I would rather see it as a continuation of a littoral vitality begun in the early nineteenth century, when new initiatives often originated from coastal reformers (with a mixed cultural background such as the journalist-entrepreneur Wang Tao), which then became legitimized as policy by the hinterland center.[26] In the late twentieth century, this littoral zone has expanded to include two powerful new centers, Taiwan and Hong Kong, whose economic supremacy over the mainland is also changing the cultural map of China. What Tu Wei-ming conceptualizes as the three Chinese cultural "universes"[27] makes increasing sense as the old national argu-ment, based on territorial and ideological grounds, of a single China represented by a single government gradually loses its relevance. With increased influence from such central littoral regions, it is not unlikely that the more prosperous parts of China—the coastal cities on the lower Yangtze River and in the provinces of Fujian and Guangdong—will become part of the economic system dominated by Hong Kong and Taiwan. At the same time, what is known as the Pacific Rim has become increasingly internationalized as a large region of intermingling econo-mies and cultures—both ancient and modern, Asian and Western. In this transnational and cosmopolitan framework, the old spatial matrix of center and periphery no longer has much validity. Even the notions of exile will have to be redefined. As we cast our gaze across the Pacific Ocean toward the future, perhaps Chinese of all regions and communi-ties may take comfort in the vision that their boundaries will no longer close them off but instead crisscross each other to form interlocking networks in which there is no single center.

A REFLECTION ON MARGINALITY

To define Chinese identity is a very difficult task. The Japanese have a clear ethnic identity. The Jewish people have been held together by the Judaic faith and the concept of being a chosen people. Americans, as people of a new nation, have developed an identity anchored upon the political faith of a constitutional republic. For most of Chinese history the Chinese were held together by their culture. In this century nationalism has also become a unifying force for the Chinese. Seldom, however, does a Chinese clearly define China as a nation or as a culture.

After two and one-half days of discussion, those who had gathered at the East-West Center to discuss the meaning of being Chinese realized that the only relevant criterion of identity is the self-identity perceived by a person. The bottom line of self-identity is the recognition of one's membership in a collective entity. The Japanese term *kyodotai*, which means an entity shared by its membership, is probably the best description of a collective body in which a person decides to participate. It is not until a person leaves the *kyodotai* that self-identity becomes a problem. Many Chinese began to be aware of their Chinese identity only after leaving China to live overseas where they were often treated as aliens by the indigenous population of their host country. Such bitter rejection trained Chinese to view non-Chinese with distrust and suspicion and only strengthened their own sense of connection with China and other Chinese. In many cases, they tended to insist upon their Chinese identity even more strongly than Chinese in China.

When discussing Chinese identity, more thought should be given to the concept of the marginality of self-identity. Marginality can be defined as one's own ambiguous status of belonging simultaneously to more than one collective entity. For either of these entities, the identity is incomplete. The term *marginal man* has been coined by anthropologists partly because anthropologists are in a field of investigation that makes them dependent upon the assistance of some informant who knows both the native culture and the vocabulary of the investigator. Very soon, however, the anthropologist will also become a marginal person, if he or she has successfully penetrated and participated in the life of the investigated. Chinese intellectuals are also mostly marginal personalities. Whether in China or abroad, they are often among the few Chinese who have exposed themselves to both Chinese and foreign (especially Western) cultures. Many feel they have to play the combined roles of informant and anthropologist; they must bear the responsibility of explaining and interpreting to each side the ideas and mentality of the other. By the same token, scholars of Chinese studies, whatever their original ethnic identity, should be regarded as marginal personalities who belong simultaneously to both the Chinese cultural world and their own heritage.

Marginality is closely related to the dichotomy of a center and its peripheries. A center and its peripheries need not be viewed as contradiction and confrontation; they are merely relative positions on a continuum. The center, be it geographic, geopolitical, social-economic, or even cultural-ideological, possesses a gravitational force which pulls from the peripheries whatever elements are scattered therein. The continuous centripetal attraction leads to an increase in the size and the mass of the center, eventually incorporating the peripheries completely to form a new, bigger center with an even more powerful gravitational force. This force, in turn, causes the formation of new spheres of peripheries by influencing elements and resources scattered around it. The relationship between a center and its peripheries, their relative bifurcation, is always temporary, always transitional.

The entire process can be envisioned as a tree-like pattern radiating from the center; adding to itself direct linkages between and among the branches, thereby increasing the density and intricacy of its network. Niches and gaps, places containing foreign elements, are gradually filled by the system, although these new components may still be alien to the original center. The final product is a solid body, a new and stronger center, which begins its own tree pattern by creating new peripheries and subsequently incorporating them into the system.

In human history, the growth and expansion of cultures can be explained by applying such an evolutionary (or expansionary) model. Chinese culture began its development in a small area in North China; it expanded to include much of North China, China proper, and then all of China. Those peripheral cultures were one after another merged into and absorbed by the continuously expanding Chinese cultural sphere. The Western world has experienced a similar process; it started on a small peninsula of Greece, expanded to the Mediterranean, then to the Atlantic, and now its gravitational forces are felt everywhere on the globe.

Along such an evolutionary process there are two noteworthy phenomena. One is that the center of the system may shift from one locality, one area, or one region to another. Former peripheries often became new centers in the expanded system. The second phenomenon is the significance of marginality that juxtaposes the two systems. As adjacent tree patterns grow into the sphere of the other, the juxtaposed areas that were formerly marginal acquire the crucial status of having a network that links both systems. The role of Philadelphia in the forming of the United States illustrates the geopolitical significance of a new center that held the New England states and the southern states together. In the intellectual history of China, neo-Confucianism emerged in the marginality of both Confucianism and Sinicized Buddhism.

If this evolutionary model is applied to Chinese culture today, it becomes apparent that there is now a wonderful opportunity for intellectuals to develop a new center, a new system that embraces both the Chinese and the Western worlds. Such a system will be one of several peripheries to the center of mainstream global culture. It will be a marginality which not only has the potential to influence the very nature of both old systems (the Chinese and the Western) but that of the entire world.

Cho-yun Hsu

Reference Matter

Glossary

Term	Characters 漢字	English equivalent, notes
Ah Q	阿Q	main character in Lu Xun's story
Amoy	廈門	Xiamen City, Fujian Province
At Middle Age	人到中年	
Ba Jin	巴金	20th century Chinese writer, b. 1904
baba	峇峇 (a Malay word)	"Straits (Malay) born"
baba-peranakans	(a Malay word)	locally born Chinese
Bai	白	the Bai people, ethnic group
Bai Fengxi	白峰溪	
Bai Hua	白樺	contemporary Mainland Chinese writer
baihua	白話	vernacular speech
Bei Dao	北島	contemporary Chinese poet
Beidahuang	北大荒	the Great Northern Wilderness (northeast China)
Beijing	北京	capital of China (lit., northern capital)
Beijing Daxue chuban she	北京大學出版社	Beijing University Press
Beijing Daxue you pai fenzi fandong yanlun huiji	北京大學右派分子反動言論彙集	*Collection of Speeches and Writings by Beijing University's Rightist Reactionary Elements*

In this volume, ethno-linguistic dialects of vernacular Chinese have been rendered by several different romanization systems, in part out of respect for the preferences of individual authors.

Chinese and Japanese characters (Hanzi 漢字) and brief explanatory notes in this glossary are intended to clarify and standardize. The list of terms was compiled by David S. K. Chu (朱小康), Tu Wei-ming (杜維明), and Wang Penglin (王鵬林), with the cooperation of some of the authors. Multi-lingual word processing was done in Microsoft Word 5.1 and Apple Chinese Language Kit for the Macintosh.

Beiping (Peiping)	北平	name for Beijing, 1927–1949, when Nanjing was the Republican capital
Bianzheng gonglun	邊政公論	*Frontier Affairs Review*
bun tong	半統 (bantong)	half-caste, mixed race
Butterfly, The	蝴蝶	
"Buyao pa wusi"	"不要怕五四"	"fear not May Fourth (1919)"
Call of the Great Northern Wilds (Wilderness), The	北大荒的召喚	
Cao Rulin	曹汝霖	Chinese foreign minister attacked by students of the May 4th Movement, 1919
ch'eng	誠	affection
Ch'ing	(see Qing)	
ch'un	群	group(s)
Chan	禪	new Buddhism
Chao-chou	(see Chaozhou)	
Chaozhou	潮州	district of Guangdong Province
Chen Chi-nan	陳其南	
Chen Duxiu	陳獨秀	first generation Communist leader
Chen Kaige	陳凱歌	contemporary Mainland movie director
Chen Ruiqing	陳瑞晴	
Chen Yizi	陳一咨	former assistant to ex-Premier and Party General Secretary Zhao Ziyang; in exile
Chen, Jack	陳依範	writer of Chinese-Trinidad descent
Cheng-hsueh chu i	政學芻議	*Comments on Political Issues*
Chengdu	成都	capital of Sichuan Province
chi	己	self
Chi-cheng T'u-shu Kung-ssu	集成圖書公司	Jicheng Publishing Company
chia	家 (jia)	family
Chiang Ching-kuo	蔣經國	son of Chiang Kai-shek; the late ruler of Taiwan
Chiang Kai-shek	蔣介石	Nationalist Chinese leader, d. 1975
chiao	橋 (qiao)	bridge
chiao	僑 (qiao)	sojourner, a person living abroad
Chiao, Chien	喬健	anthropology professor, Chinese University of Hong Kong
chin tong	正唐 (zheng tang)	pure Tang people
Chin, Frank	趙健秀	contemporary Chinese-American playwright, actor
Ching, Frank	秦家聰	contemporary Chinese-American journalist, writer
chixin baoguo	赤心報國	to serve one's country loyally
chongzhen wusi jingshen	重振五四精神	rekindle the spirit of May Fourth (1919)
Chou	(see Zhou)	
Chow Tse-tsung	周策縱	professor of Chinese studies, University of Wisconsin
Chu	楚	an ancient name for Hubei Province
Chu Hsi	朱熹 (Zhu Xi)	Confucian Chinese thinker, 1130–1200

Chu, Godwin C.	朱謙	a senior fellow, East-West Center
Chuang Ying-chang	莊英章	
chucai jinyong	楚才晉用	"brain drain"
chuguo bing	出國病	disease of going abroad
chuguo chao	出國潮	tide of going abroad
chuguo re	出國熱	fad, fever of going abroad
chung chien jen	中間人	middle man; broker; intermediary person
Chung-kuo che-hsueh shih ta-kang	中國哲學史大綱	*An Outline of the History of Chinese Philosophy*
Chung-kuo wen-hua yao-i	中國文化要義	*The Essential Features of Chinese Culture*
Chung-Ni	仲尼 (Zhongni)	another name for Confucius
Confucius	孔夫子 (Kongfuzi)	Confucius
Da Qiu Zhuang	大邱莊	a village near Tianjin Municipality
da guanhua	大官話	big-official language, speech, airs
Dai Qing	戴晴	writer-journalist formerly at *Guangming Daily*, Beijing
Dali	大理	a district of Yunnan Province
dangjia	當家	the family manager
danwei	單位	work unit (in the PRC)
Deng Xiaoping	鄧小平	paramount Chinese leader since 1978, b. 1904
Di	狄	western barbarians
Diaoyutai	釣魚台	off-shore islands in South China Sea
Ding Ling	丁玲	Communist woman writer, 1904–1986
Du Fu	杜甫 (Tu Fu)	Tang Dynasty "sage-poet," 712–770
"Dui dangzhi ji danghua jiaoyu de pipan"	對黨制及黨化教育的批判	"Criticism of Party Rule and Party Education"
Er-hai	洱海	a lake in Yunnan Province
Ershiyi Shiji	二十一世紀	*Twenty-First Century* (a Hong Kong magazine)
Everlasting Spring	永遠是春天	
Ex-Wife, The	前妻	
fangzhu	放逐	send into exile, banish
Fei Hsiao-t'ung	費孝通 (Fei Xiaotong)	social anthropologist, b. 1910
fen lei	分類	classification; categorizaton; similar to the concept of attribute
fen-hsiang	分香	to divide incense
fengjian mixin	封建迷信	feudal superstition
fenjia	分家	family division
Fu-chou	(see Fuzhou)	
Funeral, The	葬禮	
Funü fanshen ge	婦女翻身歌	*Song of Women's Emancipation*
fuqiang	富強	prosperous and strong; national wealth and power
Furxi	伏羲	

Gan of Bii	比干	loyal minister of the Shang dynasty
gen	根	roots
genshen yemao	根深葉茂	to have deep roots and luxuriant leaves
genwai zhuifei	根外追肥	foliage dressing
Gift Offering to the Bureau Chief, A	給局長送禮	
Girls' Dorm, The (Co-eds' Dorm, The)	女大學生宿舍	
gongshi	共識	common awareness, shared concerns
gongsuo	公所	social institution
Gu Hongming	辜鴻銘	Chinese poet
Guan Yu	關羽	a general in the *Romance of the Three Kingdoms*, deified as god of war
guan-xi	(see guanxi)	
Guangdong	廣東	southern coastal province adjacent to Hong Kong
Guangxi	廣西	southern Chinese province (and Zhuang Autonomous Region)
Guangxu	光緒	Qing dynasty emperor, reigned 1875–1908
guanhua	官話	official language
guanxi	關係	personal connections, network
guiqiao	歸僑	returned overseas Chinese
Guiqulai	歸去來	*Homecoming*
Guizhou	貴州	a province in southwestern China
guojia	國家	the state, nation, country
Guomindang	國民黨 (Kuomingtang, KMT)	Nationalist Party
guominxing	國民性	national character
Hahn	(see Han)	
Haiwai Zhonghua	海外中華	Overseas China, Overseas Chinese communities
Hakka	客家 (Kejia)	Guest People; an ethnic group in south China
Half of Man Is Woman	男人的一半是女人	
Han	漢	ethnic Chinese; Chinese Dynasty (206 B.C.–A.D. 220)
Han Jinchun	韓錦春	
Han Shaogong	韓少功	contemporary Mainland Chinese writer
Hang Ying	航鷹	
Hanjen ti chia tsu chih: shi lun "yu kuan-hsi, wu tsu chih" ti she hui	漢人的家族制: 試論"有關係, 無組織"的社會	*The Lineage System of the Han People: Preliminary Discussion on a Society of "Connections without Organization"*
Hanren	漢人	Chinese person, people
"Hanwen 'minzu' yi ci de chuxian ji qi chuqi shiyong qingkuang"	漢文民族一詞的出現 及其初期使用情況	"The emergence of the term 'minzu' in Han (Chinese) language and usage"

Hanzi	漢字	Chinese script, characters
hao hsiung ti ming suan chang	好兄弟明算賬	among good brothers, neat accounts are a must
He Shang	河殤	*River Elegy* (1988 TV documentary series)
Heilongjiang	黑龍江	province in northeastern China
Herland (Distant Herland, A)	遠方有個女兒國	
Hokkien	福建 (Fujian)	Fujian dialect, people
Hongfan Shudian	洪範書店	name of bookstore in Taipei
Hsia, C. T.	夏志清	professor, Columbia University
Hsiang-tu chung-kuo	鄉土中國	*Peasant China*
Hsiao, Hsin-Huang	蕭新煌	contemporary Taiwan sociologist, Academia Sinica
Hsien ch'ieh tuan chung jih she hui chi kou yen chiu ti chien t'ao: tai wan yen chiu ti i hsieh chi shi	現階段中日社會結構研究的檢討：台灣研究的一些啟示	*An Examination of Research on the Present Stage of Social Structures of China and Japan: Some Revelations from Taiwan Studies*
hsin	信	sincerity
hsu	序	order
Hsu, Cho-yun	許倬雲	professor history and sociology, University of Pittsburgh
Hsu, Francis L. K.	許烺光	Chinese-American scholar, former president of American Anthropological Association
Hu	胡	
Hu Nai-an	胡耐安	
Hu Shi (Hu Shih)	胡適	leading Chinese intellectual, liberal, 1891–1962
Hu Shih	(see Hu Shi)	
Hua	華	China, Chinese
Hua Xia	華夏	China, Cathay
Huachiao	(see huaqiao)	
Huaqiao	華僑	Chinese sojourners; overseas Chinese
Huaqiao Bangong Shi	華僑辦公室	The Overseas Chinese Affairs Office
Huaren	華人	ethnic Chinese
Huaxia	(see Hua Xia)	
Huayan	華嚴	a major school in Chinese Buddhism
Huayi	華裔	foreign citizen(s) of Chinese descent (to the PRC)
Hui	回	an ethnic minority, Sinicized Muslims
huiguan	會館	district associations; provincial or county guilds
Hunan	湖南	province in southcentral China
Hunan renmin chubanshe	湖南人民出版社	Hunan People's Press
Hwang, Henry David	黃哲倫	contemporary Chinese-American playwright
Hwang, K. K.	黃光國	psychologist at National Taiwan University
i	義	righteousness

Jejiang	浙江 (Zhejiang)	province on east coast of China
Jen tsi kuan-hsi chung jen ch'ing chih fen hsi	人際關係中人情之分析 (see jen ch'ing)	*An Analysis of Renqing in Personal Relationships*
Jen yao ch'ih chien	人妖之間	*Between Human and Demon*
jen	仁	benevolence
jen-ch'ing	人情 (renqing)	human feelings, sensibilities, obligation
jen-ch'ing wang	人情網	web of human obligations
Jiang Tingfu	蔣廷黻	diplomat-scholar, 1895–1968
Jiang Zilong	蔣子龍 (Chiang Tsi-Lung)	Chinese writer
Jiang, P. L.	江炳倫	
Jiangsu	江蘇	eastern coastal province
jiaoxin	交心	to surrender the hearts
jiaxiang	家鄉	native place, home town
jiazhang	家長	family or household head
Jihng hua yuarn	鏡花緣	*The Destinies of the Flowers in the Mirror*
Jin	金	Jurchen dynasty, 1115–1234
jiuguo	救國	to save the country
Jiushi niandai	九十年代	*The Ninties* (a Hong Kong monthly)
Ju	儒 (ru)	Confucian scholar, Confucian humanism
Ju Yanan	居延安	Mainland Chinese scholar
Jurchen	女真	the predecessor of Manchu
kan-ch'ing	感情	interpersonal feelings, emotion, affection
Kang	康	
Kang Youwei	康有為	Chinese thinker and reformer, 1857–1927
Kanji	漢字 (see Hanzi)	Japanese script based on Chinese
keai	可愛	lovable
Khitan	契丹 (Kitan)	a Mongolian tribe
King, Ambrose Yeo-chi	金耀基	sociology professor, administrator, Chinese University of Hong Kong
Kingston, Maxine Hong	湯婷婷	contemporary Chinese-American writer
ko-jen pen-wei	個人本位	individual based
Ku Hung-ming	(see Gu Hongming)	
Kuan-ch'a She	觀察社	Observation Society
Kuan-hsi chu i	關係芻議	preliminary discussion on kuan-hsi
kuan-hsi	(see guanxi)	
kuan-hsi hsüeh	關係學	"relationology"
kuan-hsi pen-wei	關係本位	relation based
kuan-hsi wang	關係網	web of personal networks
Kuan-hsi: dang dai zhong guo de she hui xing tai	關係: 當代中國的社會形態	*Kuan-hsi: The Social Mode of Behavior in Contemporary China*
Kunming	昆明	capital of Yunnan Province
Kuomingtang	(see Guomindang)	

la	拉	to make, pull, get (guanxi)
Lai, Chuen-yan	黎全恩	sociologist, Chinese University of Hong Kong and University of Victoria
Lai, Him Mark	麥禮謙	Chinese-American historian
Lee, Leo Ou-fan	李歐梵	professor of Chinese literature, U.C. Los Angeles
Lei Zhen	雷震	Taiwan writer
Li Dazhao	李大釗	first generation Communist leader
Li Ying	李英	
li	理	propriety
li	禮	ritual
Li, Jiequan	李傑泉	
Li, Victor Hao	李浩	legal scholar; former president, East-West Center
Liang Qichao	梁啟超 (Liang Chi-chao)	Chinese thinker and reformer, 1873–1929
Liang Sou-ming	梁漱溟 (Liang Shuming)	philosopher and rural reformer, 1893–1988
Liang Tee Tue	(see Liang Qichao)	
Liao	遼	Kitan dynasty (916–1125)
Lih of Chern	陳氏厲公	Duke of Li of Chen in the *Spring and Autumn Annals*
Lii Rurzhen	李汝珍	Chinese writer during the Qing Dynasty
Lin Biao	林彪	Communist military leader, Mao Zedong's designated successor; d. 1971
Lin Yu-sheng	林毓生	professor of Chinese history, University of Wisconsin
Lin Zexu	林則徐	Chinese statesman of Opium War fame
Lirn	林(烈)	a character in the *Flowers in the Mirror*
Liu Bin Yin	(see Liu Binyan)	
Liu Binyan	劉賓雁	contemporary Mainland investigative reporter; exiled
Liu Gang	劉剛	
Liu Jisheng	劉濟生	
Liu Kwang-ching (K. C.)	劉廣京	emeritus professor of Chinese history, U.C. Davis
Liu Pin-yen	(see Liu Binyan)	
Liu Xiaofeng	劉小楓	
Liu Zaifu	劉再復	contemporary Mainland Chinese literary critic
liufang	流放	send into exile, banish
Liuwang huayu yu yishixingtai	流亡話語與意識形態	*Exile Discourse and Ideology*
liuwang	流亡	go into exile, exiled
liuxue jiuguo	留學救國	to save country by study abroad
liuxuesheng	留學生	Chinese students in foreign countries
liuxuesheng wenxue	留學生文學	literature of or by Chinese students abroad

Lo Huimin	羅彗民	
loufan	老番 (laofan)	barbarians; Caucasians
Lowe, Paidee	劉裔昌	author of *Father and Glorious Descendant*
Lu Hsün	(see Lu Xun)	
Lu Wenting	陸文婷	
Lu Xing'er	陸星兒	
Lu Xun	魯迅	Chinese writer, 1881–1936
Lu-chou Ch'u-pan-she	綠洲出版社	Luzhou Publishing House
Luk Tak-chuen	陸德椿	lecturer, Hong Kong Baptist College
Lukang	鹿港	
"Lun biandi hanren ji qi yu bianjiang jianshe zhi guanxi"	論邊地漢人及其 與邊疆建設之關係	"On the Relationship between Frontier Han Chinese and the Development of Frontier Land"
lun	倫	order
luodi shenggen	落地生根	falling to the ground and striking root
luoye guigen	落葉歸根	the Chinese abroad as fallen leaves that must return to their roots in the soil of China
Ma	馬	a prominent merchant family in Sydney
Ma Huan	馬歡	Chinese historian who accompanied Cheng He on maritime expedition, 15th century
Man	滿	the Manchu people, ethnic group
Man	蠻	the southern barbarians
Manchu	滿洲	Manchuria
Mao Zishui	毛子水	scholar of Chinese literature, National Taiwan University
Marxist Old Lady (Old Lady Marxism)	馬列主義老太太	
Mazu	媽祖, 馬祖 (Ma-Tsu)	goddess of the sea worshipped in south China coast and Taiwan; off-shore islands opposite Taiwan
Meiji	明治	lit., enlightened rule; period of reign of Japanese Emperor Mutsuhito, 1868–1912
Meilan	美蘭	
Meng	蒙	the Mongols
Miao-Yao	苗瑤	the Miao-Yao peoples, ethnic groups
Mien, ch'ih yu chung kuɔ jen hsing wei chih fen hsi	面，恥與中國人行 為之分析	*Analysis of Face, Shame, and Behavior of the Chinese*
mien-tsu	面子	face, reputation
Min Chia	(see Minjia)	
min	民	(the) common people
Ming	明	Ming Dynasty, 1368–1644
Mingbao yuekan	明報月刊	*Mingbao Monthly* (Hong Kong)
Mingli lun	名理論	*Discourse on Logic*

Minjia	民家	the civilians; old name for the Bai people
Minzhu Zhongguo	民主中國	*Democratic China* (a dissident magazine published in North America)
Minzu yanjiu	民族研究	*Nationality Studies* (journal)
minzu	民族	nationality, ethnic group
Mirng	(see Ming)	
Morning in Shanghai	上海的早晨	
Naihe	奈河	a river in the underworld
Nan Chao	(see Nanzhao)	
Nanjing	南京	a city in Jiangsu Province
Nanyang	南洋	South Seas, i.e., Chinese term for Southeast Asia
Nanzhao	南詔	ancient kingdom in today's southwest China
ngo de jonggokyan	我地中國人	we overseas Chinese (Cantonese dialect)
ngo de wuakiu	我地華僑	we Chinese nationals
Nieh Hualing	聶華苓	Chinese-American writer, former co-director of Writers Workshop, Iowa
Niuyue ke	紐約客	New Yorkers
No! ("*NO!*")	″不！″	
Old Lady Meng	孟仙姑	
Old Man Zhang	老張頭	*Laozhangtou*
Ouxiang puohuai lun	偶像破坏論	*On Iconoclasm*
ouxiang puohuai	偶像破坏	idol smashing
Pai Hsien-yung	白先勇	Taiwan Chinese writer
Pan Kuang-tan	潘光旦 (Pan Guangdan)	Mainland Chinese sociologist and eugenicist, 1899–1967
pangen cuojie	盤根錯結	tangled roots and twisted branches
Panyu	番禺	district of Guangdong Province
pao	報	newspaper
Pao-sheng Ta-li	保生大力	
Park Chun Hee	朴正熙	South Korean leader
Park, Robert	帕克	American sociologist, 1864–1944
Peking	(see Beijing)	
People's Daily	人民日報 (*Renmin ribao*)	official Communist Chinese daily
peranakan	(a Malay word)	native-born Chinese who lost their mother tongue but maintained some Chinese cultural characteristics
pieh	別	differentiation, distinction
Pingtung	屏東	a city in Taiwan
pinyin	拼音 (Hanyu pinyin)	Mainland Chinese romanization system, adopted internationally
po-te-hi	布袋戲 (butaixi)	glove puppet theater
pu shih ch'i lun	不失其倫	Every role relation is properly in order
Pudong	浦東	district of Shanghai Municiipality

qi guan yan	氣管炎	tracheitis (a pun on item below)
qi guan yan	妻管嚴	a wife controls (her husband) strictly (a pun on item above)
Qian Gechuan	錢歌川	professor of English literature in Taiwan
Qian Xuantong	錢玄同	Chinese philologist
Qianshan wai shui changliu	千山外水長流	*Beyond the Myriad Mountains Flows the River*
Qiaowu Weiyuan Hui	僑務委員會	The Overseas Chinese Affairs Commission
qiaowu zhengce	僑務政策	policy toward overseas Chinese
Qin Bo	秦波	
Qing	清	Manchu dynasty, 1644–1911
Qingming	清明	memorial festival in the spring (Grave Sweeping)
Qingpu	清浦	a district of Shanghai Municipality
qiugu	求古	in search of antiquity
rencai wailiu	人才外流	talent outflow, "brain drain"
Renmin chuban she	人民出版社	People's Publishing House
Renmin wenxue	人民文學	*People's Literature*
renmin	人民	the people
Rong	戎	the northern barbarians
sa dai sheng ba	三代成峇	in three generations a Chinese will become a baba
Sangqing yu taohong	桑青與桃紅	*Mulberry Green and Peach Red*
Shaanxi	陝西	province in northwestern China
Shandong	山東	province in eastern China
Shang	商	historical dynasty, c. 16th century– 11th century B.C.
Shanghai	上海	most populous municipality, east coast of China
shangwu	商務	commerce, commercial
She	畬	the She people, ethnic minority
she-hui pen-wei	社會本位	society based
Shehui Kexue chuban she	社會科學出版社	Social Sciences Publishing House
Shenzhen	深圳	special economic zone in Guangdong
shenzhou	神州	divine country, China
shidafu	士大夫	scholar-officials
shigen qunzu	失根群族	"wandering intellectuals" away from their roots
Shijie jingji daobao	世界經濟導報	*World Economic Herald* (Shanghai)
Shijie Ribao	世界日報	*World Journal* (U.S. daily in Chinese)
shu	恕	reciprocity
shu huan shu, lu huan lu	數還數，路還路	money is money; kuan-hsi is kuan-hsi
Si Maqian	司馬遷	the "Grand Historian" of China, d. 85 B.C.
Sichuan	四川	province in southwestern China, most populous

Singapore	新加坡	city-state in southeast Asia with majority Chinese population
sinke	新客 (xinke)	new arrivals
sinkheh	(see sinke)	
Su Huih	蘇蕙	creator of an ingenious poetic diagram
Su Xiaokang	蘇曉康	co-author of *River Elegy*; in exile
Suigan lu sanshiba	隨感錄三十八	*Random Thoughts Number Thirty-Eight*
Sun Jingxuan	孫靜軒	
Sun Yat-sen	孫逸仙 (孫中山)	founder of the Chinese Republic, d. 1924
sung ko jen-ch'ing	送個人情	to give a human obligation, send gifts
t'a chi wo i ko jen-ch'ing	他給我一個人情	he gave me a human obligation; he did me a favor
t'a pu shih jen	他不是人	he/she is not jen (human)
T'ien Hou	天后	Empress of Heaven
Ta Li	(see Dali)	
ta ch'ien wo i ko jen-ch'ing	他欠我一個人情	He owes me a human obligation, favor
Ta-hsueh	大學 (Daxue)	*The Great Learning*
Tai, Jeanne	戴靜	American freelance writer and translator, of Hong Kong Chinese descent
Taipei	台北	capital of Taiwan
Taiping	太平	great peace, peaceful
Tairwan	(see Taiwan)	
Taishan	台山	district of Guangdong
Taiwan	台灣	island province across from southeast China; a.k.a. Formosa
Tan, Amy	譚恩美	Chinese-American author
Tang	唐	Tang dynasty (618–907); China
Tangren	唐人	Chinese persons
tanwei (danwei)	(see danwei)	
Tao Yuanming	陶淵明	Chinese poet
Tarng	(see Tang)	
Teochew	(see Chaozhou)	
Tiananmen	天安門	Gate of Heavenly Peace in Beijing
Tiantai	天台	a major school in Chinese Buddhism
Tiarn	天 (tian)	heaven
tien-hsia i-chia	天下一家	all the world belongs to one family
Tirngtirng	亭亭	a character in the *Flowers in the Mirror*
Tongjan (Cantonese)	(see Tangren)	
totok	(a Malay word)	unassimilated Chinese migrants
ts'a-hsu	差序	differentiated and graded relations
Ts'ung chia chih hsi t'ung k'an chung kuo wen hua ti hsien tai i i	從價值系統看中國文化的現代意義	the modern meaning of the Chinese culture as viewed from its value systems
Tsai, Shih-shan Henry	蔡石山	scholar of Chinese-American studies in the U. S.

Tseng, Wen-shing	曾文星	psychology professor, University of Hawaii
Tso, King K.	曹景鈞	lecturer in political science, Chinese University of Hong Kong
tsou hou men	走後門	to go through the back door
Tsou, Tang	鄒讜	Chinese-American professor of political science, University of Chicago
Tu Fu	(see Du Fu)	
Tu Weiming	杜維明	professor of Chinese history and philosophy, Harvard University
Tujia	土家	the Tujia people, ethnic group
tzu chia jen	自家人	persons of same circle or closely related in some way
Vice Minister Jiao	焦副部長	
Wang Gungwu	王賡武	historian, vice chancellor of Hong Kong University
Wang Luxiang	王魯湘	co-author of *River Elegy*; in exile
Wang Meng	王蒙	contemporary Mainland Chinese writer
Wang Ruoshui	王若水	former *People's Daily* editor; Marxist humanist
Wang, Ling-chi	王靈智	professor of ethnic studies, U.C. Berkeley
Wang, Peter (Cheng-fang)	王正方	
Wang, Wayne	王穎	Chinese-American movie director
Wei	魏	Northern or Later Wei dynasty (386–534)
Wei River	渭河	a tributary of Yellow River in present-day Shaanxi Province
Wei Yuan	魏源	
wei jen yu chi	為仁由己	achieving the highest virtue is in the hands of *chi* (self)
'Wenhua Zhongguo' chutan	'文化中國'初探	Probing 'Cultural China'
Wenhua Zhongguo	文化中國	Cultural China
wenhua fansi	文化反思	cultural self-reflection
Wenxing Shudian	文星書店	Wenxing Press
wenxue de "gen"	文學的根	the "roots" of literature
Wern	文 (王)	King Wen of the Zhou dynasty
Wern of Luu	魯文公	Duke Wen of the Lu in the *Spring and Autumn Annals*
Wern Yiin	文隱	a character in the *Flowers in the Mirror*
Wo canjiale wusi yundong	我參加了五四運動	I took part of the May Fourth Movement
wo ch'ien t'a i ko jen-ch'ing	我欠他一個人情	I owe him a human obligation, favor
Wong, Jade Snow	黃玉雪	Chinese-American writer
Wu Zuguang	吳祖光	contemporary Mainland Chinese writer
Wu, David Yen-ho	吳燕和	anthropology professor, Chinese University of Hong Kong

Wu, Empress	武則天 (Wu Zetian)	Tang Dynasty usurper of the throne, famous for her lasciviousness and statecraft, 625–705
Wuhan	武漢	a city in Hubei Province
Wusi huiyi lu	五四回憶錄	*Memoirs of May Fourth*
Wusi yiwang	五四憶望	Looking back on May Fourth
Wusi yundong de jinxi	五四運動的今昔	*The May Fourth Movement: Its Past and Present*
wusi de huoju wansui	五四的火炬万歲	Long live the torch of May Fourth
Xi'an	西安 (Sian, Si-an)	ancient Chinese capital
Xia	夏	historical period, 21st–16th centuries B.C.
Xiangei luosha he qiao de anhunqu	獻給羅莎和喬的安魂曲	*Requiem for Rosa and Joe*
xiao	孝	filiality, mourning
xiao guanhua	小官話	language of petit officials
Xin qingnian	新青年	*New Youth* (magazine of May Fourth era)
Xinjiang	新疆 (Sinkiang)	an autonomous region in northwestern China
Xinshi chao shiji	新詩潮詩集	Collection of New Poems
Xinwenxue shiliao	新文學史料	*Historical Materials on New Literature*
xungen	尋根	searching for roots
xungen wenzu	尋根問祖	searching for one's roots and ancestors
yamen	衙門	office of traditional Chinese government
Yan Jiaqi	嚴家其	ex-director, Political Science Institute, Chinese Academy of Social Sciences (Beijing); exiled; b. 1942
Yan Poxi	嚴婆惜	
Yan'an	延安	area of Shaanxi Province, cradel of Communist movement
Yang Guifei	楊貴妃	concubine of Emperor Xuanzhong, Tang Dynasty; A.D. 719–756
Yang Lien-sheng	楊聯陞	
yangwu yundong	洋務運動	Westernization movement, late 19th century
Yantse	揚子	Yangtze (River)
Yarn Luh	顏路	father of Yan Hui, Confucius's best disciple
Yarn Yuan	顏淵	a student of Confucius
Yarnluor	閻羅	lord of the underworld
Yazhou wenhua	亞州文化	*Asian Culture* (periodical)
Yellow Earth	黃土地	contemporary Mainland movie
Yen Ching-hwang	顏清湟	historian, University of Adelaide, S. Australia
Yi	夷	the eastern barbarians

Yi	彝	the Yi people, ethnic group
Yibusheng zhuyi	易卜生主義	Ibsenism
Yiin Yuarn	尹元	a character in the *Flowers in the Mirror*
Yin, Chien-chung	尹建中	
Ying-huan sheng-lan	瀛環勝覽	title of Ma Huan's work
yishu daigen	移樹帶根	to remove a tree with its roots
Yong, C. F.	揚進發	
Youhuo	誘惑	*Temptation*
Youjian zonglü	又見棕櫚	*Again the Palm Trees*
Youlian chubanshe	友聯出版社	Youlian Publishing House
Yu Guangzhong	余光中	Chinese poet
Yu Guangzhong shixuan	余光中詩選	*Selected Poems of Yu Guangzhong*
Yu Kwang-chung	(see Yu Guangzhong)	
Yu Pingbo	俞平伯	Chinese scholar
Yu Ying-shih	余英時	professor of Chinese history, Princeton University
Yü Lihua	於梨華	Chinese writer
Yuan	元	Mongol dynasty, 1271–1368
yundong	運動	movement, campaign
Yung Wing	閎容	Yale graduate, earliest Chinese student in U.S., mid-19th century
Yunnan	雲南	province in southwestern China
Zang	藏	the Tibetan people, ethnic group
Zha Jianying	查建英	
zhancao chugen	斬草除根	to eliminate the weeds, one must pull out their roots
Zhang Chengzhi	張承志	Chinese writer
Zhang Shenfu	張申府	
Zhang Siyuan	張思遠	
Zhang Taiyan	章太炎	Chinese statesman, late 19th century
Zhang Xian	張弦	
Zhang Xianliang	張賢亮	Chinese writer
Zhaxi Dawa	扎西達瓦	
zhishifenzi	知識分子	intellectuals, intelligentsia; a North American periodical
zhong	中	China
Zhongguo	中國	China
Zhongguo minzu zhi	中國民族誌	*Chinese Ethnography*
zhongguoren	中國人	Chinese person, people
Zhonghua minguo	中華民國	Republic of China
zhonghua minzu	中華民族	the Chinese people, the Chinese nation
Zhonghuar shujur	中華書局	China Publishing House
Zhongshan	中山	district of Guangdong
Zhou	周 (Chou)	dynasty, 11th–3rd centuries B.C.
Zhou Enlai	周恩來	the late Mainland Chinese premier, d. 1976
Zhou Erfu	周而復	Chinese writer

Zhu Hong	朱虹	researcher, Institute of Foreign Literature, Chinese Academy of Social Sciences
Zhuang	壯	the Zhuang people, ethnic minority
zhuangyuan	狀元	the highest rank
zhuigen qiuyuan	追根求源	pursuing one's roots and looking for one's origins
Zhujiang	珠江	Pearl River, south China
Ziyou zhongguo	自由中國	Free China
zongjiao	宗教	religion
zu	族	tribe, clan
zuguo	祖國	ancestral homeland
"Zulei yishi zhi chuangzao yu zai chuangzao"	族類意識之創造與再創造	"The Construction and Reconstruction of Ethnic Identity"
Zuojia	作家	*Writer* (periodical)

Notes

1. Tu Wei-ming

I am indebted to David Chu, Rosanne Hall, and Nancy Hearst for searching criticisms of early versions of this paper.

[1] Daniel K. Gardner, *Chu Hsi and the Ta-hsüeh: Neo-Confucian Reflection on the Confucian Canon* (Cambridge: Harvard University Press, 1986), pp. 96–97 with minor modifications.

[2] Herbert Passin, "The Occupation—Some Reflections," *Daedalus* 119 (3) (Summer 1990): 125.

[3] Since the founding of the Republic in 1912, at least eleven constitutional texts have been composed. In the People's Republic of China, four significantly different constitutions were implemented between 1954 and 1982. See Andrew Nathan, *Chinese Democracy* (Berkeley: University of California Press, 1986), pp. 107–32.

[4] Kwang-chih Chang, *The Archaeology of Ancient China*, 4th ed. (New Haven: Yale University Press, 1986).

[5] Owen Lattimore, *Inner Asian Frontiers of China* (London: Oxford University Press, 1940).

[6] Lynn Pan, *Sons of the Yellow Emperor: A History of the Chinese Diaspora* (Boston: Little, Brown, 1990).

[7] According to David Nivison, a Stanford University philosopher-Sinologist, "Of the many claims I have made in this study, the only one that will interest many readers will be the dating of the Chou [Zhou] conquest to 15 January 1045 B.C." David S. Nivison, "The Dates of Western Chou," *Harvard Journal of Asiatic Studies* 43 (2) (December 1983): 564. Subsequently, on the basis of new evidence, Professor Nivison changed the date to 1046 B.C. Also

see Edward L. Shaughnessy, "On the Authenticity of the *Bamboo Annals*," *Harvard Journal of Asiatic Studies* 46 (1) (September 1986): 149–80.

[8] For a recent reference to the "Central Country Complex," see Lucian Pye, "China: Erratic State, Frustrated Society," *Foreign Affairs* 69 (4) (Fall 1990): 62.

[9] Erik Zürcher, *The Buddhist Conquest of China* (Leiden: Brill, 1959).

[10] Arthur Wright, *Buddhism in Chinese History* (Stanford: Stanford University Press, 1959).

[11] Passin, "The Occupation—Some Reflections," 125.

[12] Mark Elvin, *The Pattern of the Chinese Past* (Stanford: Stanford University Press, 1973).

[13] Peter Ward Fay, *The Opium War, 1840–1842* (Chapel Hill: University of North Carolina Press, 1975).

[14] Chow Tse-tsung, *The May Fourth Movement: Intellectual Revolution in Modern China* (Cambridge: Harvard University Press, 1960). For a thought-provoking attempt to come to terms with the intellectual ethos of May Fourth, see Vera Schwarcz, *The Chinese Enlightenment: Intellectuals and the Legacy of the May Fourth Movement of 1919* (Berkeley: University of California Press, 1986).

[15] A seminal term in Alexis de Tocqueville's *Democracy in America* is used by Robert Bellah and his coauthors to characterize the individualistic ethos of contemporary American culture. See Robert Bellah et al., *The Habits of the Heart* (Berkeley: University of California Press, 1985).

[16] The blue ocean and the "Yellow Earth" are used in *River Elegy* to contrast the open, dynamic, and exploratory spirit of the West and the closed, stagnant, and insular mentality of China. For an informed discussion on this unusual cultural phenomenon, see Su Xiaokang and Wang Luxiang, eds., *Deathsong of the River: A Reader's Guide to the Chinese TV Series Heshang*, trans. Richard W. Bodman and Pin P. Wang (Ithaca: East Asia Program, Cornell University, 1991).

[17] Frederic E. Wakeman, Jr., "All the Rage in China," *New York Review of Books*, 2 March 1989, 19–21.

[18] In 1988, mainland China's per capita income was US $330, while the average for sixteen countries in western Africa was $340. "1990 World Population Data Sheet," Population Reference Bureau, Washington, DC. The statistics, of course, tell only part of the story, but the distorted picture was deliberately used to evoke a profound sense of crisis.

[19] For example, Yan Jiaqi, a prominent leader of the Federation for a Democratic China, is an articulate critic of the "dragon mentality." In his *Shijie jingji daobao* (World Economic Herald, Shanghai) interview with Dai Qing, "China Is No Longer a Dragon" (21 March 1988), he specifically berates the symbolism of the dragon.

[20] Yu-sheng Lin, *The Crisis of Chinese Consciousness: Radical Antitraditionalism in the May Fourth Era* (Madison: University of Wisconsin Press, 1979).

[21] Tu Wei-ming, "A Confucian Perspective on the Rise of Industrial East Asia," 167th Stated Meeting Report, *Bulletin of the American Academy of Arts and Sciences* 42 (1) (October 1988): 32–50.

[22] S. Gordon Redding, *The Spirit of Chinese Capitalism* (Berlin: de Gruyter, 1990).

[23] Lucian Pye, *Asian Power and Politics: The Cultural Dimensions of Authority* (Cambridge: Harvard University Press, 1985).

[24] Peter Berger and Hsin-Huang Michael Hsiao, eds., *In Search of an East Asian Development Model* (New Brunswick, NJ: Transaction Books, 1988).

[25] Tu Wei-ming, "The Rise of Industrial East Asia: The Role of Confucian Values," *Copenhagen Papers in East and Southeast Asian Studies* (April 1989): 81–97.

[26] Edwin O. Reischauer, "The Sinic World in Perspective," *Foreign Affairs* (January 1974): 341–48.

[27] Roderick MacFarquhar, "The Post-Confucian Challenge," *The Economist* 274 (9 February 1980): 67–72.

[28] S. N. Eisenstadt, "Varieties of Political Development: The Theoretical Challenge," in S. N. Eisenstadt and Stein Rokkan, eds., *Building States and Nations: Models and Data Resources*, vol. I (Beverly Hills: Sage Publications, 1973), pp. 41–72; and S. N. Eisenstadt, "Post-Traditional Societies and the Continuity of Reconstruction of Tradition in Post-Traditional Societies," in S. N. Eisenstadt, ed., *Post-Traditional Societies* (New York: Norton, 1974), pp. 1–27.

[29] Peter L. Berger, "An East Asian Development Model?," in Berger and Hsiao, eds., *In Search of an East Asian Development Model*, pp. 3–11.

[30] Tu Wei-ming, "The Search for Roots in East Asia: The Case of the Confucian Revival," in Martin Marty and R. Scott Appleby, eds., *Fundamentalisms Observed* (Chicago: University of Chicago Press, 1991), pp. 740–81.

[31] See Wang Gungwu, "The Culture of Chinese Merchants," Working Paper No. 57, Joint Center for Asia-Pacific Studies (University of Toronto and York University, 1990) in Wang Gungwu, *China and the Chinese Overseas* (Singapore: Times Academic Press, 1991), pp. 181–97.

[32] Ezra F. Vogel, *The Four Little Dragons: The Spread of Industrialization in East Asia* (Cambridge: Harvard University Press, 1991), p. 74.

[33] Statement by one Singapore leader as quoted in ibid., p. 79.

[34] Ibid.

[35] For example, the concern over the government's efforts to boost Mandarin prompted Singapore's former foreign minister, S. Rajaratnam, to raise

the issue of possible racial disharmony as a result of emphasis on Chineseness. *Far Eastern Economic Review*, 24 January 1991, 19.

[36] Vogel, *The Four Little Dragons*, pp. 81–82.

[37] The term "cultural China" (*wenhua Zhongguo*) is relatively new. A similar concept, "overseas China" (*haiwai Zhonghua*), was used to designate Chinese communities outside mainland China. Since the term carries the political connotation of a Chinese-style commonwealth encompassing the mainland, Hong Kong, Taiwan, and Singapore, it has generated much controversy on both sides of the Taiwan Straits. I propose adopting the term "cultural China," applied loosely, and invite the participation of all those trying to understand and bring understanding to China and Chinese culture—thus the idea of a community defined by participation in an intellectual discourse. See Tu Wei-ming, " 'Wenhua Zhongguo' chutan" (Probing "cultural China"), *Jiushi niandai* (The Nineties) 245 (June 1990): 60–61.

[38] For scholarly treatments of the subject, see Wang Gungwu, *A Short History of the Nanyang Chinese* (Singapore: Eastern University Press, 1959); Edgar Wickberg, *The Chinese in Philippine Life, 1850–1898* (New Haven: Yale University Press, 1965); G. William Skinner, *Chinese Society in Thailand* (Ithaca: Cornell University Press, 1957); and James L. Watson, *Emigration and the Chinese Lineage: The Mans in Hong Kong and London* (Berkeley: University of California Press, 1975).

[39] Fiji has been independent since 1970. Almost 50 percent of its total population (770,000) is of Asian Indian origin. In the past decade or so, the government has encouraged the importation of thousands of agricultural laborers from mainland China and also has made efforts to woo back many Fijian Chinese who had left the islands because of past political turmoil. In time, if these policies continue, the population of Chinese origin may exceed 3 percent. I am indebted to Sitiveni Halapua, the Director of the Pacific Islands Development Program, East-West Center, for this insight.

[40] For example, although *River Elegy* had become a major topic of discussion in the Chinese mass media throughout the first and second symbolic universes in the summer of 1988, references to the cultural phenomenon in English-language publications, including Frederic Wakeman's thoughtful piece in the *New York Review of Books* (see note 17), did not begin to appear until the spring of 1989. Bodman and Wang's translation of the text of *River Elegy*, which they render as *Deathsong of the River*, was published in 1991 (see note 16).

[41] Edward Said, *Orientalism* (New York: Vintage, 1979).

[42] John K. Fairbank, *Trade and Diplomacy on the Chinese Coast: The Opening of the Treaty Ports, 1842–1854* (Cambridge: Harvard University Press, 1953).

[43] Paul A. Cohen, *Discovering History in China: American Historical Writing on the Recent Chinese Past* (New York: Columbia University Press, 1984).

[44] Chang Hsin-pao, *Commissioner Lin and the Opium War* (Cambridge: Harvard University Press, 1964).

[45] Joseph R. Levenson, *Confucian China and its Modern Fate: A Trilogy* (Berkeley: University of California Press, 1968).

[46] Chiew Seen Kong, "Nation-Building in Singapore: An Historical Perspective," in John S. T. Quah, ed., *In Search of Singapore's National Values* (Singapore: Times Academic Press, 1990), p. 6.

[47] Yan Jiaqi, as a political scientist, has been a consistent and articulate advocate of a federated China. See *Toward a Democratic China: The Intellectual Biography of Yan Jiaqi*, trans. David S. K. Hong and Denis C. Mair (Honolulu: University of Hawaii Press, 1992), pp. 159–60, 269–70.

[48] Pye, "China: Erratic State, Frustrated Society," 58.

[49] Ibid.

[50] Ibid.

[51] I thank sociologist Ambrose King of the Chinese University of Hong Kong for illuminating discussions on this issue.

[52] Ernest W. Nicholson, *God and His People: Covenant and Theology in the Old Testament* (Oxford: The Clarendon Press, 1986).

[53] For a typical example of these patterns, see Clarence E. Glick, *Sojourners and Settlers: Chinese Migrants in Hawaii* (Honolulu: University of Hawaii Press, 1980), pp. 172–81.

[54] For the intriguing subject of networking among Chinese based on religious affiliation, see the pioneering work of Kristofer Schipper, "The Cult of Pao-sheng Ta-ti and Its Spreading to Taiwan—A Case Study of *Fen Hsiang*," in E. B. Vermeer, ed., *Development and Decline of Fukien Province in the Seventeenth and Eighteenth Centuries* (Leiden: Brill, 1990), pp. 397–416. Professor Schipper notes: "The spreading of the Pao-sheng Ta-ti has remained regional on the Chinese mainland, and its outposts reach no further, to my knowledge, than Fu-chou in the north and the Ch'an-chou region in the south. However, because of the wide-scale emigration from the area of origin to Taiwan and South-East Asia, hundreds of temples dedicated to the saint can be found from Taipei to Singapore" (p. 398).

[55] Edgar Wickberg, "Some Comparative Perspectives on Contemporary Chinese Ethnicity in the Philippines," *Yazhou wenhua* (Asian Culture), Singapore, 14 (April 1990): 24.

[56] Ibid.

[57] Ibid., 25.

[58] Ibid.

[59] Ibid., 27.

[60] Ibid., 29.

[61] True to her word, Singapore recognized the People's Republic of China only after Indonesia had done so, in 1990.

[62] Remarks by Wang Gungwu at the conference "The Meaning of Being Chinese," East-West Center, 24–26 October 1990. See conference proceedings, Institute of Culture and Communication, East-West Center.

[63] Issues concerning the legal, political, and economic status of Chinese in the diaspora were explored at the first international conference on overseas Chinese, entitled *Luodishenggen* (falling to the ground and sprouting roots), sponsored by the Asian American Studies Program of the University of California, Berkeley (Miyako Hotel, San Francisco, 26–29 November 1992).

[64] Ibid.

[65] *Shijie ribao* (World Journal), 14 October 1990, 19.

[66] The publication of *Twenty-First Century* (a bi-monthly intellectual journal modeled after the proposed *Cultural China*) clearly indicates that the "transnational Chinese intellectual community" is alive and well. Actually, the original proposal was to name the new journal *Cultural China*. See *Ershiyi shiji* (Hong Kong: Institute of Chinese Studies, Chinese University of Hong Kong, 20 October 1990).

[67] It is interesting to note that scholars from the mainland as well as official pronouncements from Taipei and Beijing continue to use *Zhongguoren* as a generic term for overseas Chinese, even though many overseas Chinese self-consciously identify themselves as *huaren* rather than *Zhongguoren*, for they do not consider themselves politically connected in any way with *Zhongguo* (the Chinese state, either the mainland or Taiwan).

[68] On the annual memorial day, Qingming, this popular demonstration mourning the death of Premier Zhou Enlai not only challenged the authority of the so-called Gang of Four, Mao's closest allies, but also foreshadowed the reform era. The demonstration has been hailed by several intellectual historians in the People's Republic of China as the first spontaneous mass movement since 1949.

[69] Chen Yizi's estimate of 40 million (in public speeches as well as private correspondence) is unusually high, but Chen claimed, on a number of public occasions, that the official figure of 20 million did not take into consideration malnutrition as a principal cause of death. Western demographers agree: see Judith Banister, *China's Changing Population* (Stanford: Stanford University Press, 1987), p. 85.

[70] A well-known dissident journalist, Liu Binyan, and an eminent Marxist theorist, Wang Ruoshui, openly admitted that they began to question the authority and legitimacy of the Party only in late 1984.

[71] *Mencius*, 5A:5.

[72] See Diane B. Obenchain, "Ministers of the Moral Order: Innovations of

the Early Kings, the Duke of Chou, Chung-Ni, and Ju" (Ph.D. dissertation, Harvard University, 1988). See also Benjamin Schwartz, *The World of Thought in Ancient China* (Cambridge: Harvard University Press, 1985), pp. 85–99, 255–320; and Tu Wei-ming, "The Structure and Function of the Confucian Intellectual in Ancient China," in Tu Wei-ming, *Way, Learning, and Politics: Essays on the Confucian Intellectual* (Singapore: Institute of East Asian Philosophies, 1989), pp. 13–28.

[73] Stevan Harrell, "Introduction," in Jonathan N. Lipman and Stevan Harrell, eds., *Violence in China: Essays in Culture and Counterculture* (Albany: State University of New York Press, 1990), p. 1. Harrell adds, "Whether Chinese culture is more violent than other cultures is difficult to judge, but it is visibly not less violent than many."

[74] Quoted in Andrew J. Nathan, "A Culture of Cruelty," *The New Republic* 203 (5) (30 July–6 August 1990): 32.

[75] Lu Xun, "Suigan lu sanshiba" (Random thoughts, no. 38), *Xin qingnian* (New Youth) 5 (5) (15 November 1918): 515–18. For an analysis of Lu Xun's "complex consciousness," see Leo Ou-fan Lee, *Voices from the Iron House: A Study of Lu Xun* (Bloomington: Indiana University Press, 1987).

[76] Quoted in Jonathan D. Spence, *The Search for Modern China* (New York: Norton, 1990), p. 342.

[77] Ibid.

[78] Nathan, "A Culture of Cruelty," 35.

[79] Ibid., 32.

[80] Mark Elvin, "The Double Disavowal: The Attitudes of Radical Thinkers to the Chinese Tradition," in Y. M. Shaw, ed., *China and Europe in the Twentieth Century* (Taipei: Institute of International Relations, 1986), pp. 112–37. For his more recent view on the extinction of Confucianism, see Mark Elvin, "The Collapse of Scriptural Confucianism," *Papers on Far Eastern History* 41 (Canberra: Australian National University, March 1990).

[81] Tu Wei-ming, "Iconoclasm, Holistic Vision, and Patient Watchfulness: A Personal Reflection on the Modern Chinese Intellectual Quest," *Daedalus* 116 (2) (Spring 1987): 94.

[82] Su Xiaokang, "Traditional Resources and Modernization: A Talk with Professor Tu Wei-ming in Paris," *Minzhu Zhongguo* (Democratic China) 1 (2) (June 1990): 52–55.

[83] Tu Wei-ming, "Toward a Third Epoch of Confucian Humanism: A Background Understanding," in Irene Eber, ed., *Confucianism: Dynamics of Tradition* (New York: Macmillan, 1986), pp. 3–21. For an awe-inspiring encounter with Confucian humanism as a living tradition in the third symbolic universe, see Wm. Theodore de Bary, *Neo-Confucian Orthodoxy and the Learning of the Mind-and-Heart* (New York: Columbia University Press, 1981), *The Liberal*

Tradition in China (Hong Kong: Chinese University Press, 1983), *East Asian Civilizations: A Dialogue in Five Stages* (Cambridge, MA: Harvard University Press, 1987), *Learning for One's Self* (New York: Columbia University Press, 1991), and *The Trouble with Confucianism* (Cambridge: Harvard University Press, 1991).

[84] Edwin O. Reischauer, *Toward the Twenty-First Century: Education for a Changing World* (New York: Knopf, 1973), pp. 63–64.

[85] Professor Ying-shih Yu of Princeton, perhaps in jest, proposed this as the theme to underscore the intellectual and political significance of the periphery in cultural China. This is reminiscent of Ernst Cassirer's famous statement, "Its center was everywhere; its periphery nowhere." See E. Cassirer, "Giovanni Pico della Mirandola," *Journal of the History of Ideas* 3 (1943): 337. I am indebted to Professor Yu for this information.

2. Mark Elvin

[1] Lii Rurzhen, *Jihng hua yuarn* (Hong Kong: Zhonghuar shujur, 1958). References give both the chapter and page numbers.

[2] Arthur Smith, *Chinese Characteristics* (New York: Revell, 1900), esp. 65, 269, 273, and 277.

[3] An alternative description could be Chinese horizontal, wind-driven sailmills. The term used in the text supports either meaning.

3. Vera Schwarcz

I am greatly indebted to Mark Elvin and to Cho-yun Hsu for their suggestions about ways to expand and substantiate the theme of the "River of Forgetting." Owing to time constraints I have been able to incorporate only a few of their many insightful recommendations.

[1] Yu Guangzhong, *Yu Guangzhong shixuan* (Selected poems of Yu Guangzhong) (Hong Kong: Hongfon Shudian, 1981), 256.

[2] The discussion of the text of "Threshold" is based upon my attendance at the opening performance at the dance-theater experimental work at La MaMa on 14 June 1989. The following afternoon, I conducted a lengthy, taped interview with the artists: choreographers Sui-Fai Pun (from Hong Kong) and Yin Mei (People's Republic of China); scriptwriter Liang Tee Tue (Taiwan); set designers Corrin Chui-yi Chan and Sylvia Fung-yi Chan (New York); and costume designer/producer Eleanor San-san Wong (New York).

[3] Leon Grinberg and Rebecca Grinberg, *Psychoanalytic Perspectives on Migration and Exile* (New Haven: Yale University Press, 1989), 8–9.

[4] Ibid., 14.

[5] Choreographer Sui-fai Pun and scriptwriter Liang Tee Tue of "Threshold"

both referred to Yu Guangzhong's poem "The River of Forgetting" as a source of inspiration for their work.

[6] Yu Kwang-chung, *Acres of Barbed Wire* (Taipei: Mei Ya Publications, 1971).

[7] Yu Guangzhong retells the myth of Lethe in the preface to "Wang Quan" in *Yu Guangzhong shixuan*, 256.

[8] The tale of Old Lady Meng is retold by another contemporary writer unable to forget, Zhang Xianliang, in his latest novel, *Getting Used to Dying* (New York: Harper Collins, 1991).

[9] Yu Guangzhong, 257–58.

[10] For a fuller discussion of the origins of the May Fourth Movement of 1919, see Vera Schwarcz, *The Chinese Enlightenment* (Berkeley: University of California Press, 1986), 12–54.

[11] For an analysis of the etymological and cultural meanings of *zachor* in Jewish history, see Yousef Hayim Yerushalmi, *Zachor: Jewish History and Jewish Memory* (Seattle: University of Washington Press, 1982).

[12] The theme of China's spiritual continuity and the role of conscious remembrance in it is the subject of Stephen Owen's *Remembrances: The Experience of the Past in Classical Chinese Literature* (Cambridge: Harvard University Press, 1986); and as well as in Pierre Ryckmans, *The Chinese Attitude Towards the Past* (Canberra, Australia: The 47th George Morrison Lecture in Ethnology, 1986). Ryckmans's first footnote acknowledges the unique communality of Chinese and Jewish strategies for maintaining "spiritual continuity."

[13] Bei Dao, "Huida" (The answer), *Xinshi chao shiji*, vol. 1 (Beijing: Beijing Daxue chuban she, 1985), 13.

[14] "Ouxiang puohui lun" (On iconoclasm) is the title and the theme of an essay published by *New Youth* editor Chen Duxiu in August 1918. This work as well as the theme of cultural iconoclasm is discussed at length in Schwarcz, *Chinese Enlightenment*, 94–144.

[15] For a thorough introduction to the origins of Gu Hongming see Lo Huimin, "Ku Hung-ming: Schooling," *Papers on Far Eastern History* (September 1988).

[16] Gu Hongming (Ku Hung-ming), "Returned Students and Literary Revolution—Literacy and Education," *Millard's Review* (16 August 1919): 436.

[17] For a further discussion of the link between 1919 and 1989 see Vera Schwarcz, "Memory, Commemoration and the Plight of Chinese Intellectuals," *Wilson Quarterly* (Autumn 1989): 120–129.

[18] Hu Shi, Preface to *The Chinese Renaissance* (Chicago: University of Chicago Press, 1934), ix–x.

[19] Grinberg and Grinberg, 21.

[20] This 1917 essay by Hu Shi is quoted and analyzed at length in Jerome B.

Grieder, *Hu Shih and the Chinese Renaissance* (Cambridge: Harvard University Press, 1970), 160–61.

[21] A new edition of Zhang Shenfu's translation of Wittgenstein's *Tractatus* was recently issued under the title *Mingli lun* (Discourse on logic) (Beijing: Beijing Daxue chuban she, 1988).

[22] These and other translations from European literature into Chinese are discussed in Joseph Levenson, *Revolution and Cosmopolitanism: The Western Stage and the Chinese Stages* (Berkeley: University of California Press, 1971).

[23] Ibid., 35.

[24] Sun Jingxuan, "A Spectre Prowls Our Land," in Barme and Milford, eds., *Seeds of Fire* (New York: Noonday Press, Farrar, Straus and Giroux, 1989), 121–124.

[25] The role of historical consciousness in the shaping of Chinese cultural identity has been thoughtfully analyzed in a special issue of *Extrême-Orient Extrême-Occident* edited by Yves Chevrier of the Centre Chine, Paris. For an overview of this theme see Chevrier, "La servante-maîtresse: condition de la référence à l'histoire dans l'espace intellectuel chinois," *Extrême-Orient Extrême-Occident* 9 (1987): 119–44.

[26] Sun Jingxuan, 121.

[27] "Chongzheng wusi jingshen" (Rekindle the spirit of May Fourth), *Ziyou zhongguo* 16 (9) (May 1957): 10.

[28] Liu Jisheng, "Wusi de houju wansui" (Long live the torch of May Fourth), in *Beijing daxue you pai fenzi fandong yanlun huiji* (Collection of speeches and writings by Peking University's rightist reactionary elements) (Beijing: Renmin chuban she, 1957), 163.

[29] Zhang Shenfu, "Wusi yundong de jinxi" (The May Fourth Movement: its past and present), *Xinwenxue shiliao* 3 (May 1979): 46–48.

[30] Yu Pingbo, "Wusi yiwang" (Looking back on May Fourth), *Wusi huiyi lu* (Beijing: Shehui Kexue chuban she, 1979), 1001.

[31] Mao Zishui, "Buyao pa wusi" (No need to fear May Fourth), *Wo canjiale wusi yundong* (I took part in the May Fourth Movement) (Taipei: Wenxing shudian, 1979), 7.

[32] The Chinese scholars were in Beijing to attend the May Fourth commemorative conferences. As a participant in those conferences, I also witnessed the euphoric mood among overseas Chinese intellectuals during the confluence of the seventieth anniversary of May Fourth and the Beijing student movement of 1989. In Beijing I was privileged to have conversations with Professor Chow Tse-tsung, as well as Dr. Cheng Fangzhen, another keen observer-participant in the Chinese intellectual scene. Chow Tse-tsung is the author of the pioneering study, *The May Fourth Movement* (Stanford: Stanford University Press, 1960).

[33] Lu Xun, "Diary of a Madman," in *Selected Works*, vol. 1 (Beijing: Foreign Languages Press, 1979), 18.

[34] Ba Jin, "A Cultrev [Cultural Revolution] Museum," *Seeds of Fire*, 381.

[35] Ibid., 382–84.

[36] Hu Shi, "Yibusheng zhuyi" (Ibsenism), *Xinqingnian* 4 (6) (June 1918): 492.

[37] Interview notes with "Threshold" scriptwriter, Liang Tee Tue, 15 June 1990.

[38] Wu Zuguang, "An Old Chinese Story," in Barme and Milford, eds., *Seeds of Fire*, 407.

[39] Havel's 1990 New Year speech was quoted and analyzed by Timothy Garton Ash, "Eastern Europe: The Year of Truth," *New York Review of Books*, 15 February 1990, 18.

[40] Franz Kafka, *The Great Wall of China*, trans. Willa and Edwin Muir (New York: Shocken Books, 1948), 162.

[41] Lu Xun, "The Great Wall," in *Selected Works*, vol. 2, 167.

4. Myron L. Cohen

[1] For present purposes I define the late traditional period in China as the Qing dynasty, the era of Manchu rule from 1644 to 1911.

[2] See the articles in David Johnson, Andrew J. Nathan, and Evelyn S. Rawski, eds., *Popular Culture in Late Imperial China* (Berkeley: University of California Press, 1985).

[3] See James Watson's "Standardizing the Gods: The Promotion of T'ien Hou ('Empress of Heaven') along the South China Coast, 960–1960," in Johnson, Nathan, and Rawski, eds., *Popular Culture in Late Imperial China*, 292–324. See also Watson, "The Structure of Chinese Funerary Rites: Elementary Forms, Ritual Sequence, and the Primacy of Performance," in James L. Watson and Evelyn S. Rawski, eds., *Death Ritual in Late Imperial and Modern China* (Berkeley: University of California Press, 1988), 3–19.

[4] See the essays in Kwang-Ching Liu, ed., *Orthodoxy in Late Imperial China* (Berkeley: University of California Press, 1990).

[5] Evelyn S. Rawski, "The Imperial Way of Death: Ming and Ch'ing Emperors and Death Ritual," in Watson and Rawski, eds., *Death Ritual in Late Imperial and Modern China*, 228–353.

[6] See, for example, Watson, "The Structure of Chinese Funerary Rites" and Arthur P. Wolf, "The Origins and Explanation of Variation in the Chinese Kinship System," in Kwang-chih Chang, Kuang-chou Li, Arthur P. Wolf, and Alexander Chien-chung Yin, eds., *Anthropological Studies of the Taiwan Area: Accomplishments and Prospects* (Taipei: Department of Anthropology, National Taiwan University, 1989), 241–60.

[7] G. William Skinner, "Marketing and Social Structure in Rural China," Parts I and II. *Journal of Asian Studies* 24 (1964–65): 3–43, 195–228.

[8] The major work in English on this subject remains Howard S. Levy, *Chinese Footbinding: The History of a Curious Erotic Custom* (New York: Bell Publishing, 1967).

[9] On this subject see G. William Skinner, "Introduction: Urban Social Structure in Ch'ing China," in G. William Skinner, ed., *The City in Late Imperial China* (Stanford: Stanford University Press, 1977), 521–54.

[10] For example, many of the non-Han groups regarded as "raw savages" during the Qing had already taken to wearing Han-style clothing.

[11] The Bai are discussed by David Wu in this volume and in his article "Chinese Minority Policy and the Meaning of Minority Culture: The Example of Bai in Yunnan, China," *Human Organization* 49 (1) (Spring 1990): 1–14. Two important earlier studies are C. P. Fitzgerald, *The Tower of Five Glories: A Study of the Min Chia of Ta Li, Yunnan* (London: Cresset, 1941); and Francis L. K. Hsu, *Under the Ancestors' Shadow* (New York: Columbia University Press, 1948).

[12] The Manchus imposed their hair style on all Chinese men shortly after their conquest of the country. See Philip A. Kuhn, *Soulstealers: The Chinese Sorcery Scare of 1768* (Cambridge: Harvard University Press, 1990), 53–59.

[13] For one interpretation of the implications of the bureaucratic model in Chinese popular religion, see Emily Martin Ahern, *Chinese Ritual and Politics* (Cambridge: Cambridge University Press, 1981). A view of popular religion as a whole is provided by Arthur P. Wolf, "Gods, Ghosts, and Ancestors," in Arthur P. Wolf, ed., *Religion and Ritual in Chinese Society* (Stanford: Stanford University Press, 1974), 131–83. For an analysis of Chinese popular religion in a local setting, see P. Steven Sangren, *History and Magical Power in a Chinese Community* (Stanford: Stanford University Press, 1987).

[14] On the contrasts between "heterodoxy" and the dominant form of popular religion, see Myron L. Cohen, "Souls and Salvation: Conflicting Themes in Chinese Popular Religion," in Watson and Rawski, eds., *Death Ritual in Late Imperial and Modern China*, 180–202.

[15] Translated in S. Robert Ramsey, *The Languages of China* (Princeton: Princeton University Press, 1989), 3.

[16] See Chang-tai Hung, *Going to the People: Chinese Intellectuals and Folk Literature, 1918–1937* (Cambridge: Council on East Asian Studies, Harvard University, 1985), 158–60, and Prasenjit Duara, "Knowledge and Power in the Discourse of Modernity: The Campaigns Against Popular Religion in Early Twentieth-Century China," *Journal of Asian Studies* 50, (1) (February 1991): 67–83. The small number of folklorists who are the subject of Hung's book might be held to represent a countercurrent during the May Fourth era of antitraditionalism. While sharing the pronounced anti-Confucianism of other Chinese intellectuals, they held that the gap between the masses and China's

modern elite had to be bridged. Key to this effort was the recording, publication, and analysis of folk literature, which they saw as a form of traditional creativity suppressed by the old Confucian elite. Among the folklorists there was an even smaller group who viewed popular religion with sympathy and emphasized its importance for people in the countryside. Nevertheless, they also shared the view that these beliefs were superstitions that would have to be eliminated as China developed. For them as for other Chinese intellectuals, popular traditions were to have no role in the construction of a new nationalism.

Increasing use of the new term "peasant" (*nongmin*, introduced from Japan) during and following the May Fourth era was another expression of the growing hostility of China's political and intellectual elites to traditional culture. This term, which replaced those best translated as "farmer," was more a designation of a category of culturally backward people than a word for a particular occupation. Its use identified the rural Chinese—who appeared to embrace most strongly traditional beliefs and practices—as being culturally unfit to participate in the construction of modern China, except under the guidance and leadership of those who were more enlightened. On this see Myron L. Cohen, "Cultural and Political Inventions in Modern China: The Case of the Chinese 'Peasant,' " *Dædalus* 122 (2) (Spring 1993): 151–70.

[17] See E. J. Hobsbawm, *Nations and Nationalism since 1780: Programme, Myth, Reality* (Cambridge: Cambridge University Press, 1990). Although China does not figure importantly in Hobsbawm's analysis, its traditional culture matches all his criteria for the "popular proto-nationalism" that elsewhere contributed to the construction of modern nation-state ideologies.

[18] The destruction or conversion of village temples toward the end of the Qing dynasty as decreed by the government is described in Prasenjit Duara, *Culture, Power, and the State: Rural North China, 1900–1942* (Stanford: Stanford University Press, 1988), 148–55.

[19] See Julian F. Pas, ed., *The Turning of the Tide: Religion in China Today* (Hong Kong: Oxford University Press, 1989).

[20] For a discussion of Mazu as a case illustrating the Taiwan government's present policy of actively embracing and interpreting elements of popular religion, see P. Steven Sangren, "History and the Rhetoric of Legitimacy: The Ma Tsu Cult of Taiwan," *Comparative Studies in Society and History* 30 (4) (October 1988): 674–97.

5. Ambrose Yeo-chi King

[1] The concepts of *mien-tsŭ* and *jên-ch'ing* are dealt with in my two papers: Ambrose Y. C. King, "Jên tsi kuan-hsi chung jên ch'ing chih fen hsi" (An analysis of *jên-ch'ing* in interpersonal relationships), in *Collected Papers of the First*

International Sinological Conference (Taipei: Academia Sinica, 1980), 413–42; and "Mien, ch'ih yu chung kuo jên hsing wei chih fen hsi" (*Mien, ch'ih* and the Chinese social behavior), in *Collected Papers of the Second International Sinological Conference* (Taipei: Academia Sinica, 1986), 39–54.

[2] The concept was originally developed by Schutz. See Alfred Schutz and Thomas Luckmann, *The Structure of the Life-World*, trans. R. M. Zarner and H. T. Engelhardt, Jr. (Evanston, Ill.: Northwestern University Press, 1973), 99–182.

[3] Liu Pin-yen, "Jên yao ch'ih chien" (Between human and demon), *People's Literature* (September 1976): 34–35.

[4] Fox Butterfield, *China: Alive in the Bitter Sea* (London: Coronet Books, 1983), 74–75.

[5] J. Bruce Jacobs, "A Preliminary Model of Particularistic Ties in Chinese Political Alliance: *Kan-ch'ing* and *Kuan-hsi* in a Rural Taiwanese Township," *China Quarterly* 78 (June 1979): 237–73.

[6] Charles A. Moore, "Introduction: The Humanistic Chinese Mind," in C. A. Moore, ed., *The Chinese Mind* (Honolulu: University of Hawaii Press, 1967).

[7] Hu Shih, *Chung-kuo che-hsueh shih ta-kang* (An outline of the history of Chinese philosophy) (Shanghai: Commercial Press, 1919), 116.

[8] Tu Wei-ming, "Confucian Humanism in a Modern Perspective," in Joseph P. L. Jiang, ed., *Confucianism and Modernization: A Symposium* (Taipei: Freedom Council, 1987), 71.

[9] Francis L. K. Hsu, "Psychosocial Homeostasis and Jên: Conceptual Tools for Advancing Psychological Anthropology," in *American Anthropologist* 73 (1) (1971).

[10] Liang Sou-ming, *Chung-kuo wen-hua yao-i* (The essential features of Chinese culture) (Hong Kong: Chi-cheng T'u-shu Kung-ssu, 1974), 94.

[11] Ambrose Y. C. King, "The Individual and the Group in Confucianism: A Relational Perspective," in Donald J. Munro, ed., *Individualism and Holism: Studies in Confucian and Taoist Values* (Ann Arbor: University of Michigan Press, 1985), 57–72.

[12] Yu Ying-shih, *Ts'ung chia chih hsi t'ung k'an chung kuo wen hua ti hsien tai i i* (The modern meaning of the Chinese culture as viewed from its value systems) (Taipei: Times Publishing Co., 1984), 62.

[13] Pan Kuang-tan, *Cheng-hsueh chu yen* (Comments on political issues), (Shanghai: Kuan-ch'a She, 1948), 133.

[14] Robert H. Silin, *Leadership and Values* (Cambridge: Harvard University Press, 1970), 36.

[15] Fei Hsiao-t'ung, *Hsiang-tu chung-kuo* (Peasant China) (Taipei: Lu-chou Ch'u-pan-she, 1967), 20–22.

[16] Hu Shih, 116.

[17] Richard H. Solomon, *Mao's Revolution and the Chinese Political Culture* (Berkeley: University of California Press, 1971).

[18] Ambrose Y. C. King and Michael Bond, "The Confucian Paradigm of Man: A Sociological View," in Wen-shing Tseng and David Wu, eds., *Chinese Culture and Mental Health* (New York: Academic Press, 1985), 29–46.

[19] Wm. Theodore de Bary, "Individualism and Humanitarianism in Late Ming Thought," in de Bary, ed., *Self and Society in Ming Thought* (New York: Columbia University Press, 1970), 149.

[20] Fei Hsiao-t'ung, 26–27.

[21] Ibid.

[22] Barbara E. Ward, "Sociological Self-Awareness: Some Uses of the Conscious Models," *Man* (N.S.) (1) (1966): 201–15.

[23] Steve Duck and Daniel Perlman, *Understanding Personal Relationships: An Interdisciplinary Approach* (London: Sage, 1985).

[24] John Clyde Mitchell, ed., *Social Networks in the Urban Situation* (Manchester: Manchester University Press, 1969), 13.

[25] Chien Chiao, *Kuan-hsi chu i* (Preliminary discussion on *kuan-hsi*), Special Bulletin No. 10 (Taipei: Institute of Ethnology, Academia Sinica, 1982), 345–50. This is one of the pioneering works on *kuan-hsi*. I have benefited greatly from this paper and from discussing it with the author.

[26] W. La Barre, "Some Observations on Character Structure in the Orient," II, *Psychiatry* 9: 215.

[27] Chie Nakane, *Japanese Society* (New York: Penguin, 1970), 1.

[28] Ibid., 14.

[29] Chuang Ying-chang and Chen Chi-nan, "Hsien ch'ieh tuan chung jih she hui chieh kou yen chiu ti chien t'ao: tai wan yen chiu ti i hsieh chi shi" (A review on the present stage's studies on the social structure of China and Japan), in *The Sinicization of Research in Social and Behaviour Science*, Special Bulletin No. 10 (Taipei: Institute of Ethnology, Academia Sinica, 1982), 281–310.

[30] Wang Sung-hsing, *Han jên ti chia tsu chih: shih lun yu "kuan-hsi, wu tsu chih" ti she hui* (The lineage of the Han people), unpublished.

[31] Jacobs.

[32] Ibid.

[33] *People's Daily*, 8 May 1979, 4.

[34] Butterfield, 141.

[35] Godwin Chu and Ju Yanan, *The Great Wall in Ruins: Cultural Change in China* (Honolulu: East-West Center, 1990). Chu and Ju's study drew a stratified probability sample of 2,000 respondents, including 1,199 from metropolitan Shanghai, 304 from two towns in Qinpu, and 497 from twenty villages in four of the twenty rural districts. The findings of the survey give us an overall picture of what contemporary Chinese culture looks like.

[36] Ibid., 66.

[37] Ibid.

[38] Ibid., 132.

[39] Ezra F. Vogel, "From Friendship to Comradeship," *China Quarterly* 21 (1965): 46–60.

[40] Franz Schurmann, *Ideology and Organization in Communist China*, 2d ed. (Berkeley: University of California Press, 1970), iii.

[41] Luk Tak-Chuen, "Kuan-hsi: dang dai zhong guo de she hui xing tai" (*Kuan-hsi:* the social mode of behaviour in contemporary China), M.Phil. thesis, The Chinese University of Hong Kong, 1988; and King K. Tsao, "Microfoundation of Structural and Historical Macroanalysis: Prolegomenon to the Study of Chinese Human Relationships (*Guanxi*)," qualifying paper for Ph.D. program, University of Chicago, 1988, 43–56.

[42] Andrew G. Walder, *Communist Neo-traditionalism: Work and Authority in Chinese Industry* (Berkeley: University of California Press, 1986); and "Organized Dependency and the Culture of Authority in Chinese Industry," *Journal of Asian Studies* (1983): 51–76.

[43] Tang Tsou, *The Cultural Revolution and Post-Mao Reforms* (Chicago: University of Chicago Press, 1986), 86–88.

[44] Ibid., 220.

[45] Thomas B. Gold, "After Comradeship: Personal Relations in China Since the Cultural Revolution," *China Quarterly* 104 (1985): 673.

[46] Ezra F. Vogel, *One Step Ahead in China* (Cambridge: Harvard University Press, 1989), 407.

[47] Ibid., 405.

[48] Ibid., 409.

[49] See King, "Jên tsi kuan-hsi chung jên ch'ing chih fen hsi."

[50] L. S. Yang, "The Concept of 'Pao' as a Basis for Social Relations in China," in J. K. Fairbank, ed., *Chinese Thought and Institutions* (Chicago: University of Chicago Press, 1957), 292.

[51] Silin, 43.

[52] Ibid., 162.

[53] John H. Weakland, "The Organization of Action in Chinese Culture," *Psychiatry* 13 (1950): 361–70.

[54] Silin, 43.

[55] Chu and Ju, 37.

[56] Ibid., 55.

[57] D. R. De Glopper, "Doing Business in Lukang," in Arthur P. Wolf, ed., *Studies in Chinese Society* (Stanford: Stanford University Press, 1978), 314–15.

[58] Talcott Parsons, *The Structure of Social Action* (New York: Free Press, 1949), 550–51.

[59] Max Weber, *The Religion of China*, trans. H. H. Gerth (New York: Free Press, 1951), 48.

[60] Ibid.

[61] See G. William Skinner, "Chinese Peasants and the Closed Community: An Open and Shut Case," *Comparative Studies in Society and History* 13 (July 1971): 277.

[62] Fei Hsiao-t'ung, 82.

[63] De Glopper, 306, 317.

[64] K. K. Hwang, "Face and Favor: The Chinese Power Game," *American Journal of Sociology* 92 (4) (1987).

[65] Chu and Ju, 58.

[66] Ibid., 37, 67.

6. Wang Gungwu

References in these notes have been confined to books and articles in English. For readers who are interested in writings or sources in Chinese and other languages, many of the books mentioned here contain very full bibliographies, including published documents and monographs in Chinese.

[1] See Wang Gungwu, *Community and Nation: Essays on Southeast Asia and the Chinese* (Kuala Lumpur: Allen and Unwin, 1981); and Wang Gungwu, *China and the Chinese Overseas* (Singapore: Times Publishing, 1991).

[2] See Yen Ching-hwang, *Coolies and Mandarins: China's Protection of Overseas Chinese During the Late Ch'ing Period (1851–1911)* (Singapore: Singapore University Press, 1985).

[3] Jennifer Cushman and Wang Gungwu, eds., *Changing Identities of the Southeast Asian Chinese since World War II* (Hong Kong: Hong Kong University Press, 1988).

[4] See Ma Huan, *Ying-yai Sheng-lan: The Overall Survey of the Ocean's Shores*, J. V. G. Mills, trans. and ed. (Cambridge: Cambridge University Press, 1970); Wang Gungwu, "Ming Foreign Relations: Southeast Asia," in Frederick W. Mote and D. C. Twitchett, eds., *The Cambridge History of China: The Ming Dynasty*, part 2, vol. 8 (Cambridge: Cambridge University Press, forthcoming); and Sarasin Viraphon, *Tribute and Profit: Sino-Siamese Trade 1652–1853*, Harvard East Asian Monographs, 76 (Cambridge: Harvard University Press, 1977).

[5] See Leonard Blussé, *Strange Company: Chinese Settlers, Mestizo Women and the Dutch in VOC Batavia* (Dordrecht, Holland: Foris Publications, 1986), 73–96; Tan Chee Beng, *The Baba of Melaka: Culture and Identity of a Chinese Peranakan Community in Malaya* (Petaling Jaya, Malaysia: Pelanduk Publications, 1988).

[6] Wang Gungwu, "Patterns of Chinese Migration in Historical Perspec-

tive," in R. J. May and William J. O'Malley, eds., *Observing Change in Asia: Essays in Honour of J. A. C. Mackie* (Bathurst, Australia: Crawford House Press, 1989), 33–48.

[7] Wang Sing-wu, *The Organisation of Emigration, 1848–1888* (San Francisco: Chinese Materials Center, 1978); Sucheng Chan, *This Bittersweet Soil: The Chinese in California Agriculture, 1860–1910* (Berkeley: University of California Press, 1986).

[8] C. F. Yong, *The New Gold Mountain: The Chinese in Australia, 1901–1921* (Richmond, Australia: Raphael Arts, 1977), 35–96.

[9] Wang Gungwu, "The Study of Chinese Identities in Southeast Asia," in Cushman and Wang, eds., *Changing Identities*, 1–21.

[10] See Linda Y. C. Lim and L. A. Peter Gosling, eds., *The Chinese in Southeast Asia* (Singapore: Maruzen Asia, 1983).

[11] Shih-shan Henry Tsai, *The Chinese Experience in America* (Bloomington: Indiana University Press, 1986), 151–92; Edgar Wickberg, ed., *From China to Canada: A History of the Chinese Communities in Canada* (Toronto: McClelland and Stewart, 1982), 204–67; David Chuenyan Lai, *Chinatowns: Towns within Cities in Canada* (Vancouver: University of British Columbia Press, 1988); C. Y. Choi, *Chinese Migration and Settlement* (Sydney: Sydney University Press, 1975); and James Jupp, ed., *The Australian People* (Sydney: Angus and Robertson, 1988); see essays by K. K. Shum, 307–11, and K. H. Chin, 317–23.

[12] Jack Chen, *The Chinese in America* (San Francisco: Harper and Row, 1980); Francis L. K. Hsu, *The Challenge of the American Dream: The Chinese in the United States* (Belmont, California: Wadsworth Publishing, 1971); and Peter S. Li, *The Chinese in Canada* (Toronto: Oxford University Press, 1988).

[13] Yen Ching-hwang, *A Social History of the Chinese in Singapore and Malaya, 1800–1911* (Singapore: Oxford University Press, 1986); and Loh Kok Wah, *Beyond the Tin Mines* (Singapore: Oxford University Press, 1988).

[14] See Lim and Gosling, eds., *Chinese in Southeast Asia*. For the case of Malaysia, see Jomo Kwame Sundaram, *A Question of Class: Capital, the State, and Uneven Development in Malaysia* (Singapore: Oxford University Press, 1986).

[15] Tsai, *Chinese Experience*, 1–55, 119–50; Li, *Chinese in Canada*, 43–82.

[16] Edward Wickberg, *The Chinese in Philippine Life, 1850–1898* (New Haven: Yale University Press, 1965), 168–206.

[17] See Lea E. Williams, *Overseas Chinese Nationalism: The Genesis of the Pan-Chinese Movement in Indonesia, 1900–1916* (Glencoe: Free Press, 1960); Antonio S. Tan, *The Chinese in the Philippines, 1898–1935: A Study of their National Awakening* (Quezon City: privately published, 1972); and

Yen Ching-hwang, *The Overseas Chinese and the 1911 Revolution, with Special Reference to Singapore and Malaya* (Kuala Lumpur: Oxford University Press, 1976).

[18] See Tan Liok Ee's essay in Leo Suryadinata, ed., *Ethnic Chinese in the ASEAN States* (Singapore: Inst. of Southeast Asian Studies, 1989), 166–202; and Douglas Murray, "Chinese education in Southeast Asia," *China Quarterly* (20) (1964): 67–95.

[19] Chai Hon Chan, *Education and Nation-building in Plural Societies: The Malaysian Experience* (Canberra: Australian National University, Development Studies Centre, 1977); and Tan Liok Ee, "Chinese Independent Schools in West Malaysia: Varying Responses to Changing Demands," in Cushman and Wang, eds., *Changing Identities*, 61–74.

[20] J. A. C. Mackie, "Changing Patterns of Chinese Big Business in Southeast Asia," in Ruth McVey, ed., *Industrializing Elites in Southeast Asia* (Ithaca: Cornell University Press, forthcoming); and L. A. Peter Gosling, "Changing Chinese Identities in Southeast Asia: An Introductory Review," in Lim and Gosling, eds., *Chinese in Southeast Asia*, vol. 2, 1–15.

[21] Y. C. Wang, *Chinese Intellectuals and the West, 1872–1949* (Chapel Hill: University of North Carolina Press, 1966).

[22] See Harold Z. Schiffrin, *Sun Yat-sen and the Origins of the Chinese Revolution* (Berkeley: University of California Press, 1968); Jerome B. Grieder, *Hu Shih and the Chinese Renaissance: Liberalism in the Chinese Revolution, 1917–1937* (Cambridge: Harvard University Press, 1970); see also essays in *Chinese Students' Monthly* (New York, 1909–1921).

[23] The literature is growing but an analytical study is yet to come. Some idea of the riches awaiting the scholar can be seen in Him Mark Lai, *A History Reclaimed: An Annotated Bibliography of Chinese-Language Materials on the Chinese in America* (Los Angeles: Asian American Studies Center, University of California, 1986).

[24] There is a vast literature in Chinese, especially since the 1920s. For background, see Victor Purcell, *The Chinese in Southeast Asia* (London: Oxford University Press, 1951, rev. ed. 1965); and Wang Gungwu, *A Short History of the Nanyang Chinese* (Singapore: Eastern Universities Press, 1959).

[25] Tsai, *Chinese Experience*, 151–92; and Wickberg, ed., *From China to Canada*, 221–71, delineate the formation of new kinds of Chinese communities in North America after World War II. Developments in the 1980s have yet to be systematically studied, but the variety of writings reflecting the recent changes (whether by the locally born or those who migrated from Southeast Asia, China, Taiwan, or Hong Kong) suggests a degree of pluralism and polycentrism that is new.

[26] Loh Kok Wah, *The Politics of Chinese Unity in Malaysia* (Singapore:

Maruzen Asia, 1982); Judith Strauch, *Chinese Village Politics in the Malaysian State* (Cambridge: Harvard University Press, 1981); and Sundaram, *Question of Class*, 205–82.

[27] See Charles A. Coppel, *Indonesian Chinese in Crisis* (Kuala Lumpur: Oxford University Press, 1983); Richard J. Coughlin, *Double Identity: The Chinese in Modern Thailand* (Hong Kong: University of Hong Kong Press, 1960); Cristina Blanc Szanton, "Thai and Sino-Thai in Small Town Thailand: Changing Patterns of Interethnic Relations" in Lim and Gosling, eds., *Chinese in Southeast Asia*, vol. 2, 99–125.

[28] The turning point came during the 1960s. It began even before the Cultural Revolution, but *huayi* stopped returning to China altogether once the Cultural Revolution was launched. On the contrary, many *guiqiao* left China during the disastrous decade 1966–1976.

7. David Yen-ho Wu

[1] See Han Jinchun and Li Yifu, "Hanwen 'minzu' yi ci de chuxian jiqi chuqi shiyong qingkuang" (The emergence of the term 'minzu' in Han (Chinese) language and usage), *Minzu yanjiu* 2 (1984): 36–43; David Y. H. Wu, "Zulei yishi zhi chuangzao yu zaichuangzao" (The construction and reconstruction of ethnic identity), paper presented at the Conference of Ethnic Relation and Regional Development, Academia Sinica, Taipei, 1 September 1989.

[2] Cited in Hu Nai'an, *Zhongguo minzu zhi* (Chinese ethnography) (Taipei: Shangwu, 1964).

[3] Jiequan Li, "Dui dangzhi ji danghua jiaoyu de pipan" (Criticism of party rule and party education), *Mingbao yuekan* (September 1990): 34–37.

[4] David Y. H. Wu, *The Chinese in Papua New Guinea* (Hong Kong: Chinese University Press, 1982).

[5] Many Chinese communities, for lack of an alternative Chinese word, still call themselves *huaqiao* to this day.

[6] Leo Suryadinata, "Government Policy and National Integration in Indonesia," *Southeast Asian Journal of Social Science* 12(2) (1988): 111–131.

[7] Stevan Harrell, "Introduction," in Jonathan N. Lipman and Stevan Harrell, eds., *Violence in China* (Albany: State University of New York Press, 1990), 1–25.

[8] Tao Yunkui, "Lun biandi hanren ji qi yu piajiang jianshe zhi guanxi" (On the relationship between frontier Han Chinese and the development of frontier land), *Bianzheng gonglun* 2 (1–2) (1943): 28–34.

[9] See David Y. H. Wu, "Chinese Minority Policy and the Meaning of Minority Culture: The Example of Bai in Yunnan, China," *Human Organization* 49 (1) (March 1990): 1–13.

[10] See David Y. H. Wu, "Ethnicity and Culture Change," *Proceedings of the Second International Conference of Sinology* (Taipei: Academia Sinica, 1990).

[11] Francis L. K. Hsu, *Under the Ancestors' Shadow* (Stanford: Stanford University Press, 1963).

[12] See C. P. Fitzgerald, *The Southern Expansion of the Chinese People* (Canberra: Australian National University Press, 1972).

[13] David Y. H. Wu, "Culture Change and Ethnic Identity among Minorities in China," in Chien Chiao and Nicholas Tapp, eds., *Ethnicity and Ethnic Groups in China* (Hong Kong: New Asia College, 1989), 11–22.

[14] Chee-Beng Tan, "Peranakan Chinese in Northeast Kelantan with Special Reference to Chinese Religion," *Journal of the Malaysian Branch of the Royal Asiatic Society* 55 (part 1) (1982): 26–52; Chee-Beng Tan, *The Baba of Melaka* (Petaling Jaya, Malaysia: Pelanduk Publications, 1988).

[15] Tao, 28–34.

[16] Tao, 23.

[17] Tan, *The Baba of Melaka*.

[18] William H. Newell, *Treacherous River: A Study of Rural Chinese in North Malaya* (Kuala Lumpur: University of Malaya Press, 1962).

[19] Newell, 99.

[20] David Y. H. Wu, "Adaptation and Change: The Chinese in Papua and New Guinea," diss., Australian National University, May 1974.

[21] See David Y. H. Wu, "Ethnicity and Adaptation," *Southeast Asian Journal of Social Science* 5 (1–2) (1974): 95.

[22] *Far Eastern Economic Review*, 15 October 1987, 52–53.

[23] Wang Gungwu, "The Study of Chinese Identities in Southeast Asia," in Jennifer W. Cushman and Wang Gungwu, eds., *Changing Identities of the Southeast Asian Chinese since World War II* (Hong Kong: Hong Kong University Press, 1988), 1–22.

8. Zhu Hong

This paper was first given as a talk at the Humanities Research Centre, Australian National University Canberra, 1988. The paper was completed at the Bunting Institute, Harvard-Radcliffe, 1991.

[1] *Harvard University Gazette*, October 5, 1990.

[2] Charles Dickens, *Dombey and Son*, Chapter 21.

[3] See Margery Wolf, *Revolution Postponed: Women in Contemporary China* (Stanford: Stanford University Press, 1985), 20. See also Delia Davin, *Women-Work: Women and the Party in Revolutionary China* (Oxford: Oxford University Press, 1976).

[4] *Di Wang Quan Mo Shu* (Shanghai: Guji, 1989).

[5] Charles Dickens, *Bleak House*, Chapter 16.

[6] Bette Bao Lord, *Legacies: A Chinese Mosaic* (New York: Knopf, 1990).

[7] *New York Times*, January 10, 1992.

9. L. Ling-chi Wang

[1] One of the earliest and most comprehensive statements against the Chinese for their "nonassimilability" was given by the California governor John Bigler in his special message to the legislature on April 23, 1852, *California Senate Journal, 3rd Session, 1852*, 373–78; for an extended version of this perspective, see Willard B. Farwell, *The Chinese at Home and Abroad: Together with the Report of the Special Committee of the Board of Supervisors of San Francisco, on the Conditions of the Chinese Quarter of That City* (San Francisco: A.L. Bancroft, 1885). For the most complete recent explication of how the presumed Chinese nonassimilability affected their mistreatment and exclusion, see Gunther Barth, *Bitter Strength: A History of the Chinese in the United States, 1850–1870* (Cambridge: Harvard University Press, 1964).

[2] Representative of the assimilationist perspective is the work of the Chinese American sociologist Rose Hum Lee, *The Chinese in the United States of America* (Hong Kong: University of Hong Kong Press, 1960). Lee's assimilationist view was heavily influenced by Robert E. Park and Ernest Burges, *Introduction to the Science of Society* (Chicago: University of Chicago Press, 1921) and William Carlson Smith, *Americans in the Making: The Natural History of the Assimilation of Immigrants* (New York: Appleton-Century, 1939). For more recent application of the assimilation theory in popular media, see "Success Story of One Minority in the United States," *U.S. News and World Report* (December 26, 1966), 73–78; "Asian American: A 'Model Minority,' " *Newsweek* (December 6, 1978), 39–41; Robert Oxnam, "Why Asians Succeed Here," *New York Times Magazine* (November 30, 1986), 74ff.; Anthony Ramirez, "America's Super Minority," *Fortune* (November 24, 1986), 148ff.; Keith Osajima, "Asian Americans as the Model Minority: An Analysis of the Popular Press Image in the 1960s and 1980s," in Gary Y. Okihiro et al., eds., *Reflections on Shattered Windows* (Pullman: Washington State University Press, 1988), 165–74; Peter Kwong, *The New Chinatown* (New York: Hill and Wang, 1987), 57–80.

[3] Victor and Brett de Bary Nee, *Longtime Californ': A Documentary Study of an American Chinatown* (1972: reissue; Stanford, Calif.: Stanford University Press, 1986), 200–201; Huang Zhengwu, *Huaqiao yu Zhongguo Geming* (Overseas Chinese and the Chinese Revolution) (Taipei: Guofang Yanjiuyuan, 1963); and Jian Yongjing, ed., *Huaqiao Kaiguo Geming Shiliao* (A Brief History of Overseas Chinese in the 1911 Revolution) (Taipei: Zhengzhong, 1977),

are typical examples of this perspective. For a comprehensive and critical assessment of China's relations with the *huaqiao*, see Wang Gungwu, *China and the Chinese Overseas* (Singapore: Times Academic Press, 1991).

[4] Shih-shan Henry Tsai, *China and the Overseas Chinese in the United States, 1868–1911* (Fayetteville: University of Arkansas Press, 1983), 104–46.

[5] For an excellent example of life in a permanent Chinese settlement in the United States but unassimilated, see the novel by Louis Chu, *Eat a Bowl of Tea* (New York: Lyle Stuart, 1961). However, this life style was sharply criticized by assimilationist Rose Hum Lee in her book.

[6] See the work of Tsai; and Stephen Fitzgerald, *China and the Overseas Chinese: A Study of Peking's Changing Policy, 1949–1970* (Cambridge: Cambridge University Press, 1972).

[7] For general works on the history of Chinese overseas, see H.F. MacNair, *The Chinese Abroad: Their Position and Protection* (Shanghai: Commercial Press, 1924); Victor Purcell, *The Chinese in Southeast Asia* (London: Oxford University Press, 1965); Wang, *China and the Chinese Overseas*; Lynn Pan, *Sons of the Yellow Emperor: A History of the Chinese Diaspora* (Boston: Little, Brown, 1990); Li Xisuo, *Jindai Zhongguo de Liuxuesheng* (Modern Chinese Studying Abroad) (Beijing: Renmin Chubanshe, 1987).

[8] Two excellent examples of this kind of debate are: Jennifer Cushman and Wang Gungwu, eds., *Changing Identities of the Southeast Asian Chinese since World War II* (Hong Kong: Hong Kong University Press, 1988), and the special issue of *Daedalus* on which this volume is based.

[9] Barbara Vobejda, "Asians, Hispanics Giving Nation More Diversity," *Washington Post*, June 12, 1991, p. A3.

[10] Mary R. Coolidge, *Chinese Immigration* (New York: Henry Holt, 1909), 109–82, 498–501.

[11] Ping Chiu, *Chinese Labor in California, 1850–1880: An Economic Study* (Madison: State Historical Society of Wisconsin, 1963).

[12] Leigh Bristol-Kagan, *Chinese Migration to California 1851–1882: Selected Industries of Work, the Chinese Institutions and the Legislative Exclusion of a Temporary Labor Force* (Ph.D. diss., Harvard University, 1982), 12.

[13] Zhuang Guoto, *Zhongguo Fengjian Zhengfu de Huaqiao Zhengce* (Overseas Chinese Policies of the Feudal Government of China) (Xiamen: Xiamen University, 1989), 61–86; Tsai, 8–11; Yen Ching-hwang, *Coolies and Mandarins: China's Protection of Overseas Chinese during the Late Ch'ing Period, 1851–1911* (Singapore: Singapore University Press, 1985), 19–31.

[14] Coolidge, 15–25, 55–68; Elmer Clarence Sandmeyer, *The Anti-Chinese Movement in California* (Urbana: University of Illinois Press, 1939), 25–39.

[15] Coolidge, 53–59.

[16] L. Eve Armentrout Ma, *Revolutionaries, Monarchists, and Chinatowns: Chinese Politics in the Americas and the 1911 Revolution* (Honolulu: University of Hawaii Press, 1990).

[17] Renqiu Yu, *To Save China, To Save Ourselves: The Chinese Hand Laundry Alliance of New York* (Philadelphia: Temple University Press, 1992), 77–99; Peter Kwong, *Chinatown, New York: Labor and Politics, 1930–1950* (New York: Monthly Review Press, 1979), 101–110; Zheng Ruiyan, *Huaqiao yu Kang Ri Zhanzheng* (Overseas Chinese and the Sino-Japanese War) (Chengdu: Sichuan University Press, 1988).

[18] Lin Jinzi, *Jindai Huaqiao Touzi Guonei Qiye Shi Ziliao Xuanji* (Selected Sources for the Modern History of Overseas Chinese Investments in China's Enterprises) (Fuzhou: Fujian Renmin Chubanshe, 1989).

[19] Zhang Cunwu, *Guangxu Sanshiyinian Zhong-Mei Gongyue Fenchao* (1905 Sino-American Treaty Conflict) (Taipei: Zhongyang Yanjiuyuan Xiandaishi Yanjiusuo, 1966).

[20] Liu Boqi, *Meiguo Huaqiao Shi* (History of the Chinese in the United States) (Taipei: Li Ming Wenhua, 1976), 449–54; Harold Z. Schriffrin, *Sun Yat-sen and the Origins of the Chinese Revolution* (Berkeley: University of California Press, 1970), 98–139. A recent example of the extraterritorial reach of the Guomindang is the assassination of Chinese American journalist Henry Liu in his home in Daly City, California, on October 15, 1984. For documents and reports related to the case, see Jiangnan Shijian Weiyuanhui, ed., *Jinian Jiangnan* (Remembering Henry Liu) (San Francisco: Committee to Obtain Justice for Henry Liu, 1985); and for a full account of the case, see David E. Kaplan, *Fires of the Dragon* (New York: Atheneum, 1992).

[21] 78th Congress, 1st Session, 1943. *House Report 732* "Repealing the Chinese Exclusion Laws"; Fred W. Riggs, *Pressures on Congress: A Study of the Repeal of Chinese Exclusion* (New York: King's Crown Press, 1950).

[22] David M. Reimers, *Still the Golden Door: The Third World Comes to America* (New York: Columbia University Press, 1985), 67–90; James T. Fawcett and Benjamin V. Carino, eds., *Pacific Bridges: The New Immigration from Asia and the Pacific Islands* (Staten Island, N.Y.: Center for Migration Studies, 1987).

[23] Sucheng Chan, *Asian Americans: An Interpretive History* (Boston: Twayne, 1991), 37.

[24] Kwong, 25–44; Timothy Fong, *The Unique Convergence: A Community Study of Monterey Park, California* (Ph.D. Diss., University of California, Berkeley, 1992).

[25] Chang Pao-min, *Beijing, Hanoi, and the Overseas Chinese* (Berkeley: Institute of East Asian Studies, University of California, 1982).

[26] The most comprehensive depiction of the Chinese in the United States

as sojourners can be found in Barth, *Bitter Strength*; for an opposite interpretation of Chinese as permanent settlers, see Sandy Lydon, *Chinese Gold: The Chinese in the Monterey Bay Area* (Capitola, Calif.: Capitola Books, 1985).

[27] Robert McCellan, *The Heathen Chinese: A Study of American Attitudes toward China, 1890–1905* (Columbus: Ohio State University Press, 1971); Stuart Creighton Miller, *The Unwelcome Immigrant: The American Image of the Chinese, 1785–1882* (Berkeley: University of California Press, 1969).

[28] Shen Yimin and Tong Chengzhu, *Zhongguo Renkou Qianyi* (Population Migration in China) (Beijing: Zhongguo Tongji Chubanshe, 1992).

[29] Lydon; James W. Loewen, *The Mississippi Chinese: Between Black and White* (Cambridge: Harvard University Press, 1971); Sylvia Sun Minnick, *Samfow: The San Joaquin Chinese Legacy* (Fresno, Calif.: Panorama West, 1988).

[30] Tsai, 8–12.

[31] Christian G. Fritz, "Due Process, Treaty Rights, and Chinese Exclusion, 1882–1924," and Charles J. McClain and Lauren Wu McClain, "The Chinese Contribution to the Development of American Law," both in Sucheng Chan, ed., *Entry Denied: Exclusion and the Chinese Community in America, 1882–1943* (Philadelphia: Temple University Press, 1991), 25–56; also Christian G. Fritz, *Federal Justice in California: The Court of Ogden Hoffman, 1851–1891* (Lincoln: University of Nebraska Press, 1991).

[32] Fitzgerald, 6, 78–80; Qiu Sheru, *Huaqiao Guoji Wenti* (Citizenship Problems of Overseas Chinese) (Taipei: Zhengzhong, 1965).

[33] Wang, 222–39; Fitzgerald, 102–115, 135–36, and 141–55.

[34] Jade Snow Wong, *Fifth Chinese Daughter* (1954; reissue, Seattle: University of Washington Press, 1988); Pardee Lowe, *Father and Glorious Descendant* (Boston: Little, Brown, 1943). Robert E. Park headed a massive Survey of Race Relations in the West coast out of which several influential books on American-born Chinese and Japanese were published. Among them are: William C. Smith, *The Second Generation Oriental in America* (Honolulu: Institute of Pacific Relations, 1927) and *Americans in Process: A Study of Our Citizens of Oriental Ancestry* (Ann Arbor: Edwards Brothers, 1937); R. D. McKenzie, *Oriental Exclusion: The Effect of American Immigration Laws, Regulations, and Judicial Decisions upon the Chinese and Japanese of the American Pacific Coast* (New York: Institute of Pacific Relations, 1927); Eliot G. Mears, *Resident Orientals on the American Pacific Coast* (Chicago: University of Chicago Press, 1928); and Edward K. Strong, *The Second-Generation Japanese Problem* (Stanford: Stanford University Press, 1934). Other studies include Kit King Louis, "Problems of Second Generation Chinese," *Sociology and Social Research*, 16 (1932), 250–58, 455–62; Francisco Y. Chang, "An Accommodation Program for Second-Generation Chinese," *Sociology and Social Research*, 18 (1934), 541–53.

[35] For an interesting public debate on their dilemma in 1936, see Thomas W. Chinn, *Bridging the Pacific: San Francisco Chinatown and Its People* (San Francisco: Chinese Historical Society, 1989), 138–42.

[36] Harold R. Issacs, *Images of Asia: American Views of China and India* (New York: Harper and Row, 1973).

[37] Rose Hum Lee, "Chinese in the United States Today: The War Has Changed Their Lives," *Survey Graphic* (October 1942), 419ff.

[38] Amado Cabezas and Harold T. Yee, *Discriminatory Employment of Asian Americans: Private Industry in the San Francisco–Oakland Standard Metropolitan Statistical Area* (San Francisco: Asian-Inc., July 4, 1977); "America's Asians: The Glass Ceiling," *The Economist* (June 3, 1989), 23–26; and Richard Bernstein, "Asian Newcomers Hurt by Precursors' Success," *New York Times* (July 10, 1988), 12.

[39] When the Korean War began, the U.S. Treasury Department issued regulations, pursuant to the Trading with the Enemy Act, prohibiting Chinese Americans from sending remittances to relatives in China. See Kwong, 1979, 147.

[40] Lee, 103–12; for an unusual account of one of the stranded students, Qian Xuesen, see William L. Ryan and Sam Summerlin, *The China Cloud: America's Tragic Blunder and China's Rise to Nuclear Power* (Boston: Little, Brown, 1967).

[41] Victor and Brett de Bary Nee, "Chiang Still Runs the Show (in Chinatown)," *San Francisco Bay Guardian* (March 23, 1972), and their *Longtime Californ'*, 207–13.

[42] Chan, 158–59; L. Ling-chi Wang, "The Politics of Ethnic Identity and Empowerment: The Asian American Community Since the 1960s," *Asian American Policy Review*, 2 (Spring 1991), 46–51.

[43] William Wei, "On the Development of Asian American Studies Program," in Okihiro et al., 5–15; Sucheng Chan, *Asian Californians* (San Francisco: MTL/Boyd & Fraser, 1991), 139–43.

[44] Chinese for Affirmative Action (CAA) was founded in 1969 in San Francisco; Organization of Chinese Americans (OCA) in 1971 in Washington, D.C.; and the National Association of Chinese Americans (NACA) in 1977 in Washington, D.C.

[45] Frank Ching, *Ancestors: 900 Years in the Life of a Chinese Family* (New York: Morrow, 1988).

11. Leo Ou-fan Lee

[1] See Leo Ou-fan Lee, "The Crisis of Culture," in Anthony J. Kane, ed., *China Briefing: 1990* (Boulder, Colo.: Westview, 1990), 83–106.

[2] For a sampling of these stories, see Jeanne Tai, ed., *Spring Bamboo: A Collection of Contemporary Chinese Short Stories* (New York: Random House, 1989); see also my Introduction, xi–xii.

[3] M. M. Bakhtin, *The Dialogic Imagination*, ed. Michael Holquist (Austin: University of Texas Press, 1981).

[4] Ibid., 22.

[5] Han Shaogong, *Youhuo* (Temptation) (Changsha: Hunan renmin chubanshe, 1986). The collection includes both "Homecoming" (*Guiqulai*) and "Ba-Ba-Ba."

[6] Pai Hsien-yung, "The Wandering Chinese: The Theme of Exile in Taiwan Fiction," *Iowa Review* 7 (2/3) (Spring/Summer, 1976): 208–9.

[7] Hualing Nieh, *Sangqing yu taohong* (Hong Kong: Youlian chubanshe, 1976; most recent edition, Taipei: Hanyi, 1988). English edition, *Mulberry and Peach: Two Women of China*, trans. Jane Parish Yang (Boston: Beacon Press, 1981).

[8] Pai, 211.

[9] Ibid., 212.

[10] Ibid.

[11] C. T. Hsia, "Obsession with China: The Moral Burden of Modern Chinese Literature," in Hsia, *A History of Modern Chinese Fiction*, rev. ed. (New Haven: Yale University Press, 1971), 533–54.

[12] An excellent example of this new genre is a short story by Zha Jianying, "Xiangei luosha he qiao de anhunqu" (Requiem for Rosa and Joe), *Renmin wenxue* (People's literature) (3) (1989). In this story the peripheral existence of an old American couple assumes central symbolic significance in the meaningless life of a young Chinese woman exiled in New York.

[13] Václav Havel, *Living in Truth*, ed. Jan Vladislav (London: Faber, 1989), 113.

[14] Josef Škvorecký, "Bohemia of the Soul," *Dædalus* 119 (1) (Winter, 1990): 135.

[15] Ibid., 132.

[16] Leszek Kolakowski, "In Praise of Exile," in Kolakowski, *Modernity on Endless Trial* (Chicago: University of Chicago Press, 1990), 59.

[17] Ibid., 57.

[18] Liu Xiaofeng, "Liuwang huayu yu yishixingtai" (Exile discourse and ideology), *Ershiyi shiji* (Twenty-first century) (1) (October 1990): 115.

[19] Edward Shils, *Center and Periphery: Essays in Macrosociology* (Chicago: University of Chicago Press, 1975), 3.

[20] Ibid., 7.   [21] Havel, 42.
[22] Shils, 5.   [23] Ibid., 7.
[24] Ibid., 8–9.

[25] Han Shaogong, "Wenxue de 'gen'" (The "roots" of literature), *Zuojia* (Writer) (4) (1985): 2–5. For some of my argument related to *xungen* fiction in this paper I am also indebted to William Schafer, "Composing Roots: Dialogues of Center and Peripheries in Three Xungen Short Stories," M.A. thesis, University of Chicago, 1990.

[26] In Chinese studies, the notion of reform as a "littoral" initiative acting upon the "hinterland" was first developed by Paul A. Cohen in *Between Tradition and Modernity: Wang T'ao and Reform in Late Ch'ing China* (Cambridge: Harvard University Press, 1973), chap. 1.

[27] See Tu Wei-ming's essay in this volume.

Index

In this index an "f" after a number indicates a separate reference on the next page, and an "ff" indicates separate references on the next two pages. A continuous discussion over two or more pages is indicated by a span of page numbers, e.g., "57–59." *Passim* is used for a cluster of references in close but not consecutive sequence.

Library of Congress Cataloging-in-Publication Data

The living tree : the changing meaning of being Chinese today / edited
by Tu Wei-ming.
    p.   cm.
   Includes bibliographical references and index.
   ISBN 0-8047-2191-2 (cloth)—ISBN 0-8047-2137-8 (pbk.)
   1. Chinese—Ethnic identity.   2. National characteristics,
Chinese.   3. Nationalism—China.   1. Tu, Wei-ming.
DS730.L596   1994
305.8'00951—dc20   93-41416
                                           CIP
                                          Rev.

♾ This book is printed on acid-free paper.